PROGRAMMING DISTRIBUTED APPLICATIONS WITH COM AND MICROSOFT® VISUAL BASIC® 6.0

Ted Pattison

PUBLISHED BY
Microsoft Press
A Division of Microsoft Corporation
One Microsoft Way
Redmond, Washington 98052-6399

Library of Congress Cataloging-in-Publication Data
Pattison, Ted, 1962–
      Programming distributed applications with COM and Microsoft Visual
   Basic 6.0 / Ted Pattison.
          p.   cm.
      Includes index.
      ISBN 1-57231-961-5
      1. Electronic data processing--Distributed processing.
   2. Application software--Development.   3. COM (Computer
   architecture)   4. Microsoft Visual BASIC.   I. Title.
   QA76.9.D5P38   1998
   004'.36--dc21   98-39267
                                                          CIP

Printed and bound in the United States of America.

   2 3 4 5 6 7 8 9   MLML   3 2 1 0 9

Distributed in Canada by ITP Nelson, a division of Thomson Canada Limited.

A CIP catalogue record for this book is available from the British Library.

Microsoft Press books are available through booksellers and distributors worldwide. For
further information about international editions, contact your local Microsoft Corporation office
or contact Microsoft Press International directly at fax (425) 936-7329. Visit our Web site at
mspress.microsoft.com.

Acquisitions Editor: Ben Ryan
Project Editor: Kathleen Atkins
Manuscript Editor: Ina Chang
Technical Editor: Donnie Cameron

To my lovely and loving wife, Amy.

Special thanks to my parents, who have always given me every opportunity to be both happy and successful.

Contents

Foreword

1998 marks the fifth anniversary of the first public appearance of the Component Object Model. Five years after the fact, no two people completely agree about what COM is, exactly. Some view COM as a superior way to export functionality from DLLs that has at least some chance of withstanding two or three production cycles without producing absolute chaos. Some people view COM as a communications technology that can vastly reduce the cost of developing distributed applications. Others simply view COM as that thing that makes MTS work. Still others view COM as a confusing mess of ill-documented technologies that seems to exhibit no regular structure or form, much like a mural painted by five different artists on five different canvases who never looked at each other's brushstrokes until the final work was stitched together. While there is merit to each of these viewpoints, none of them capture the essence of what COM is really about: that is, *tough love*.

The most fundamental principle of COM is the separation of interface from implementation. If the interface is sufficiently well-defined (that's the *tough* part), the implementation is free to do whatever it chooses in a consequence-free environment of love and acceptance (that's the *love* part).

Being a COM developer implies collaboration with others. As in any other relationship, each party has his or her own habits, preferences, and annoying mannerisms. For a relationship to be successful, each party has to set boundaries so that everyone in the relationship knows what is and isn't acceptable. This is often done via the unspoken social contract that we all live by, but in more intimate relationships, the parties tend to explicitly verbalize their likes and dislikes to let everyone know what it takes to make them happy. In COM (where all relationships are intimate), we set these boundaries as interfaces in IDL.

Of course, having boundaries implies that individuals might have to change their behavior *somewhat* to avoid completely offending the other parties involved. If the required changes in behavior prove to be too much to bear, the relationship is doomed. If one party cannot agree to respect everyone's boundaries, the collaboration with that individual will be difficult, at best. This applies as much in COM as it does in everyday life.

COM has flourished largely because it is so adaptable to a broad spectrum of programming styles and applications. Part of COM's success lies squarely at the feet of the Visual Basic programmer. More than any other development culture, the Visual Basic world understands the value of components and reusability. Unlike many of their C++ counterparts, Visual Basic programmers see that the whole is often greater than the sum of its parts. C++ programmers (myself included) tend to think that the goal is to build infrastructure. Visual Basic programmers think that the goal is to solve problems. Granted, infrastructure is important, but the pragmatism of the average Visual Basic programmer is refreshing when compared to the machismo-laden C++ culture in which I have spent the last 10 years of my life.

In this book, Ted has captured the essence of COM and MTS programming and has written perhaps the most accurate and approachable text on MTS programming available today. Rather than simply parroting the SDK documentation and proclaiming that "stateless objects equal scalability," Ted has looked at the COM and MTS programming models and distilled the fundamental principles into a very readable (and short) text. In an age when authors seem to get paid by the pound, this book is a breath of fresh air. I am sure that this book will help many more developers achieve their personal COM and MTS epiphanies than any of its predecessors.

Don Box
Redondo Beach, California
August 1998
http://www.develop.com/dbox

Acknowledgments

First and foremost, I must acknowledge the place where I learned about COM. I work for a company in Los Angeles called DevelopMentor, which is for all practical purposes the center of the COM universe. DevelopMentor is a community of the brightest and most enthusiastic group of computer scientists I have ever encountered—a peer group of the highest level of technical integrity, practiced in heated intellectual debate. At DevelopMentor, unsound ideas are blasted out of the air like slow ducks on the opening day of hunting season. In my humble opinion, the ability of this group to research and to teach others about the most significant aspects of Microsoft Windows development is unparalleled in the industry. I would like to thank Mike Abercrombie, Lorrie Trussell, and all the other good people at DevelopMentor who keep the company afloat on a day-to-day basis.

A very special thanks goes to Don Box. (Don is our technological forefather and lead mentor at DevelopMentor.) Don, I can say that I have learned every significant aspect of COM programming from you either directly or indirectly. Thanks for writing the foreword to my book. Thanks for your outstanding quality assurance checks on so many of my chapters. And finally, thanks for coaching me in my writing style by teaching me that sentences should never be written passively and that a preposition is a terrible thing to end a sentence with.

Many others at DevelopMentor deserve special acknowledgment. Thanks to Martin Gudgin, Keith Brown, Jason Masterman, Brian Randell, and Tim Ewald for reviewing chapters, finding bugs, and making excellent suggestions. I'd like to express my gratitude to all the other instructors at DevelopMentor who have taught me so much, including Chris Sells, Fritz Onion, George Shepherd, Joe Hummel, Brian Meso, Brent Rector, Calvin Caldwell, Ken Getz, Ron Sumida, Brad Needham, Andrew Harrison, Mark Taparauskas and, of course, Fred Wesley. And one more thing—while I must share credit with this entire crew, I'd like to point out that any technical inaccuracies in this manuscript are mine and mine alone.

I would like to thank Mitch Argon and the people at QuickStart Technologies for giving me my first job, where I was paid to learn how I could make businesses more productive and competitive through the use of computer technology. It was nirvana getting my hands on the original beta for Microsoft Access four months before version 1.0 shipped in the early 90s. I enjoyed my time at QuickStart, and I learned a lot by working with motivated and talented individuals like Marc Huynen, Matt Chamberlain, and Ryan Reed. The three years I spent there started me out on the path I am following today.

I would like to thank everyone at the Moore Literary Agency for their support and assistance. Thanks especially to Claire Horne for helping me create and shop the proposal for this book. I appreciate her hard work, and I have always been impressed by the knowledge and experience she has in her field.

Thanks to Joshua Trupin of *MIND* and Joseph Flanigen of *Microsoft Systems Journal* for publishing my articles. I'd also like to thank the other people at these excellent publications who helped me get my words into print, including Joanne Steinhart, Terry Dorsey, Joan Levinson, Laura Euler, and Eric Maffei.

Thanks to Jim Fawcette and everyone I have worked with at Fawcette Technical Publications. Thanks to Lee The and the other people who edited my articles for *VBPJ*. I'd also like to thank all the hardworking people who put the VBITs conferences together, including Tena Carter, Timothy Haight, Ann ODonnell, Janet Brandt, Daryl Haggard, and Robert Scoble.

So many folks at Microsoft deserve my thanks as well. At the risk of alienating myself from the entire UNIX community, I would like to give one big broadcast thanks to everyone at Microsoft who has ever given me or anyone else at DevelopMentor technical assistance, beta software, and the all-important inside scoop. In particular, I would like to thank Carolyn Duffy, Sean Alexander, Chris Flores, Rajiv Saxena, Bill Vaughn, and John Roskill on the Microsoft Visual Basic team. I would also like to thank Ben Willet, Sara Williams, Brian Staples, and Frank Redmond III.

I am very appreciative of Microsoft Press for helping me put this book together. This includes my original acquisitions editor, David Clark; my current acquisitions editor, Ben Ryan; and a very talented editing and production team. Many thanks to Kathleen Atkins, for doing an excellent job as lead editor and project manager. I was also very lucky to have Ina Chang as the manuscript editor, Shawn Peck as the copy editor, and Donnie Cameron as the technical editor. I hope to work with all of them again in the future.

Finally, I would like to recognize my favorite technical writers in the industry by listing the books that have influenced the way I look at COM and software development. I'd like to thank them all for their contributions to the collective literature on which every Windows developer depends. These are the books I found myself picking up time after time as I wrote this manuscript. I can highly recommend these books to anyone involved in building distributed applications with Visual Basic and C++.

Doing Objects in Microsoft Visual Basic 5.0
    Deborah Kurata

Design Patterns: Elements of Reusable Object-Oriented Software
    Erich Gamma, Richard Helm, Ralph Johnson, John Vlissides, Grady Booth

Hitchhiker's Guide to Visual Basic & SQL Server, Sixth Edition
William Vaughn

Inside SQL Server
Ron Soukup

Principles of Transaction Processing
Philip P. Bernstein and Eric Newcomer

Advanced Windows
Jeffrey Richter

Visual Basic Programmer's Guide to the Win32 API
Dan Appleman

Inside OLE
Kraig Brockschmidt

Inside COM
Dale Rogerson

Understanding ActiveX and OLE
David Chappell

Essential COM
Don Box

Effective COM
Don Box, Keith Brown, Tim Ewald, Chris Sells

Introduction

Any developer who wants to create LAN-based, WAN-based, and Web-based applications using Microsoft Windows NT Server as a foundation must use many separate pieces of software. Some of these pieces will be supplied by Microsoft, and you or your company will write other pieces. Still other pieces can come from third-party software vendors. Component Object Model (COM) is the glue that binds all of these pieces together. It enables programmers and companies to distribute and reuse their code efficiently. The more you know about COM, the easier it will be for you to put these systems together.

THE PURPOSE OF THIS BOOK

I believe that COM is the most important thing that a Microsoft Windows programmer can learn. Whether you're creating a desktop application that relies on ActiveX controls or an MTS application that runs business objects in an N-tier architecture, COM ties it all together. Whatever programming language or languages you're using, understanding COM is a prerequisite. However, learning about COM isn't easy. Just ask anybody who's taken the time to really get up to speed.

The creators of COM claim that they made it as simple as possible and no simpler. For a programmer with an IQ of 184 and a ponytail, who spends 14 hours a day writing software, COM might seem simple. To the rest of us, COM looks like several challenging high-level concepts and thousands of grungy details. People who learned COM using C++ in the early days speak of the six months of fog they walked through in search of the light. Microsoft Visual Basic has whittled down the required details from thousands to merely hundreds, but as you read through this book, you'll find that every time you peel back another layer of COM, another daunting level of complexity appears.

The early days of COM are now fondly remembered as the days of pain and suffering. The brave developers who became productive in COM between 1993 and 1995 had to hack their way to productivity by studying the few available resources. Only the most hardcore C++ programmers became COM-literate by reading and re-reading the COM Specification and Kraig Brockschmidt's *Inside OLE*. Today several development tools and frameworks enable you to benefit from COM without having to ride the intense learning curve that was required only a few years ago.

A thriving community of C++ programmers now eats, breathes, and sleeps the way of COM. Some C++ programmers write COM code by hand, while others use a productivity framework such as the Active Template Library. You can find excellent books, such as *Essential COM* by Don Box and *Inside COM* by Dale Rogerson, which explain the critical aspects of COM that you need to understand to be productive.

LEARNING COM FROM THE VISUAL BASIC PERSPECTIVE

I started my trek through COM in the spring of 1995, when resources about COM for Visual Basic programmers didn't exist. Everything I read and studied about COM was written by C++ programmers for C++ programmers. I had to learn C++ just to learn COM. Fortunately, I became associated with a talented group of computer scientists at DevelopMentor who were willing to teach me about COM and C++ at the same time.

While learning C++ was profoundly important to my understanding of COM, it seemed odd to me that there were no COM resources for the non-C++ crowd. C++ takes a long time to learn. It's an intimidating mixture of assembly language and advanced object-oriented syntax. Learning C++ seemed like a fairly unrealistic requirement for Visual Basic programmers who wanted to learn about COM. After all, if Microsoft wanted to preach COM as a language-independent technology, the rest of us needed better resources. This was my primary motivation for writing this book.

WHO THIS BOOK IS FOR

This book is for intermediate and advanced Visual Basic programmers who want to learn about COM. Many programmers create distributed applications using Microsoft Transaction Server (MTS) and Microsoft Message Queue (MSMQ), and many of them want to use Visual Basic instead of C++. These programmers need to understand how COM ties everything together. They also need to know how to create components that are both efficient and extensible.

This book is also for programmers who are interested in the interoperability between Visual Basic and C++ and who need to make Visual Basic components and C++ components talk to one another. I have provided C++/COM programmers with enough information about the way Visual Basic deals with COM to allow them to peacefully coexist in an environment with Visual Basic programmers.

From the time Microsoft engineers started working on the ideas behind COM in 1988 until COM first shipped in a product in 1993, COM went through quite an evolution. In this book, I'll trace this evolution and describe key decisions that the COM architects made along the way. You'll see that many low-level details, such as the way C++ compilers work and the way the remote procedure call (RPC) transport moves packets across the network, have a significant impact on the way you create distributed applications with Visual Basic. To understand why COM was designed the way it was, you must look at many of these details and think long and hard about them.

These details are essential for readers who are interested in Visual Basic/C++ interoperability as well as for those who care only about Visual Basic but still want to create distributed applications that are efficient and extensible.

Many Visual Basic programmers don't have the motivation or aptitude to learn about COM at this level. Visual Basic can extend a modest amount of COM functionality to these programmers without their needing any knowledge of the underlying technology, but they won't be able to create large information systems with MTS and MSMQ. This book is most definitely not for them.

What Background Do You Need?

I'll assume that you have some background with object-oriented programming and creating applications that use classes. It doesn't matter whether you learned about classes using Visual Basic, C++, or Java. It's just important that you understand why you would design a class using encapsulation and that you understand the relationship between a class and an object.

Most readers of this book will have some background in database programming. It's hard to imagine that an intermediate Visual Basic programmer could have gotten by without being involved in at least one database-oriented application. When I describe writing transactions for MTS objects, I'll assume that you have a moderate comfort level with ActiveX Data Objects (ADO) and writing SQL statements. If you don't have this background, you should acquire it on your own. The ADO code and the SQL presented in this book are not overly complicated. For those of you who already know Data Access Objects (DAO) or Remote Data Objects (RDO), the online help for ADO will probably be all you need. Those of you who need additional help can find many other excellent resources on these topics.

It's helpful but not essential that you have some background in computer science or a low-level language such as C. It would be impossible for me to tell you about COM without talking about things such as pointers, memory addresses, stack frames, and threads. If you don't have this background, please take the time to contemplate what's going on at a lower level. Occasionally your temples might begin to throb. But the time and effort you invest will be more than worthwhile.

WHAT'S ON THE CD?

The CD included with this book contains the source code for several Visual Basic applications. These applications contain working examples of the code I use throughout this book. As a Visual Basic programmer, I've always felt that my understanding was boosted by hitting the F5 key and single-stepping through an application line by line. I'd like you to have the same opportunity. The Samples.htm file will give you a synopsis of all the applications and what they do.

The Setup directory on the CD contains the files and instructions for setting up the SQL Server database that you need to run the Market application. The Setup.htm file can walk you through the steps. Any other applications that have additional setup instructions will have a Setup.htm file in their directory. I hope you find these sample applications valuable.

UPDATES AND OTHER INFORMATION

In my work as an instructor and a writer, I'm continually improving and creating new Visual Basic applications that relate to COM and MTS programming. You're free to download the most recent collection of samples from my Web site, *http://www.sublimnl.com*. At this site, you'll also find other information relating to this book, including a listing of any bugs and inaccuracies. If you'd like to send me feedback, mail it to me at *tedp@sublimnl.com*. I hope you enjoy this book.

Chapter 1

An Overview of Distributed COM

This chapter briefly describes what the Component Object Model (COM) is, where COM came from, and why you need to understand this technology to work in a distributed Windows NT environment. It introduces COM as both a distributed technology and a programming discipline through which you can write extensible, object-oriented software based on plug-compatible components. This chapter also describes the limitations of systems built using a two-tier architecture and explains the advantages of introducing a layer of business objects between user applications and data access code. In addition, this chapter explains how Microsoft server-side components, such as Microsoft Transaction Server (MTS), Microsoft Message Queue Server (MSMQ), Internet Information Server (IIS), and Active Server Pages (ASP), fit into the big picture of developing distributed N-tier applications.

WHAT IS COM?

The term *COM* means many different things to many different people. On the one hand, the *Component Object Model* is a specification for writing reusable software that runs in component-based systems. On the other hand, COM can be thought of as a sophisticated infrastructure that allows clients and objects to communicate across process and host computer boundaries. Many developers who are already COM-savvy see it as a new programming style and a set of disciplines required to work in a Microsoft-centric environment. Business managers and system designers see COM as technology that's solving many of the problems the industry has experienced in maintaining and extending large information systems. COM is all of these things and more.

COM is a model based on binary reuse. This means that software (components) adhering to COM can be reused without any dependencies on source code. Developers can ship their work as binary files without revealing their proprietary algorithms. The reuse of code in a binary form also eliminates many compile-time problems that occur when systems are assembled according to a development style based on source code reuse. Binary reuse makes it far easier to incorporate small changes into a system. For instance, a minor bug fix or a performance modification can be made to a dynamic link library (DLL). The DLL can then be recompiled and replaced in the field without adversely affecting any of the client applications that use it. Systems based on source code reuse must typically recompile every line of code in the entire application. This requirement makes maintaining and extending software cumbersome and expensive.

The principles of binary reuse allow you to construct COM-based applications using language-independent components. When several teams are building components for a single system, each team can choose its programming language independently. Today's list of COM-enabled languages includes C++, Visual Basic, Java, Delphi, and even COBOL. Each team can select a language that matches its programming expertise and that gives it the best mix of flexibility, performance, and productivity. For instance, if one team requires low-level systems code, it can use C++ for the flexibility of the language. Another team writing and extending business logic for the same application can elect to use Visual Basic for its high levels of productivity. The ability to mix and match languages makes it easier for companies to make the best possible use of their existing pools of programming talent.

COM is based on object-oriented programming (OOP). This means that COM is a story about clients communicating with objects. COM exploits the OOP paradigm to achieve higher levels of reuse than is possible with other models of binary reuse. COM clients and COM classes typically live in separate binary files, as shown in Figure 1-1. COM specifies an infrastructure that enables clients to bind to objects at run time.

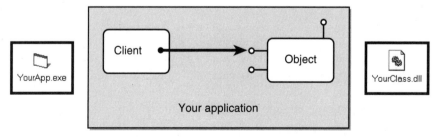

Figure 1-1. *Object-oriented binary code reuse is one of COM's primary reasons for being.*

COM is *interprocess-capable*. This means that clients can create objects in separate processes and on remote computers. Thus COM serves as core technology in Microsoft's strategy for distributed computing. While both OOP and distributed programming have existed for well over a decade, the synergy of the two has produced a powerful new programming paradigm. It has never been easier to write a distributed application.

Why Use Visual Basic with COM?

Of all the COM-enabled development tools on the market, Visual Basic offers the highest levels of productivity. Visual Basic 3 and Visual Basic 4 both offered modest advancements in the product's COM-awareness, but Visual Basic 5 really opened the door to make this development tool a viable option for building components for use in COM-based systems. Visual Basic 6 continues to add to the COM capabilities of this development tool.

Take a moment to consider the following questions. What is your perception of Visual Basic? Does it provide a viable option for writing the code to be used in a large information system? Why are you reading this book? Respond to the following questions by choosing Visual Basic, C++, or Structured Query Language (SQL):

- Which language is the easiest for writing business logic?
- Which language offers the lowest cost of code maintenance?
- Which language offers the fastest means to enhance an existing application?
- Which is the best language for people without a classic computer science background?

Many designers and project leads answer these questions quickly by saying, "Visual Basic." Visual Basic is in no way a cure-all language. In many cases, C++ or some other language would be a better choice for a specific component. For instance, many system-level COM interfaces can be readily accessed only through C++, which means that some components should be written with C++. However, companies have many opportunities to use Visual Basic in a distributed application. One of the greatest opportunities for Visual Basic today is writing business logic and data access code for distributed objects in the middle tier of a large information system.

Component-Based Development

Before component-based technologies such as COM were available, large applications were built by sending hundreds or possibly thousands of source files together to a compiler in a single batch job to build one executable file. This development style, with its production of *monolithic applications,* poses many problems. It requires huge executables and long build times. Furthermore, to take advantage of a modification to a single line of source code, the entire application must be rebuilt. This makes it increasingly difficult to coordinate the various programming teams working together on a large application. Maintaining and enhancing a monolithic application is awkward at best.

Component-based development solves many of the problems associated with monolithic applications. It allows development teams to ship binary files as opposed to source code. Binary components can be updated independently and replaced in the field, making it much easier to maintain and extend an application after it's been put into production. Most people agree that using COM or some other component-based technology is an absolute requirement in the development of a large information system.

Software development for the Windows operating system has always been based on binary reuse. DLLs such as the Win32 API allow a Windows programmer to re-use functions through a C-style call-level interface. Many companies and third-party vendors have also written reusable DLLs for Windows applications using the same technique. However, these C-style DLLs typically don't offer any object-oriented extensions. Standard Windows DLLs are also very difficult to use from higher-level languages such as Visual Basic. Developers at Microsoft knew they needed a technique to facilitate binary reuse with an object-oriented paradigm.

COM was built from the ground up to be object-oriented. It's based on clients, classes, and objects. Classes are defined in binary files called *servers.* These servers make it possible for clients to create and connect to objects whose code lives in a separate binary file. Figure 1-1 shows the basic relationship between a client and an object served up from a DLL. The beauty of COM is that this model makes it possible for a client to use a class that's defined inside a separate binary file. This, as you will see, is no simple undertaking.

After a client connects to an object, it simply invokes method calls as in any other OOP environment. COM fully supports the object-oriented concepts of *encapsulation* and *polymorphism* as means to achieve code reuse. COM, however, doesn't support a form of inheritance known as *implementation inheritance.* In later chapters, I describe exactly what you lose and what you don't lose with the omission from COM technology of this popular OOP feature.

If code reuse in COM were limited to in-process DLLs, clients would have no way to communicate with objects running in another process or running on another machine. Out-of-process communications would require programmers to use some interprocess communications mechanism such as dynamic data exchange (DDE) or named pipes. Fortunately, COM supports remote method calls across process boundaries. Figure 1-2 shows the relationship between a client and an out-of-process server.

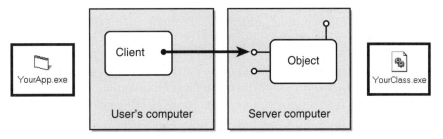

Figure 1-2. *COM has the ability to extend client-object communications across process and host boundaries.*

Notice that the client code and the object code are actually running in different processes on different machines. COM takes care of establishing an efficient and reliable communications channel between these two parties.

As you'll see, COM not only takes care of many grungy plumbing details in an efficient and reliable manner but does so in a way that's transparent to programmers. COM programming for both clients and objects is the same whether you're dealing with an in-process server or an out-of-process server. This incredibly powerful feature of COM is known as *location transparency*. All the complicated work of preparing, sending, and receiving network packets is taken care of by the distributed infrastructure of COM. The more you learn about COM, the more you will appreciate this fact.

Interface-Based Programming

Today COM is language independent, but many of the original COM design decisions were made to achieve object-oriented binary reuse in a C++ environment. The most profound decision made by Microsoft engineers is that COM needed to formalize the separation of interface from implementation. This means that COM is founded on the idea of *interface-based programming.*

The concept of interface-based programming wasn't a clever new idea thought of by Microsoft engineers. Instead, it was a programming style that had already been recognized by the academic community of computer science and by organizations that needed to build large, extensible information systems. Interface-based programming was pioneered in languages such as C++ and Smalltalk that have no formal support for the concept of a distinct, stand-alone interface. Today languages and tools such as Java and Visual Basic have built-in support for this style of programming. So while Microsoft can't be given credit for the idea, it should definitely be given credit for seeing the elegance of interface-based programming and using it as the cornerstone of COM.

An interface, like a class, is a distinct data type. It defines a set of public methods without including any implementation. In another sense, an interface defines a very specific protocol for the communications that occur between a client and an object. The act of decoupling the interface from the class or classes that implement it gives COM developers the freedom to do many things that would otherwise be impossible. A developer designing a client application against an interface can avoid creating dependencies on class definitions. This allows for an environment in which several different types of compatible objects can be used in a plug-compatible way. This promotes what is arguably the most powerful feature of OOP: *polymorphism*.

Interfaces are also the key to COM's ability to send remote method calls across host boundaries. Programmers never need to worry about which platforms or network protocols are involved. It's all taken care of behind the scenes. This condition points to one of the most enlightened observations about COM: *Interfaces are the key to seamless object distribution.*

What About OLE and ActiveX?

The first time COM showed up in a released product was with OLE2 in 1993. OLE1 was based on DDE and was generally unusable in production code for a variety of reasons. Microsoft decided to redesign OLE using an internally-developed protocol for interprocess communications. This new component technology was devised by a group of engineers that had been assembled from various internal development teams at Microsoft.

Today it's safe to say that COM is more significant than OLE, although it's equally safe to say that it's hard to define what OLE and ActiveX really mean. They are umbrella terms for a set of technologies that are based on COM. All these acronyms are confusing because people often say "OLE" or "ActiveX" when they really mean "COM." Much of the early documentation was too relaxed when it used these acronyms. Moreover, the marketing people at Microsoft made things more confusing when they attempted to change OLE from an acronym into a word. After that didn't catch on, they decided to come up with ActiveX, a new, sexier term for the Internet.

It's not just the marketing people who have contributed to the confusion in the terminology. It goes right to the heart of COM itself. For example, the main DLL that exposes COM's core library of functions is named OLE32.dll. Even in the Visual Basic integrated development environment (IDE), when you want to create a new COM DLL or a COM EXE you must select ActiveX DLL or ActiveX EXE as your project type. In the early days, Microsoft was slow to bring the term *COM* out of the closet. Things have changed. Now people are beginning to use *COM* correctly in more writings and product documentation, but you still expect some degree of confusion. This book will use the term *COM* correctly and use those other terms only when absolutely necessary.

Distributed COM

From the beginning, COM was designed to extend process boundaries. The earlier releases of COM made this possible only when the client process and the server process were running on a single computer. With the release of Microsoft Windows NT 4, support was added to COM that allowed this interprocess communication to extend computer boundaries. This new wire protocol made it possible to deploy distributed objects in a networked environment as depicted in Figure 1-2. This was a significant milestone in Microsoft's strategy for enterprise computing.

At first, Microsoft struggled to get a marketing term to signify that COM could finally be used in a distributed system. *DCOM* won out over *Network OLE* when Windows NT 4 was first shipped in August 1995. Today, however, neither of these terms is in style. *Distributed COM* is currently the proper term to use when talking about the remoting facilities of COM, although some COM developers think that COM itself is a distributed technology and that the word *Distributed* in front of COM is redundant.

COM's distributed capabilities are based on an interprocess mechanism known as *Remote Procedure Call* (RPC). RPC is an industry standard that has matured on many different platforms. Microsoft's implementation is known as MS-RPC. Together COM and RPC have a symbiotic relationship. COM offers RPC an object-oriented feel. RPC offers COM the ability to serve up distributed objects. I'll explain in later chapters how COM leverages RPC to transparently send request and response packets between clients and objects. All the while, clients still invoke methods as usual, as if the objects were very close at hand.

Distributed COM introduces several new requirements that aren't issues when a client and an object run on the same computer. First, Distributed COM must provide an infrastructure for remote object creation and activation. A client must be able to create and use objects that run on computers down the hall or across the country. And with these distributed objects also comes a pressing need for security. COM and Windows NT must provide a robust security layer so that all access to a remote server process is authenticated and authorized. Chapter 8 addresses how these two important requirements are met.

THE MOVE FROM TWO-TIER TO N-TIER ARCHITECTURE

One of the best reasons, these days, for using Distributed COM is to assist companies who are moving their information systems from a two-tier architecture to an N-tier architecture. This transition requires the design and creation of a middle tier of *business objects*. These business objects are placed between client applications and database servers. Distributed COM can serve as the foundation for these types of systems. Before examining the requirements of an N-tier architecture, let's look at two-tier systems and their strengths and limitations.

Figure 1-3 shows the layout of a typical two-tier information system. It's currently the most common architecture for applications built on multiuser database systems. Client applications connect directly to a *database management system* (DBMS), such as ORACLE or Microsoft SQL Server. Each client computer requires a vendor-specific library, such as an ODBC driver for ORACLE or SQL Server. Client applications are typically required to log on to the DBMS independently and maintain an exclusive connection. The client application is then responsible for preparing and sending SQL statements directly to a server. The client is also responsible for dealing with messages, errors, and streams of data returned by the database engine.

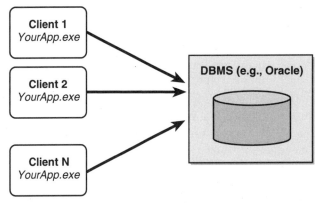

Figure 1-3. *Typical two-tier applications require each user to acquire a direct connection to a database server.*

In a two-tier system, the client application commonly maintains some or all of the application's business logic. Whenever the business logic changes, the client application must be rebuilt and redistributed to all the client desktops. This can be a fairly painful undertaking, and as a result, a fairly pressing need usually has to be present to justify the distribution of a new version. As soon as a company puts two or more client applications into production, the odds are very high that redundant code for the same business logic will spread across several applications. This creates problems with both the maintenance and the consistency of a company's business logic. These two problems are common weaknesses of a two-tier system.

Two-tier systems have benefited from the introduction of *stored procedures*. Stored procedures are routines written in a vendor-specific dialect of SQL that allow business logic and data access logic to be stored and run on the database server. All popular client/server DBMSs offer one form of stored procedures or another.

Figure 1-4 demonstrates how this logic can be shared across several client applications. Business logic can be maintained centrally by a database server. Client applications call these stored procedures by name. This makes it easy to maintain business logic simply by rebuilding stored procedures. Client applications don't care whether they are rebuilt as long as the names of the stored procedures remain the same.

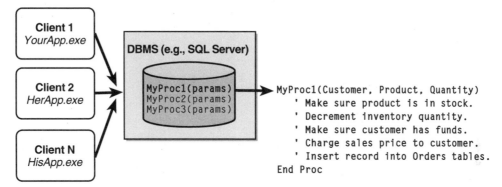

Figure 1-4. *Stored procedures give programmers a way to centralize business logic in a two-tier application.*

Stored procedures also offer improvements in performance and scalability. The SQL code in a stored procedure is parsed and normalized when it's created by a developer. Stored procedures are also optimized and saved in native machine language. When a stored procedure is called, it's all ready to go. For these reasons, it's much faster to call a stored procedure than to submit a raw SQL statement that must undergo all these steps at every single execution. The performance gains that you can attribute to the use of stored procedures are significant. Database systems can usually accommodate a client base twice the size simply by using stored procedures instead of raw SQL.

A two-tier architecture is at its best in an information system that employs a single data source. Unfortunately, the performance gains and centralization of business logic within stored procedures are usually unattainable when the system's data is spread across multiple servers. SQL Server does have *remote stored procedures,* but this feature works only when every database server uses SQL Server as its DBMS. In systems with heterogeneous data sources, a two-tier architecture begins to quickly break down, as you can see in Figure 1-5 on the following page.

Two-tier systems have been widely deployed in the industry, and consequently, the problems associated with them are very well known. Most problems arise under two circumstances: The data is being accessed by multiple client applications, and the system's data is stored across multiple database servers.

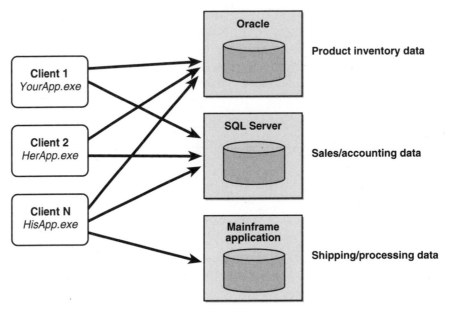

Figure 1-5. *Two-tier applications are very costly to create, maintain, and extend when data is stored in multiple, heterogeneous data sources.*

Here's a summary of the most frequently recurring problems that make a two-tier architecture hard to work with:

■ Changing business logic requires the rebuilding of client applications.

■ Changing database schema, data location, or connection information requires the rebuilding of client applications.

■ Rebuilding client applications requires costly redistribution to client desktops.

■ Database drivers must be installed and configured on the client desktops.

■ Centralized business logic in stored procedures must be written in SQL.

■ The existence of multiple DBMS's makes it difficult to maintain logic in stored procedures.

These problems of a two-tier architecture can be solved like many other problems in computer science. The answer is to add a layer of indirection. The introduction of a set of business objects can serve to decouple client applications from data access code, as shown in Figure 1-6.

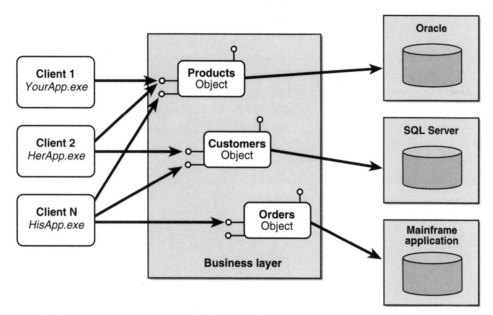

Figure 1-6. *Introducing a middle tier of business objects eliminates costly dependencies between client applications and database servers.*

Business objects are like stored procedures in that they allow you to centralize your logic and reuse it across several client applications. Unlike stored procedures, business objects make it easy to access data across several data sources, even when these data sources are of heterogeneous formats. Furthermore, these business objects can be written in languages such as Visual Basic, C++, and Java, which offer many advantages over writing and maintaining the same logic in a vendor-specific dialect of SQL.

In Windows NT–based networks, these business objects can be deployed using COM as the foundation. COM can serve as the basis for communications between the client applications and the middle-tier objects. This means that computers running the client applications need only to be COM-aware. They don't require desktop database drivers as they do in the two-tier model.

Another advantage is that COM allows a middle-tier programmer to update these business objects without requiring a recompilation and redistribution of client applications. This makes it very easy to change an application's business logic or data access code because the client applications are completely shielded from the system's infrastructure. A system's data can change storage formats, and new database servers can be brought on line painlessly. The necessary modifications are made in the middle tier, allowing client applications to remain in production unaltered.

One of the first questions that usually comes to mind is, "Where should each of these layers be deployed?" Figure 1-7 on the following page illustrates two possible scenarios for deployment. Three tiers don't always mean three computers. In a small deployment, the business code and the database server might run on the same computer. In a larger system, the data can be kept in one or more dedicated database servers while the business objects run on a separate host. Some deployment schemes offer greater scalability, reliability, and fault tolerance than others. When people speak of three-tier systems, they're speaking of three distinct *logical* levels. The physical deployment can vary and can be easily changed after a system is put into production. The location transparency afforded by COM makes it possible to make these deployment changes with few or no changes to application code.

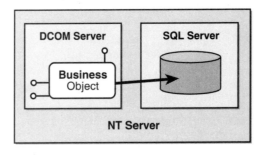

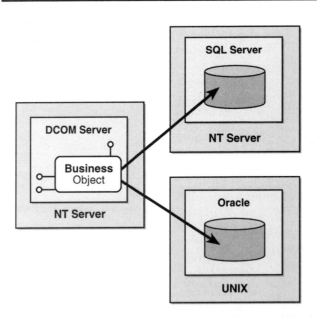

Figure 1-7. *The mapping between business objects and the data access layer can start simple and become more complex later without affecting client applications.*

Some people use the term *three-tier,* while others prefer the term *N-tier.* The term *N-tier* simply means a system has at least three tiers. Figure 1-8 shows a more complex set of physical layers. In the N-tier model, the business and data access tiers can be arbitrarily complex. The best part about this model is that the client application knows only about the business tier. All the additional complexity going on behind a visible set of business objects doesn't concern a client application. The primary design goal in a N-tier system, therefore, is to hide as much of this complexity as possible from the client applications that make up the presentation layer.

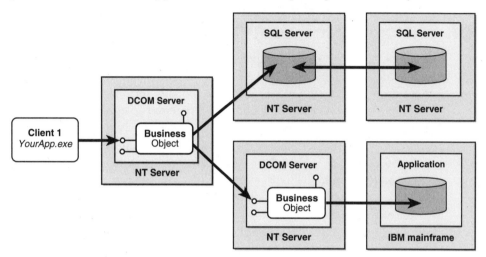

Figure 1-8. *One of the greatest strengths of an N-tier architecture is that it hides the complexity and evolution of an enterprise's Information Systems (IS) infrastructure.*

Three-Tier Costs and Benefits

Before jumping off the deep end and abandoning your existing two-tier system, you should understand the costs of designing and deploying a three-tier system. Up front, such costs include those of designing and writing code for a set of objects that model your business processes, which frequently isn't a trivial undertaking. Second, a distributed application requires lots of infrastructure support. In your old two-tier system, you had a powerful DBMS such as ORACLE or SQL Server to manage connections, pool threads, monitor transactions, and perform a host of other services that are incredibly important to system throughput and scalability. Who will be responsible for all that work in an N-tier system?

A middle-tier application running a set of business objects must provide a similar set of services. Scalable N-tier systems require sophisticated frameworks to supply these services. The cost of putting together a distributed framework might not be warranted if a two-tier system is adequate. In particular, a smaller system with a single database server and one or two client applications might be better off staying with a two-tier model.

The obvious benefit of a three-tier system is that once it is put in place, it's far easier to maintain and extend. For large and complex systems that deploy many client applications or data sources, the initial investment is recouped quickly. Future client applications can be written against a preexisting set of business objects. Database servers can be changed or brought on line with minimal impact. And most important, business logic can be modified quickly and at a much lower cost.

DISTRIBUTED DEVELOPMENT ON WINDOWS NT SERVER

The previous section of this chapter examined the costs and benefits of an N-tier design. One of the costs is in developing a sophisticated framework to handle the requirements of a distributed application. Industry reports have shown that most successful N-tier systems in production have required a large investment to put such a framework in place. These reports show companies typically spend around 40 percent of their programming efforts on the infrastructure for a distributed system. That leaves only 60 percent of their investment for writing domain-specific code, such as business logic and data access code.

Microsoft saw the disproportionate amount of money that was being spent on infrastructure in these distributed systems. It realized that companies wanted to spend more time writing business logic and less time writing complex code to take on issues such as connection management, thread pooling, and transaction monitoring. Microsoft's entire enterprise strategy is based on the assumption that companies would rather have someone else create the pieces of this essential distributed application framework.

Microsoft is building a COM-based infrastructure for creating distributed N-tier applications with Windows NT Server. Quite a few of its pieces are already in place, and many more are expected over the next few years. In the last part of 1998 and through 1999, you'll see the transition from COM to COM+. One of the biggest motives for the development of COM+ is to provide programmers all the necessary infrastructure components they need for building a distributed application.

COM+ infrastructure components will, of course, be accessible to programmers through COM. This plan builds on COM strengths, such as OOP, component-based development, and language independence. COM makes it practical to assemble systems composed of Microsoft's components and yours.

The release of the Windows NT 4 Option Pack in December 1997 was a big milestone for distributed development. In many ways it represented the first phase of COM+. The Windows NT 4 Option Pack contained the initial release of MSMQ as well as improved integration among MTS, IIS, and ASP. This has made it possible for developers to build applications that take advantage of the connection management, thread pooling, transaction monitoring, message passing, and Web integration that are built into the infrastructure of Windows NT Server.

Projected additions to COM+ are other features that would be valuable in distributed application design, such as an event service and the automatic clustering of servers for fail-over support. Microsoft is also working hard to define the roles and responsibilities of each of these components and services with greater clarity. Some components might move from one service to another, and other components and services as yet unannounced will be added. Microsoft is pioneering this idea of creating a multipurpose distributed infrastructure, so you must expect some areas of COM+ to be in a continual state of flux. A few existing components in COM will continue to be center stage in COM+.

What Is MTS?

MTS stands for *Microsoft Transaction Server.* As the name implies, MTS is the piece of software that allows applications to use a transaction monitor in the middle tier of a distributed application. However, MTS is much more than a transaction monitor; it provides Microsoft's newest run-time environment for COM objects. Distributed objects can run in the MTS environment whether or not they're involved in transactions. The name *MTS* confuses people when they learn it can be used to deploy nontransactional objects.

This naming confusion exists because MTS has been the vehicle that Microsoft has used to ship the first generation of its distributed application framework. MTS programmers benefit from automatic support for practices such as connection management, thread pooling, and security. In the future, many of the MTS elements will be considered part of the generic COM+ shell as opposed to being part of MTS. Fortunately, these changes won't affect the way you create and deploy MTS applications.

MTS provides a distributed run-time environment in which you can run your business objects by launching a surrogate process on the server and loading user-defined objects from DLLs. Figure 1-9 on the following page shows the relationship between the client applications and MTS objects running on NT Server. These middle-tier objects can be created using any COM-enabled language, such as Visual Basic, C++, or Java. As a Visual Basic programmer, you're required to create ActiveX DLLs and install them in the MTS environment to deploy your business objects.

MTS is a platform for building *online transaction processing (OLTP)* systems. Your business objects access data in various data sources such as a DBMS from across the network. The transaction monitor built into MTS makes it easy for you to define a transaction across multiple data sources. MTS uses *declarative transactions,* which hide proprietary transaction APIs from MTS programmers. As you'll see in later chapters, MTS makes writing transactions far easier than writing explicit transactions using ODBC, ActiveX Data Objects (ADO), or Transact SQL.

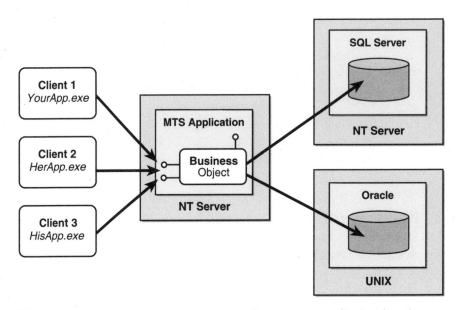

Figure 1-9. *MTS allows you to run business objects in Microsoft's distributed run-time environment.*

What Is MSMQ?

Another powerful component to assist in building distributed applications is *Microsoft Message Queue* (MSMQ). MSMQ is a middleware product that enables asynchronous communications between applications. This means that client applications can send messages to a server even when the server isn't running. It also means that the server can receive messages after the client application has gone away. In environments in which client applications and servers can become disconnected for any number of reasons, this capability allows the distributed application as a whole to stay up and running.

MSMQ is based on the asynchronous delivery of messages to named queues. It's a very sophisticated product that can be integrated into distributed applications, including those based on MTS. Messages model procedure calls between a client and a server except that either party can do its work in the absence of the other. For instance, in a sales order application a client could submit several orders to the queue even when the server application wasn't running. At some time later when the server was started, the server could open the queue and retrieve all the order requests that were submitted by any client. MSMQ also makes it possible to return a message receipt to the caller as if it were the response to a method call.

MSMQ also contributes to an application's scalability. As the traffic in a distributed application increases, the managers of the system need to add more computers to increase the throughput of the entire system. To make use of any additional hardware, the system must somehow distribute client requests across all the available servers. This act of using as many of the available processing cycles as possible is known as *load balancing*. A queue facilitates load balancing because a client doesn't send a request to a specific server. The queue is a single repository that holds all incoming requests. A group of servers monitors the queue and splits up the workload as it arrives.

MSMQ will continue to be a big part of COM+. Visual Basic programmers can access MSMQ services through a set of COM interfaces. MSMQ integration with MTS makes it possible for a business object to retrieve a message from a queue inside a declarative transaction. If something goes wrong during the transaction, the message is left in the queue. This means that MSMQ can ensure that all messages eventually reach their destination. MSMQ also provides advanced features that address routing efficiency, security, and priority-based messaging.

Web-Based Development

Web servers are becoming increasingly popular as a platform for building information systems. Several key benefits accrue to a company when it moves toward an HTML-based environment. First, HTML is currently the best way to create a cross-platform application. Second, applications built around a standard Web browser significantly reduce desktop configuration and deployment costs. Finally, Web-based systems can be used to reach a much larger audience than is possible with typical LAN/WAN-based architecture. In a Web-based application, all a user needs is a browser, an Internet connection, and a valid IP address.

Until recently most Web sites have only been able to participate in data publishing. Today companies are beginning to see the advantages of implementing true OLTP systems through standard Web browsers. Using IIS and ASP, you can create Web-based OLTP systems based on COM and MTS. Figure 1-10 on the following page shows how all the pieces fit together. Web applications built using this architecture can exploit the strengths of one particular browser, such as Microsoft Internet Explorer, in an intranet-style environment. Other applications can use a pure-HTML approach that can serve a larger, Internet-style, user base.

Visual Basic 6 has added a new enhancement to the IDE called the *IIS Application Designer* (IISAD). The IISAD makes it easy for programmers to write their server-side logic in Visual Basic code instead of using VBScript or JavaScript in an ASP application. When a Web client makes a request, an application built using the IISAD responds to the request just like any other Web application. The difference is that the request will execute code you have written in Visual Basic. When you use the IISAD, you'll still program against the same set of ASP objects. The IISAD has also provided an easy way for you to stream HTML back to the client. As with ASP applications, the IISAD makes it possible to build a pure-HTML solution that leverages the MTS business objects you have running in the middle tier.

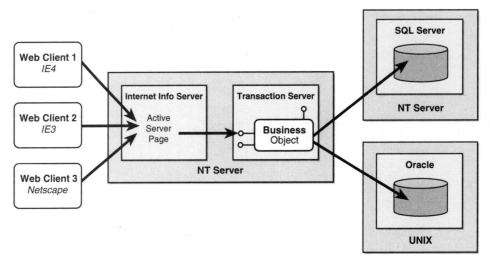

Figure 1-10. *The integration between MTS and IIS allows Web clients to run MTS objects through browser-independent HTML.*

HOW DO YOU GET UP TO SPEED AND STAY AFLOAT?

As you can see, you're expected to know a mountain of information. You should start by getting a solid understanding of COM: how it works and why. Everything that Microsoft is working on is based on COM. Lots of things will start falling into place once you understand how this technology puts everything together.

You must expect the landscape of COM and COM+ to be always changing. Keeping yourself up to speed on the technology can be daunting, but try to be optimistic and see these changes as a necessary and positive part of an evolutionary process. The good news is that the core aspects of COM won't change. These are the parts of COM that allow programmers to achieve higher levels of reusability, maintainability, and extensibility. Once you understand these core aspects, you will be prepared for whatever else comes your way.

Chapter 2

Understanding Interface-Based Programming

Getting a grasp of interface-based programming is really tough. To gain an appreciation for this style of programming, you must leave behind old habits and intuitions about writing code and look back at the evolution of object-oriented programming (OOP) and computer science over the past decade—a Darwinian saga of how the interface has made modern software designs more fit for survival. For software to survive in the ever changing jungle of the production environment, it must have three distinct characteristics: *reusability, maintainability,* and *extensibility.* This chapter provides a general overview of interface-based programming and examines these characteristics.

COM is founded on the idea of interface-based programming, a style of programming in which the interface is separate from implementation. (COM has no meaning without the concept of the interface. Interfaces, on the other hand, can exist outside the world of COM.) Interface-based programming was pioneered in languages such as C++ and Smalltalk by software engineers who discovered that using distinct interfaces could make their software, especially large applications, easier to maintain and extend. (The creators of Java saw the elegance of interface-based programming and consequently built support for it directly into their language.)

Interfaces solve many problems associated with code reuse in object-oriented programming. This chapter investigates some of these problems. In particular, when you program in a style consistent with classic OOP, a client can build inflexible dependencies on a class definition. These dependencies can make it difficult to maintain or extend the class without breaking the client. It becomes tedious or impossible to improve the code for an object over time. Certain problems are also associated with a popular OOP language feature known as *implementation inheritance*. This powerful but often misused feature is vulnerable to similar dependency problems, which compromise an application's maintainability and extensibility. Even though Visual Basic doesn't support implementation inheritance, this chapter describes its strengths and limitations in order to address some of the problems that interface-based programming was created to solve.

Visual Basic 5.0 added support for defining and implementing user-defined interfaces. This chapter shows you how to use interfaces in a Visual Basic application. After covering the basics of using interfaces, it demonstrates how to achieve *polymorphism* and *run-time type inspection,* which make interface-based programming powerful.

CLASSES, OBJECTS, AND CLIENTS

Your first stop on the road to interface awareness must be an examination of the problems that interface-based programming is meant to solve. Many of these problems have to do with the relationship between a class and the clients that use it. Think about the following questions: What is the relationship between a client and a class definition? What must a client know about a class in order to benefit from using it? What dependencies are created in the client when a programmer writes code using a class's methods and properties?

In an object-oriented paradigm, a client typically instantiates an object from a class. The client usually creates the object by using the *New* operator followed by the class name. After creating the object, the client uses it by accessing an exposed set of properties and methods through a variable that is a *class-based reference*. Here's a simple example that uses a variable based on a class type to access an object's public members:

```
Dim Dog As CDog
Set Dog = New CDog
'*** Access a property.
Dog.Name = "Snoopy"
'*** Invoke a method.
Dog.Bark
```

In this example, a class-based reference makes it possible to instantiate and communicate with a dog object. The communication between the client and the object takes place through a set of publicly accessible properties and methods that are known as an object's *public interface*. The class author must use the public interface to expose the object's functionality to the client. This is what makes an object useful. Note that the method names and property names from the public interface are hardcoded into the client. Future versions of the class must continue to supply these members in order to honor the dependencies built into the client.

One benefit of using classes is that they allow you to reuse code. Once a class has been written, you can use it in many different places in an application. Classes thus let you reduce or eliminate redundant code in an application. They also facilitate code maintenance. You can modify or remove any properties or methods that aren't publicly visible. You can also change public method implementations as long as the calling syntax of the methods isn't altered. When the implementation of a method in a class is improved, any client that uses the class will seamlessly benefit from the changes.

When you modify an existing class definition, you shouldn't change the calling syntax for accessing any public method or property because of the risk of breaking the dependencies that client code has built on the original class definition. As long as you hold the public interface constant, you can make any modifications to improve your class without breaking any client code.

To rephrase the key point of the last paragraph: Once you publish a property or a method signature in a class's public interface, you can't change or remove it. This means that you must properly design the public interface at the beginning of a project and use discipline as the class evolves. This lets you improve and extend object code without having to rewrite any client code. You can maintain a class by fixing bugs and improving method implementations.

The rules for maintaining existing members of the public interface are cut-and-dried, but what flexibility do you have when you add new functionality to a class? What can you do to safely extend an object in later versions? It's easy and safe to add new public methods and properties to a class. Old clients continue to run as before, even though they can't take advantage of the object's new functionality. However, new clients written after the class has been modified can take advantage of any members added to the public interface. This means you can improve an object safely over time in the production environment.

Problems arise in class design when you change the signature of a public method in a way that breaks an existing client. This commonly happens when you discover that the initial class design was inadequate. For instance, imagine a method that provides the behavior for a dog rolling over. The following *RollOver* method is defined with a 16-bit integer parameter to allow the client to request a specific number of rolls in each invocation.

```
' Method defined in CDog class.
Public Sub RollOver(ByRef Rolls As Integer)
    ' Implementation code goes here.
End Sub

' Client hardcodes calling syntax.
Dim Dog As CDog, Rolls As Integer
Set Dog = New CDog
Rolls = 20000
Dog.RollOver Rolls
```

What if the requirements of a dog object change weren't anticipated properly in the initial design? For instance, what if the required number of rolls exceeds the highest possible value for an integer (about 32 KB)? What if a client wants to invoke the method with the value 50,000? To accommodate a larger value, you must change the parameter type to a long integer. This creates quite a design problem. The newer clients want a 32-bit integer, but older clients, such as the one shown above, already have a dependency on the 16-bit integer.

You have only two options. One is to modify the method signature and then rewrite all the client code that calls it. The other is to leave things as they are and deal with the limitations of the original design. As you can see, poor class design results in either broken clients or nonextensible objects.

The intuitive solution to this problem is to make sure that the design of the class's public interface is full-featured and finalized before you write client code against it. But this isn't always possible, even for the most experienced class designer. If a class models a real-world entity that never changes, an experienced designer can create a robust, long-lasting design. However, in many cases it's impossible to predict how external changes will affect the requirements for an object's public interface. A designer who is creating classes for an application that is expected to run for years in a rapidly changing business environment can't possibly predict what is needed. If the business model is constantly changing, your classes must change with it. Therein lies the need for extensible objects.

The use of *class-based references* results in a layer of dependencies between clients and classes. You can lessen the impact of these dependencies on maintainability and extensibility through disciplined design and by anticipating future requirements. Don't define a method or a property in the public interface unless you're prepared to live with it forever. Most experienced designers make all data properties private and provide access to an object's state through public methods. This prevents any client dependencies on the actual data layout of the class. Be conscientious about which methods you mark as public. Any member you mark as private can be changed or removed as the class implementation evolves. Of course, you have to make some members public, or the class will be useless. Designing with class-based references always involves these trade-offs.

IMPLEMENTATION INHERITANCE

Many of the features of OOP are meant to give programmers higher levels of code reuse. Languages such as C++, Smalltalk, and Java offer a popular feature known as *implementation inheritance,* which offers one of many possible ways to achieve code reuse in an object-oriented paradigm. Some people argue that a language must offer implementation inheritance to be considered a real object-oriented language. This has led to a heated debate in both the software industry and the academic community—a debate that this book will not address. Instead, we will focus on the benefits and problems associated with this powerful feature.

In implementation inheritance, one class is defined to reuse the code of another class. The class that is reused is called the *superclass*. The class that benefits from the reuse is the *subclass*. Visual Basic doesn't currently support implementation inheritance, so I will use a Java example to illustrate what implementation inheritance looks like. Examine the following Java class *CDog*:

```
// superclass
class CDog
{
    // dog state
    public String Name;

    // dog behavior
    public void Bark()
        {/* method implementation */}
    public void RollOver(int Rolls)
        {/* method implementation */}
}
```

The class *CDog* contains a property and two methods. Assume that each method has been defined with a valuable implementation. You can reuse the state and the behavior of the class by using implementation inheritance. *CDog* will be used as a superclass. A subclass that extends *CDog* will inherit both the class properties and the method implementations. The following Java code shows the syntax required to achieve implementation inheritance:

```
// subclass
class CBeagle extends CDog
{
    // beagle state
    // Name property is inherited.
    // A color property is added.
    Public String Color;
```

(continued)

```
// beagle behavior
// Implementation of RollOver() is inherited.
// Implementation of Bark() is overridden.
public void Bark()
     {/* CBeagle-specific implementation */}
// CBeagle extends CDog by adding a new method.
public void FetchSlippers()
     {/* CBeagle-specific implementation */}
}
```

When *CBeagle* (the subclass) extends *CDog* (the superclass), it inherits all of the existing properties and method implementations. This means that *CBeagle* can reuse all of the state and behavior defined in *CDog*. You can then extend *CDog* by overriding existing methods such as *Bark* and adding methods such as *FetchSlippers* in CBeagle. You can also add new properties to the subclass definition.

You should use implementation inheritance only when a logical "is a" relationship exists between the subclass and the superclass. In this example, you can say, "A beagle is a dog," as shown in Figure 2-1. As long as the "is a" requirement is met, implementation inheritance is useful for achieving code reuse. Implementation inheritance can be especially valuable when an application contains many classes that must exhibit a common behavior. The commonality of several classes can be hoisted to a superclass. For example, once the *CDog* class has been written, it can be extended by *CBeagle*, *CTerrier*, *CBoxer*, and any other class that "is a" dog. Code written to define state and behavior in the *CDog* class can be reused in many other classes.

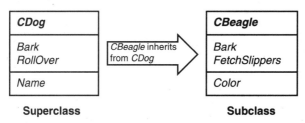

Figure 2-1. *Implementation inheritance allows one class to reuse the state and the behavior of another.*

Figure 2-2 is a graphic representation of what is known as an *inheritance hierarchy*. The hierarchy shows the relationships among the various classes in the application. This hierarchy is simple; you can create others that are far more complex. Imagine a hierarchy in which *CScottie* extends *CTerrier*, which extends *CDog*, which extends *CMammal*, which extends *CAnimal*. As you can imagine, inheritance hierarchies can become large and complex. Hierarchies containing five or more levels aren't uncommon in production code.

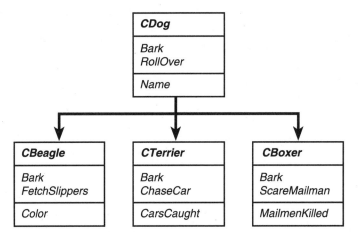

Figure 2-2. *An inheritance hierarchy shows the relationships between the superclasses and the subclasses in an application.*

When implementation inheritance is used correctly, it can be a powerful mechanism for code maintenance. When you improve the implementation of a method in a superclass, all the classes down the inheritance hierarchy automatically benefit from the changes. A bug fix to the *CAnimal* class can potentially improve hundreds of other classes. As the inheritance hierarchy becomes larger and more complex, modifications to classes at the top can have a significant impact on many classes below. This implies that a single modification can affect the behavior of many distinct object types.

What Is Polymorphism?

So far, this chapter has explained how implementation inheritance offers the implicit reuse of method implementations, which results in greater maintainability through the elimination of duplicate code. Another powerful OOP feature provided by implementation inheritance is known as *polymorphism*. This is arguably the most important concept in object-oriented programming. Polymorphism allows a client to treat different objects in the same way, even if they were created from different classes and exhibit different behaviors.

You can use implementation inheritance to achieve polymorphism in languages such as C++ and Java. For instance, you can use a superclass reference to connect to and invoke methods on subclass instances. Figure 2-3 on the following page shows how a client can use a *CDog* reference to communicate with three different types of objects. Each subclass that derives from *CDog* is type-compatible with a *CDog* reference. Therefore, a client can use a *CDog* reference when communicating with objects of type *CBeagle*, *CRetriever*, or *CBoxer*.

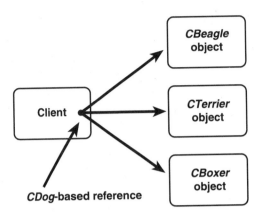

Figure 2-3. *You can achieve polymorphism by using a superclass reference to communicate with subclass instances. A client can use a* CDog *reference to communicate with any* CDog-*compatible object.*

A client can be sure that any class that extends the *CDog* class provides an implementation of the *Bark* method. The client doesn't care if the subclass uses the definition of *Bark* that was supplied by *CDog* or if the subclass has overridden this method with its own implementation. The client simply invokes the method using the calling syntax defined in the *CDog* class. However, if each subclass supplies its own implementation of *Bark*, each object type can respond in its own unique way to the same request. Examine the following Java code:

```
// Method accepts any CDog-compatible object.
Public void MakeDogBark(CDog Dog)
{
    // Different objects can respond differently.
    Dog.Bark()
}
```

If this method is invoked using a *CBeagle* object, it might have very different results than if it is invoked using a *CTerrier* object. The client code knows which method to call, but it has no idea how the *Bark* method will be carried out. The calling syntax is well defined at compile time, but the actual method implementation is not determined until run time. Polymorphism is based on the idea of *dynamic binding* as opposed to static binding. Dynamic binding provides a degree of controlled uncertainty that makes polymorphism extremely powerful. You can create applications based on *plug-compatible* objects. If thousands of lines of client code have been written to *CDog*'s public interface, you can easily replace a *CBeagle* object with a *CTerrier* object or a *CBoxer* object. Such a change has little or no impact on client code because client code has dependencies on the *CDog* class but not on any of the classes that extend it.

Problems Associated with Implementation Inheritance

So far, this chapter has explored the two biggest benefits of implementation inheritance: the implicit reuse of method implementations and polymorphism. It has not yet covered some of the potential problems with implementation inheritance. Unfortunately, implementation inheritance makes an application more susceptible to the kinds of dependency problems associated with class-based references because of the tight coupling between a subclass and its superclass.

With the proper use of encapsulation, you can hide implementation details from clients. This allows you to freely change the implementation details of the class without breaking client code. The problem with implementation inheritance is that it breaks the encapsulation of nonpublic members. Languages that offer implementation inheritance provide a *protected* level of visibility in addition to public and private. Properties and methods that are marked as protected are hidden from a client but are accessible from subclasses. Subclasses therefore have access to implementation details that have been hidden from the client. As you hardcode the names of protected properties and methods of a superclass into a subclass, another layer of inflexible dependencies is created.

Implementation inheritance is an example of a development style known as *white-box reuse*. Applications that are built on white-box reuse often experience tight coupling between the classes in the inheritance hierarchy. Once a subclass uses a protected property or method, you can't change the superclass's signature or remove it without breaking dependencies built into subclasses. This leads to fragility in applications with large inheritance hierarchies. Changing the classes at the top of the hierarchy often requires modifications to many subclasses. In some applications, changing a method signature or a property type at the top of the hierarchy can result in breaking tens or hundreds of classes down the inheritance chain. On the other hand, freezing the public and protected interfaces of key superclasses usually results in a system that can't evolve.

As in the case of simple class design, you must carefully consider whether to give a property or a method protected visibility. Proper design using implementation inheritance requires a high level of expertise and discipline to prevent what is known as the *fragile superclass scenario*. You should know whether a class will be extended by other subclasses. If you expect a class to be extended, it's as important to encapsulate implementation details from subclasses as it is to encapsulate them from clients.

This isn't to suggest that implementation inheritance isn't useful. It's powerful in appropriate development scenarios. It's best used in smaller, controlled situations. Creating a large inheritance hierarchy that can evolve along with the requirements of an application is beyond the reach of all but the most experienced object-oriented designers.

When C++ and Smalltalk were first introduced, the OOP evangelists oversold implementation inheritance as a cure-all technique to achieve code reuse. As a result, this feature has been abused by designers who haven't understood the coupling problems that accompany white-box reuse. Over the past decade, the casual use of implementation inheritance has crippled the evolution of many large systems. Experienced developers who knew that implementation inheritance was most appropriate in small doses continued to look for more flexible ways to achieve reuse on a large scale. In particular, they looked for ways to achieve reuse without compromising extensibility in larger systems. This fueled the birth of interface-based programming and a development style known as *object composition*.

SEPARATING THE INTERFACE FROM THE IMPLEMENTATION

Object composition offers another way to achieve reuse without the tendency toward tight coupling. Object composition is based on *black-box reuse,* in which implementation details of a class are never revealed to the client. Clients know only about an available set of requests. Objects never expose internal details of the response.

Black-box reuse is based on formal separation of interface and implementation. This means that the interface becomes a first-class citizen. An interface is an independent data type that is defined on its own. This is an evolution of classic OOP, in which a public interface is defined within the context of a class definition.

At this point, you are probably thinking that this is all pretty vague. You're asking yourself, "What exactly is an interface?" Unfortunately, it's hard to provide a concise definition that conveys the key concepts of an entirely new way to write software. An interface can be described in many ways. You can get up to speed pretty quickly on the syntax for defining, implementing, and using interfaces. However, the ramifications of interfaces for software design are much harder for the average programmer to embrace. Learning how to design with interfaces usually takes months or years.

At its most basic level, *an interface is a set of public method signatures*. It defines the calling syntax for a set of logically related client requests. However, while an interface defines method signatures, it can't include any implementation or data properties. By providing a layer of indirection, an interface decouples a class from the clients that use it. This means that an interface must be implemented by one or more classes in order to be useful. Once an interface has been implemented by a class, a client can create an object from the class and communicate with it through an interface reference.

You can use an interface to create an object reference but not the object itself. This makes sense because an object requires data properties and method implementations that cannot be supplied by an interface. Because it isn't a creatable entity, *an interface is an abstract data type*. Objects can be instantiated only from creatable classes known as *concrete data types*.

From a design standpoint, *an interface is a contract*. A class that implements an interface guarantees that the objects it serves up will support a certain type of behavior. More specifically, a class must supply an implementation for each method defined by the interface. When communicating with an object through an interface reference, a client can be sure that the object will supply a reasonable response to each method defined in the interface.

More than one class can implement the same interface. An interface defines the exact calling syntax and the loose semantics for each method. The loose semantics give each class author some freedom in determining the appropriate object behavior for each method. For instance, if the *IDog* interface defines a method named *Bark*, different class authors can supply different responses to the same request as long as each somehow reinforces the concept of a dog barking. The *CBeagle* class can implement *Bark* in a way that's different from either *CTerrier* or *CBoxer*. This means that *interfaces provide the opportunity for polymorphism*. Interfaces are like implementation inheritance in that they let you build applications composed of plug-compatible objects. But interfaces provide plug compatibility without the risk of the tight coupling that can occur with implementation inheritance and white-box reuse.

The Two Faces of Inheritance

Inheritance is an objected-oriented concept that models an "is a" relationship between two entities. So far, this chapter has used the term *implementation inheritance* instead of the more generic term *inheritance* because extending a superclass with a subclass is only one way to leverage an "is a" relationship. When a class implements an interface, it also takes advantage of an "is a" relationship. For instance, if a class *CBeagle* implements the interface *IDog*, it is correct to say that a beagle "is a" dog. You can use a *CBeagle* object in any situation in which an *IDog*-compatible object is required.

Interface-based programming is founded on a second form of inheritance known as *interface inheritance*. This means that inheritance doesn't require the reuse of method implementations. Instead, the only true requirement for inheritance is that a subclass instance be compatible with the base type that's being inherited. The base type that's inherited can be a class or a user-defined interface. In either situation, you can use the base-type references to communicate with objects of many different types. This allows both forms of inheritance to achieve polymorphism.

Both implementation inheritance and interface inheritance offer polymorphism, but they differ greatly when it comes to their use of encapsulation. Implementation inheritance is based on white-box reuse. It allows a subclass to know intimate details of the classes it extends. This allows a subclass to experience implicit reuse of a superclass's method implementation and data properties. Implementation inheritance is far more powerful than interface inheritance in terms of reusing state and behavior. However, this reuse comes with a cost. The loss of encapsulation in white-box reuse limits its scalability in large designs.

As the term *black-box reuse* suggests, interface inheritance enforces the concepts of encapsulation. Strict adherence to the encapsulation of implementation details within classes allows for more scalable application designs. Interface-based programming solves many problems associated with white-box reuse. However, to appreciate this style of programming, you must accept the idea that the benefits are greater than the costs. This is a struggle for many programmers.

When a class implements an interface, it takes on the obligation to provide a set of methods. Subclass authors must write additional code whenever they decide to implement an interface. When you compare this with implementation inheritance, it seems like much more work. When you inherit from a class, most of your work is already done, but when you inherit from an interface, your work has just begun. At first glance, implementation inheritance looks and smells like a cheeseburger, while interface inheritance looks like a bowl of steamed broccoli. You have to get beyond the desire to have the cheeseburger to reach a higher level of interface awareness. The key advantage of interface inheritance over implementation inheritance is that interface inheritance isn't vulnerable to the tight coupling that compromises the extensibility of an application.

Using Interfaces with Visual Basic

Visual Basic 5.0 was the first version of the product to support user-defined interfaces. You can achieve the benefits of interface-based programming with a Visual Basic project by following these three required steps:

1. Define an interface.

2. Implement the interface in one or more creatable classes.

3. Use an interface reference in a client to communicate with objects.

As you can see, the basic steps for adding interfaces to your applications are pretty easy. Using interfaces also lets you add polymorphism to your application designs. We'll use a simple example to demonstrate the Visual Basic syntax required to complete these steps.

You define a custom interface in Visual Basic by using a regular class module. It would be better if the Visual Basic IDE were to provide a separate editor for defining interfaces, but unfortunately an editor dedicated to creating interfaces isn't currently available. You use the class module editor to create both interface definitions and classes.

To define a new interface, you simply add a new class module to an existing project. Then you give it an appropriate name. If you're creating an interface to express the behavior of a dog, a suitable name might be *IDog* or *itfDog*. These are the two most common naming conventions among Visual Basic developers. If you're working in a Visual Basic project that's either an ActiveX DLL or an ActiveX EXE, you should also set the class module's instancing property to *PublicNotCreatable*. This setting makes sense because the interface will represent an abstract data type. In a Standard EXE project, class modules don't have an instancing property.

You define your interface by creating the calling syntax for a set of public methods. Don't include an implementation for any of the methods in your interface. You need only define the signatures, nothing more. In essence, you define *how* the client calls these methods, not *what* will happen. Here's an example of the *IDog* interface defined in a Visual Basic class module:

```
' Interface IDog
' expresses behavior of a dog object.

Public Property Get Name() As String
End Property

Public Property Let Name(ByVal Value As String)
End Property

Public Sub Bark()
End Sub

Public Sub RollOver(ByRef Rolls As Integer)
End Sub
```

One of the first things you notice when declaring an interface in Visual Basic is the presence of *End Sub*, *End Function*, or *End Property* after each method signature. This makes no sense. The keyword *End* usually signifies the end of a method implementation. This is a confusing idiosyncrasy of the Visual Basic IDE and an unfortunate side effect of using the Visual Basic class module for defining both classes and interfaces. Perhaps a future version of Visual Basic will provide a module type dedicated to defining interfaces that won't require *End Sub*, *End Function*, or *End Property*, but for now you just have to grin and bear it.

Another important point is that this interface can use logical properties in addition to methods. This is reasonable when you consider that a logical property is actually a set of methods, not a data property. The client can use the logical property *Name* defined in the interface above just like a regular data property, but it must be implemented in terms of a *Property Let/Property Get* method pair.

Stop and think about this: Why can't an interface contain data members? Because an interface, unlike a class, is never used to create objects. Its mission is to encapsulate a class's implementation details. The data layout of an object is among the most important details to encapsulate within a class definition. If an interface were to contain actual data members, the client would build dependencies on them. You know by this point that dependencies are bad.

Even though interfaces can't contain data properties, Visual Basic still lets you define a property in an interface, like this:

```
Public Name As String
```

However, when you define a data property in an interface, Visual Basic transparently redefines the data property as a logical property. This is simply a convenience that Visual Basic provides when you create interfaces. The *Name* property defined above still requires *Property Let* and *Property Get* in any class that implements the interface. Also note that implementing an interface has no effect on the data layout for a class definition. Any class that implements this interface should include a private data property for the physical storage of the dog's name.

After you create the interface definition, the next step is to create a concrete class that implements it. Add a second class module to your project, and give it an appropriate name. For instance, you can create a concrete class *CBeagle* that implements the *IDog* interface. You must use the keyword *Implements* at the top of a class module. This is what the statement looks like:

```
Implements IDog
```

Once a class module contains this line, every method and logical property in the interface must have an associated implementation in the class module. This requirement will be checked by Visual Basic's compiler. You can't compile your code without supplying every implementation. For instance, implementing the *Bark* method in the *IDog* interface requires this definition:

```
Private Sub IDog_Bark()
    ' Implementation code goes here.
End Sub
```

Visual Basic's mapping of interfaces requires each method implementation to use the name of the interface followed by an underscore and the method name. Visual Basic uses this proprietary syntax to create an entry point into an object when a particular interface is used. The Visual Basic compiler requires you to supply a similar implementation for each method and logical property in the interface. This guarantees that objects created from the class will provide an entry point for each interface member.

Fortunately, the Visual Basic IDE makes it easy to create the procedure stubs for the method implementations if you use the keyword *Implements* at the top of the class module. The class module's editor window has a *wizard bar* that includes two drop-down combo boxes. If you select the name of the interface in the left combo box, you can quickly generate the skeletons for the method implementations by selecting the method names in the right combo box. An example of using the wizard bar is shown in Figure 2-4. Here's a partial implementation of the *CBeagle* class that implements the *IDog* interface:

```
Implements IDog
Private Name As String

Private Property Let IDog_Name(ByVal Value As String)
    Name = Value
End Property

Private Property Get IDog_Name() As String
    IDog_Name = Name
End Property

Private Sub IDog_Bark()
    ' Implementation code goes here.
End Sub

Private Sub IDog_RollOver(ByRef Rolls As Integer)
    ' Implementation code goes here.
End Sub
```

Figure 2-4. *The wizard bar makes it easy to create the procedure stubs for implementing a user-defined interface.*

The wizard bar generates method implementations that are marked as private. This means that these method implementations aren't available to clients that use a *CBeagle* reference. They're available only to clients that use an *IDog* reference. The code above also demonstrates how the *CBeagle* class can implement the logical *Name* property by defining a private data property and implementing the *Property Let* and *Property Get* methods.

Now that you have created an interface and a class that implements it, you can use the interface to communicate with an object. For instance, a client can communicate with a *CBeagle* object through an *IDog* reference. You can use the *IDog* reference to invoke any method that the interface exposes. Here's a simple example.

```
Dim Dog As IDog
Set Dog = New CBeagle
' Access object through interface reference.
Dog.Name = "Spot"
Dog.Bark
Dog.RollOver 12
```

Once the client is connected to the object through the interface reference, it can invoke methods and access logical properties. The Visual Basic IDE provides the same IntelliSense, type checking, and debugging that are available when you use class-based references. Note that you can't use an interface after the *New* operator. An interface isn't a creatable type. You must use a concrete class such as *CBeagle* to create an object when you use the *New* operator.

Why Use Interfaces?

When Visual Basic programmers learn how to use interfaces in an application, they often wonder, "Why would I ever want to do that?" or, "Why should I care?" Programming with class-based references seems far more natural compared with the additional complexity required with user-defined interfaces. The previous example would have been far easier if the client code had programmed against a *CBeagle* class instead of the *IDog* interface. User-defined interfaces seem like extra work without any tangible benefits.

There are several significant reasons why a Visual Basic/COM programmer should care about interfaces. The first reason is that interfaces are the foundation of COM. In COM, clients can't use class-based references. Instead, they must access COM objects through interface references. As you'll see in later chapters, Visual Basic can do a pretty good job of hiding the complexities of this requirement. When you use a class-based reference, Visual Basic generates a default COM interface for the class behind the scenes. This means that you can work in Visual Basic without ever having to deal with user-defined interfaces explicitly. However, if you embrace interface-based programming, you will become a much stronger COM programmer.

Another reason you should care about interfaces is that they can offer power and flexibility in software designs. Using user-defined interfaces in Visual Basic becomes valuable when you don't have a one-to-one mapping between a class and a public interface. There are two common scenarios. In one scenario, you create an interface and implement it in multiple classes. In the other scenario, you implement multiple interfaces in a single class. Both techniques offer advantages over application designs in which clients are restricted to using references based on concrete classes. While interface-based designs often require more complexity, the sky is the limit when it comes to what you can do with them.

Consider a case in which many classes implement the same interface. For example, assume that the classes *CBeagle*, *CTerrier*, and *CBoxer* all implement the interface *IDog*. An application can maintain a collection of *IDog*-compatible objects using the following code:

```
Dim Dog1 As IDog, Dog2 As IDog, Dog3 As IDog
' Create and initialize dogs.
Set Dog1 = New CBeagle
Dog1.Name = "Mo"
Set Dog2 = New CTerrier
Dog2.Name = "Larry"
Set Dog3 = New CBoxer
Dog3.Name = "Curly"
' Add dogs to a collection.
Dim Dogs As New Collection
Dogs.Add Dog1
Dogs.Add Dog2
Dogs.Add Dog3
```

The application can achieve polymorphic behavior by treating all of the *IDog*-compatible objects in the same manner. The following code demonstrates enumerating through the collection and invoking the *Bark* method on each object:

```
Dim Dog As IDog
For Each Dog In Dogs
    Dog.Bark
Next Dog
```

As the application evolves, this collection can be modified to hold any mix of *IDog*-compatible objects, including objects created from *CBeagle*, *CTerrier*, *CBoxer*, and any other future class that is written to implement the *IDog* interface. The *For Each* loop in the previous example is written in terms of the *IDog* interface and has no dependencies on any concrete class. You don't have to modify the loop when you introduce new concrete class types into the application.

Another powerful design technique is to have a single class implement multiple interfaces. If you do this, you'll have objects that support multiple interfaces and therefore multiple behaviors. When used together with run-time type inspection, this becomes very powerful. Assume that the sample application adds another interface, *IWonderDog*, with the following method:

```
Sub FetchSlippers()
End Sub
```

Assume that the *CBeagle* class implements *IWonderDog* but that the *CTerrier* class doesn't. A client can inspect an object at run time and ask whether it supports a specific interface. If the object does support the interface, the client can call upon its functionality. If the object doesn't support the interface, the client can degrade gracefully. The following code demonstrates using the Visual Basic *TypeOf* syntax to test for *IWonderDog* support.

```
Dim Dog1 As IDog, Dog2 As IDog

Set Dog1 = New CBeagle
Set Dog2 = New CTerrier

If TypeOf Dog1 Is IWonderDog Then
    Dim WonderDog1 As IWonderDog
    Set WonderDog1 = Dog1
    WonderDog1.FetchSlippers
End If

If TypeOf Dog2 Is IWonderDog Then
    Dim WonderDog2 As IWonderDog
    Set WonderDog2 = Dog2
    WonderDog2.FetchSlippers
End If
```

When the client queries the *CBeagle* object, it finds that it's *IWonderDog*-compatible. In other words, the object supports the *IWonderDog* interface. The client can then create an *IWonderDog* reference and assign the *CBeagle* object to it by casting the *IDog* reference with the *Set* statement. Once the client has an *IWonderDog* reference, it can successfully call *FetchSlippers*. Note that there are two references but only one object. When you have multiple interfaces, code in the client becomes more complex because it takes several references to a single object to get at all the functionality.

When the *CTerrier* object is queried for *IWonderDog* compatibility, the client discovers that the interface isn't supported. This condition allows the client to degrade gracefully. Client code can enumerate through a collection of *IDog*-compatible objects and safely call *FetchSlippers* on each object that supports the *IWonderDog* interface, like this:

```
Dim Dog As IDog, WonderDog As IWonderDog
For Each Dog In Dogs
    If TypeOf Dog Is IWonderDog Then
        Set WonderDog = Dog
        WonderDog.FetchSlippers
    End If
Next Dog
```

As you can imagine, this ability to determine the functionality of an object at run time is very useful when you improve an application. If a later version of the *CBoxer* class implements the *IWonderDog* interface, the *For Each* loop shown above can take advantage of that without being rewritten. Client code can anticipate supported functionality in future versions of the object.

Extending an Object

The example above showed how to use an object that supports more than one interface. You can also employ user-defined interfaces to safely extend the behavior of an object when an existing set of method signatures has become too limiting. For instance, the *IDog* interface defines the *RollOver* method as follows:

```
Public Sub RollOver(ByRef Rolls As Integer)
End Sub
```

If you need to extend the functionality of dog objects in the application so that clients can pass larger integer values, you can create a second interface named *IDog2*. Assume that the *IDog2* interface defines the same members as *IDog* with the exception of the *RollOver* method, which is defined like this:

```
Public Sub RollOver(ByRef Rolls As Long)
End Sub
```

A new client can test to see whether an *IDog* object supports the new behavior. If the new behavior isn't supported, the client can simply fall back on the older behavior. Here's an example of how this works:

```
Sub ExerciseDog(Dog As IDog)
    If TypeOf Dog Is IDog2 Then
        ' Use new behavior if supported.
        Dim Dog2 As IDog2, lRolls As Long
        Set Dog2 = Dog
        lRolls = 50000
        Dog2.RollOver lRolls
    Else
        ' Use older behavior if necessary.
        Dim iRolls As Integer
        iRolls = 20000
        Dog.RollOver iRolls
    End If
End Sub
```

The key observation to make about this versioning scheme is that you can introduce new clients and new objects into an application without breaking older clients and older objects. A new object can accommodate older clients by continuing to support the interfaces from earlier versions. New clients deal with older objects by using the older interface when required. In a world without interfaces, extending objects often requires modifying all the clients. Modifying clients often requires modifying all the objects. The versioning scheme made possible by interface-based programming allows you to make small changes to an application with little or no impact on code that's already in production.

USING INTERFACES IN YOUR APPLICATION DESIGNS

This chapter has presented a simple application to demonstrate the core concepts of interface-based programming. How can you apply these principles in a real-world application? If you're designing a large application that uses customer objects, you can create a user-defined interface *ICustomer* and start writing lots of client code against the interface instead of to a concrete *CCustomer* class. If you create several classes that implement the *ICustomer* interface, you can achieve the plug-and-play benefits of polymorphism. Different types of customer objects exhibit different behavior, but they're all controlled through the same interface.

From a versioning standpoint, this design lets you improve the behavior of various customer objects by introducing new interfaces into the application. Interfaces such as *ICustomer2*, *ICustomer3*, and *ICustomer4* let you safely extend the behavior of customer objects. The best part about this approach is that you can revise clients and objects independently. Older clients and objects can use earlier interfaces, while newer clients and objects can communicate through newer interfaces. All of this is made possible through the run-time type inspection of interface support.

Interfaces and COM

The industry has adopted interface-based programming because of the limitations of other common techniques, such as the use of class-based references and implementation inheritance. User-defined interfaces bring a new level of complexity to both application design and programming, but their value is easy to measure in large applications. In a Darwinian sense, interface-based programming makes software more fit for survival. Interfaces make your code easier to reuse, maintain, and extend.

The next chapter presents the internals of COM. As you'll see, COM is based on the following core concepts of interface-based programming:

- *COM requires a formal separation of interface and implementation*—that is, it requires that clients communicate with objects exclusively through interface references. This ensures that clients never build dependencies on the classes that serve up objects, which in turn allows COM programmers to revise their object code without worrying about breaking client code.

- *COM clients can get run-time type information from objects*. A COM client can always query an object and ask whether it supports a specific interface. If the requested interface isn't supported, the client can discover this and degrade gracefully. This lets programmers revise components and applications independently. Older clients and older objects can work in harmony with newer clients and newer objects. Herein lies the key to versioning in COM.

This chapter showed the use of interfaces in a single application. The entire application was written in a single language, and all the source code was sent to a compiler at the same time. COM, on the other hand, must work across binary components. Moreover, COM clients and COM objects can be written in different languages and can run in different processes on different computers. COM must solve many problems at the physical level to achieve the benefits of interface-based programming.

Chapter 3

Exploring COM Internals

This chapter examines the COM architecture to show how things work at the physical level. It explains Microsoft's motivation for creating COM and its original design goals. It also explains the problems with C++ and binary encapsulation that motivated Microsoft engineers to create a standard for the physical layout of all COM interfaces. As you'll see, COM connects clients to objects using the principles of interface-based programming. This chapter explains how COM achieves language independence. Microsoft Visual Basic, for example, can map to COM by providing support in the compiler and a run-time mapping layer.

In COM, the code written for clients and the code that defines classes often live in separate binary files. COM clients can't see class definitions, but they still need to create objects. But how can a client application create an object if its server doesn't expose a visible class definition? COM provides an infrastructure in which clients can create and connect to objects without ever seeing the concrete class. This chapter explains the COM services and design requirements that make object activation possible.

THE BIRTH OF COM

The seed for COM was planted in 1988, when several different teams at Microsoft began to build object-oriented infrastructures that provided reuse based on components. When a group of engineers was assembled from various other teams to help out on the OLE2 project, the group decided they needed to draft a few high-level requirements for the new architecture they would be building.

These Microsoft engineers came up with four high-level requirements for their new component architecture. First, the architecture had to be *component-based* because maintaining and enhancing code in large, monolithic applications is difficult. Systems based on binary components are much easier to assemble, maintain, and extend.

Second, the architecture had to be based on the *object-oriented paradigm*. Most of the binary reuse in Windows had been based on traditional DLLs, which don't commonly include object-oriented extensions. This type of binary reuse can't benefit from the encapsulation that can be achieved with a class-based design.

Third, the architecture had to be *language independent*. It would be far more powerful if each component author could select a language independently of other component authors. Every programming language requires programmers to make trade-offs in productivity, flexibility, and performance. The ability to choose a language on a component-by-component basis offers many advantages over having to use a single language for an entire application.

Finally, the architecture had to address *interprocess communication*. It was essential to compose systems of clients and objects that ran on different machines so that the architecture could be a foundation for distributed technologies. The engineers also knew that if they could hide the details of interprocess communication from the majority of programmers, their architecture would foster much higher productivity.

The efforts of these engineers debuted in production code with Microsoft's second major release of Object Linking and Embedding (OLE), a technology that allows users to embed or link documents produced in one type of application in a document of another application. Anyone familiar with Microsoft Windows and Microsoft Office has seen an example of a Microsoft Excel spreadsheet or chart embedded in a Microsoft Word document. OLE allowed Microsoft to promote a document-centric approach to computing rather than the application-centric approach that was most common in business software.

OLE requires interprocess communication among applications. The original version of OLE was based on an interprocess mechanism called Dynamic Data Exchange (DDE). This initial release was plagued with resource and performance problems, which resulted in limited acceptance within the industry. Microsoft knew that OLE's features were valuable conceptually but also that making this technology usable in a production environment would mean optimizing the underlying infrastructure. In essence, OLE needed a whole new plumbing system to be viable.

OLE2 shipped with the first generation of COM in 1993. OLE and COM are distinct entities: OLE is a technology for linking and embedding documents, while COM is an architecture for building component-based systems. Unfortunately, the two are often assumed to be one and the same. Because COM was an essential piece of the OLE2 project, many people use the term *OLE* when they mean *COM*. Just remember that OLE and COM are very different conceptually. And be prepared to deal with the confusion.

INITIAL COM DESIGN REQUIREMENTS

Systems built from binary components offer several advantages over monolithic systems. You can revise and replace individual components in the field without affecting other parts of the system. This development style allows component suppliers to improve and revise their code far more effectively. It also allows reuse of generic components in many applications.

From the beginning, the Windows operating system has been based on the principle of binary code reuse. The Windows API is a call-level interface made up of thousands of functions written in C and assembly language. The Win32 API is available to all applications through a series of operating system DLLs. A client can link to a DLL at run time and call exported functions. Languages such as C, C++, and Visual Basic can link to DLLs as long as they have the definitions of functions and structures from a C header file at compile time. The main limitation of this type of DLL is that it's simply a collection of global functions and data structures that don't contain classes or objects and therefore don't offer an object-oriented solution.

Binary reuse alone wasn't hard to achieve on the Windows platform. However, moving binary reuse into an object-oriented paradigm proved more challenging. C++ was one of the first and most popular object-oriented programming (OOP) languages for Windows developers. It provides support for powerful OOP features that are missing in C, such as encapsulation, polymorphism, and inheritance. Unfortunately, C++ was designed to create monolithic applications and is therefore tricky to use for component-based development.

It's possible to export a C++ class from a DLL, but with many limitations. Most of the problems arise because the ANSI C++ standard defines the requirements only for the compilation process. The original designers of C++ assumed that all of the source code for an application would be compiled and linked at the same time. Therefore, the C++ standard doesn't specify how objects should be laid out in memory. This leads to severe problems in component-based development.

The lack of a binary standard causes compatibility problems among C++ compilers. Compiler vendors such as Microsoft, Symantec, and Borland have implemented C++ features such as exceptions, function overloading, and run-time type information (RTTI) in proprietary ways. This means that using these features creates vendor-specific dependencies among binary components. For instance, you can't throw an exception from a class in a DLL built with the Borland compiler and catch it in a client application built with the Microsoft compiler. The only way to use all of the advanced C++ features in component-based development is to standardize all development on a compiler from a single vendor. This is clearly not an acceptable solution in open software design.

The intuitive solution to this problem is to get rid of all the C++ features that create vendor-specific dependencies. It seems reasonable that if all C++ development is restricted to using a set of C++ features that are compatible across all major compiler vendors, the language can be used for building binary components. This solves some of the problems, but not all of them. There is one remaining problem with C++ that turns out to be the biggest one of all.

The problem is that *C++ doesn't support encapsulation at the binary level* because the language was designed for building monolithic applications. When a C++ class author marks a data member as private, it is off-limits to client code, as you would expect. However, this encapsulation is enforced only in the syntax of the language. Any client that calls *New* on a class must have knowledge of the object's data layout. The client is responsible for allocating the memory in which the object will run. This means that the client must have knowledge of each data member for a class regardless of whether it is marked public, protected, or private.

These layout dependencies aren't a problem in a monolithic application because the client always recompiles against the latest version of the class. But in component-based development, this is a huge problem. The layout of a class within a DLL can't change without breaking all the clients that use it. The following C++ code shows a client and two versions of a class in a DLL.

```
// In SERVER.DLL - Version 1
// Each object will require 8 bytes of memory.
class CDog{
private:
    double Weight;
}


// In CLIENT.EXE
// Compiled against Version 1 of DLL
// Client allocates 8 bytes for object.
CDog* pDog = new CDog;


// In SERVER.DLL - Version 2
// Each object will require 16 bytes of memory.
// Replacing older DLL will break client.
class CDog{
private:
    double Weight;
    double Age;
}
```

When the first version of the DLL is replaced in the field by the second version, a big problem arises. The client application continues to create objects that are 8 bytes in size, but each object thinks that it's 16 bytes. This is a recipe for disaster. The newer version of the object will try to access memory that it doesn't own, and the application will likely fail in strange and mysterious ways. The only way to deal with this is to rebuild all client applications whenever the object's data layout changes. This eliminates one of the biggest benefits of component-based development: the ability to modify one binary file without touching any of the others.

How can you replace the DLL without breaking any of the client applications that use it? The object's data layout must be hidden from the client. The client must also be relieved of the responsibility of calling the C++ *New* operator across a binary firewall. Some other agent outside the client application must take on the responsibility of creating the object. Over the past decade, many C++ programmers have wrestled with the problems of using C++ in component-based development, and the C++ community has devised a few techniques for solving this problem.

One popular technique for solving the binary encapsulation problem is to use a handle-based approach. You can see a great example of this in Windows SDK applications and the Win32 API. The client deals with handles to objects such as windows, files, and device contexts. The client calls a global function to create an object. The client receives an integer identifier, which acts as a logical pointer to an entity such as a window object. The client communicates with the window by calling other global functions in the Win32 API and passing the handle to indicate which window to act on. The operating system responds by performing the desired operation on the window. The downside to this approach is that the client code doesn't have an object-oriented feel. Therefore, it doesn't meet one of the main requirements of COM.

Abstract Base Classes as Interfaces

Another technique for solving the binary encapsulation problem with C++ is the use of *abstract base classes*. In C++, an abstract base class is used to define method signatures that don't include any implementation. (This should sound familiar.) Here's an example of what an abstract base class looks like in C++:

```
class IDog{
    virtual void Bark() = 0;
    virtual void RollOver(int rolls) = 0;
};
```

A C++ member function (such as a method) that's marked with the *=0* syntax is a pure virtual function. This means that it doesn't include an implementation. It also means that the class that defines it isn't a creatable type. Therefore, the only way to use an abstract base class is through inheritance, as shown on the following page.

```
class CBeagle: public IDog{
    virtual void Bark()
        {/* Implementation */}
    virtual void RollOver(int Rolls);
        {/* Implementation */}
};
```

C++ programmers who use abstract base classes and a little extra discipline can achieve the reusability, maintainability, and extensibility benefits that we covered in Chapter 2. The extra discipline required is to avoid the definition of both data storage and method implementations inside an abstract base class. As a result, an abstract base class can formalize the separation of interface from implementation. A C++ client application can communicate with a *CBeagle* object through an *IDog* reference, which allows the client application to avoid building any dependencies on the *CBeagle* class.

You should see that a C++ abstract base class can be used as a logical interface. Even though the language has no real support for interface-based programming, advanced techniques in C++ allow you to reap the most significant benefits. In fact, C++ programmers were the ones who pioneered the concepts of interface-based programming by using abstract base classes in large component-based applications. This technique has been used in numerous projects and is described in depth in *Large-Scale C++ Software Design,* by John S. Lakos. The principles of interface-based programming as implemented in C++ have had a profound effect on the development of COM.

Creating a Binary Standard

The creators of COM concluded that if they removed vendor-specific features of the C++ language and used abstract base classes, they could achieve object-oriented binary reuse. DLLs could hold class definitions. Client applications could use objects created from these DLLs as long as they communicated through abstract base classes. DLLs could be revised and replaced in the field without adversely affecting the client applications that used them. Arriving at this series of conclusions was a big milestone for the Microsoft engineers. They had devised a way to achieve binary reuse in an object-oriented paradigm using C++.

A language that offers polymorphism must provide a way to dynamically bind clients to different versions of the same method signature. A client application can contain code programmed against a generic data type, and any type-compatible object can be plugged in at run time. Different languages and compilers approach this requirement of *dynamic binding* in different ways. Because of its low-level nature, C++ happens to have one of the fastest binding techniques available. Dynamic binding in C++ is based on a highly efficient dispatching architecture that relies on the use of *virtual functions*.

The C++ compiler and linker make dynamic binding possible by generating an array of function pointers called a *vTable*. (The *v* stands for *virtual*.) A vTable represents a set of entry points into an object. Each method defined in an abstract base class has one entry point. If the client knows the calling syntax and acquires the function pointer of a particular method, it can access the object without any knowledge of the concrete class from which it was created.

Figure 3-1 shows what a vTable looks like in memory. Note that an object can have more than one vTable. This simply means that an object can expose more than one interface. vTables are automatically created and populated by the C++ compiler on the object side. The C++ compiler can also generate the client-side binding code that invokes methods through the vTable function pointers. It's fortunate that all popular C++ compilers treat vTables in the same way at the physical level. Whether vTable compatibility between compilers was fate or a stroke of good luck is irrelevant. The Microsoft engineers decided to take this physical layout and make it the standard for all COM objects.

Sometime after the completion of the OLE2 project, a team of engineers drafted the COM Specification, a document that defines the rules for COM programming. The rules state that COM objects must adhere to a specific memory layout. Each COM object must implement one or more COM interfaces. COM clients can communicate with objects only through these interfaces. COM obtains information about an object and a list of the interfaces the object supports from a *coclass*. A coclass is a visible concrete COM implementation that can be used by external COM clients to create

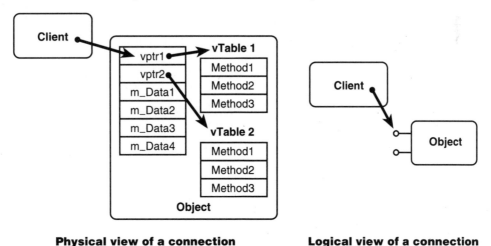

Physical view of a connection   **Logical view of a connection**

Figure 3-1. *In both C++ and COM, clients are dynamically bound to objects through the use of vTables. Each physical vTable represents a logical interface implemented by the object.*

objects. Coclasses are packaged for distribution in binary files called COM servers. A server must also support the COM infrastructure for creating and activating objects. As you will see, a server does this by exposing well-known entry points to the system.

COM and Language Independence

In COM, clients and objects must communicate through vTables. This means that COM objects as well as COM clients must be savvy in their use of function pointers. Luckily, the compiler helps C++ programmers by doing most of the work behind the scenes. C programmers aren't so lucky. To create a COM object in C, you must simulate a C++-style vTable by manually creating and populating an array of function pointers. On the client side, you must manually acquire the function pointer and explicitly invoke the method through it. This makes straight C unattractive for writing COM code by hand.

But what about Visual Basic and Java programmers? Many developer tools and languages such as these have no built-in support for dealing with function pointers. To create or use COM objects, a development tool or language must follow the rules in the COM Specification, which state that vTable binding must be used to conduct all client-object communications. Many higher-level tools and languages need assistance to be able to participate in COM programming.

Visual Basic provides this assistance by adding support to its compiler and adding a Visual Basic–to–COM mapping layer in the run-time engine. After all, the COM Specification defines the rules clearly. The Visual Basic team knew exactly what it would take to make objects vTable-compliant. On the client side, the Visual Basic compiler creates the vTable binding code that is required to access a COM object. Fortunately, when a language or a tool uses a mapping layer, it can hide many of the underlying details from its programmers. This is why Visual Basic is so much easier to use than C++ for programming COM.

Introducing Interface Definition Language (IDL)

In COM, clients bind to objects at run time. However, to properly communicate with an object, a client must know a few things at compile time. In particular, it must have the following pieces of information:

- The type of object it wants to create and use (the coclass)
- The interface or interfaces it will use to communicate with the object
- The calling syntax for each method in the interface or interfaces

To achieve language independence, COM must provide a universal way for servers to publish information about the interfaces and the coclasses they contain.

COM has standardized on a language called *interface definition language (IDL)*. IDL provides a way to define a set of interfaces and coclasses in a manner that is language-neutral. This means that any COM-capable language can be used to implement or use the definitions from an IDL source file. The IDL source file must be fed to the Microsoft IDL (MIDL) compiler. The MIDL compiler generates a few source files used by C and C++ programmers and a special binary database called a *type library*.

A type library is a catalog that describes interfaces, coclasses, and other resources in a server. Each interface is defined with a set of methods; each coclass is defined with one or more interfaces. Type library files have many possible extensions, including .tlb, .dll, .exe, .olb, and .ocx. When you create a server with Visual Basic, the type library is generated without the use of IDL and is automatically bundled into the server's binary image.

A development tool such as Visual Basic requires the use of a type library for building a client application against a COM server. The type library provides the information that Visual Basic needs at compile time to create the client-side vTable binding code. You can import a type library into a Visual Basic project by opening the References dialog box from the Project menu. This dialog box presents a list of all the type libraries registered on your developer workstation.

Using IDL

C++ and Java developers create type libraries using IDL. In COM, IDL is the one and only official language for describing what's inside a server. When the COM team began formalizing the COM Specification, it became obvious that C++ and C couldn't be used to define COM interfaces. C and C++ weren't designed to define functions that extend process boundaries, and they therefore allow parameter definitions that are extremely vague. For instance, if a C++ method defines a parameter as a pointer, what does the pointer actually point to? What data must actually move between the client process and the object process? A mere pointer can't define what needs to be moved between the two processes. IDL solves this problem by using syntax that describes method parameters without ambiguity.

IDL looks a lot like C, but it adds a few object-oriented extensions. It also allows the specification of attributes for entities such as type libraries, coclasses, interfaces, methods, and parameters. Here is a watered-down example of what IDL looks like:

```
library DogServerLib
{
    interface IDog {
        HRESULT Bark();
        HRESULT RollOver([in] int Rolls);
    };
    interface IWonderDog{
        HRESULT FetchSlippers();
```

(continued)

```
    };
        coclass CBeagle {
            interface IDog;
            interface IWonderDog;
        };
}
```

This example shows how type libraries, the interface, and coclasses are defined in an IDL source file. Note that each method definition has a return value of type HRESULT. COM requires this standard return value to allow detection of dead objects or network failures in a distributed environment. Chapter 5 describes in more detail how HRESULTs work.

When C++ or Java programmers want to create a COM object, they must first define the appropriate IDL and feed it to the Microsoft IDL (MIDL) compiler. Visual Basic programmers, on the other hand, don't go through this process because the Visual Basic IDE creates type libraries directly from Visual Basic code. Visual Basic programmers never have to work with IDL.

You can live a productive life as a Visual Basic/COM programmer without ever seeing or understanding IDL. However, if you learn the basics of IDL, you will be a better COM programmer. This is especially true if you are concerned with interoperability among components written in different languages, such as Visual Basic and C++. With an understanding of IDL, you can see exactly what Visual Basic is doing behind the scenes. A COM utility named *Oleview.exe* can help you reverse-engineer a type library into a readable text-based version of IDL. Figure 3-2 shows how you can use this utility to examine the IDL of coclasses and interfaces built into your ActiveX DLLs and ActiveX EXEs. Be sure you set *Oleview.exe* to expert mode when attempting to read a type library. If you don't do this, you won't see the type libraries in the left-side tree view control of *Oleview.exe*.

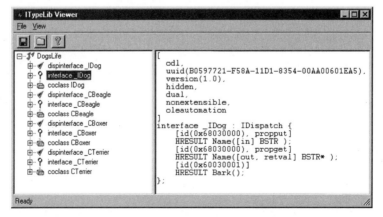

Figure 3-2. OleView.exe *lets you examine and modify many aspects of your COM servers. This example shows how* Oleview.exe*'s type library viewer lets you reverse-engineer IDL from a COM server created with Visual Basic.*

How Does Visual Basic Map to COM?

COM requires that every object implement at least one interface. Visual Basic makes things easy for you by creating a default interface in each creatable class. All of the public methods and properties from a class are placed in a *default interface*. For instance, assume that you have a class *CCollie* with the following public interface:

```
Public Name As String

Public Sub Bark()
    ' implementation
End Sub
```

Visual Basic creates a *hidden* interface named *_CCollie* from the public properties and methods of the class module. The fact that this interface is marked *hidden* in the type library means that other Visual Basic programmers can't see it in the Object Browser or through IntelliSense. (Visual Basic also hides any type name that begins with an underscore "_".) Visual Basic then creates a coclass named *CCollie* that implements *_CCollie* as the *default interface*. The basic IDL looks like this:

```
[hidden]
interface _CCollie{
    [propget] HRESULT Name([out, retval] BSTR* Name);
    [propput] HRESULT Name([in] BSTR Name);
    HRESULT Bark();
};

coclass CCollie {
    [default] interface _CCollie;
};
```

This transparent one-to-one mapping allows Visual Basic classes to be COM-compliant without any assistance from the programmer. Naive Visual Basic programmers have no idea what's really going on. Any Visual Basic client can write the following code to use this class:

```
Dim Dog As CCollie
Set Dog = New CCollie

Dog.Name = "Lassie"
Dog.Bark
```

In the code above, the variable declared with the type *CCollie* is transparently cast to the *_CCollie* reference. This makes sense because a client must communicate with an object through an interface reference. This also makes COM programming easy in Visual Basic. As long as there is a logical one-to-one mapping between a class and the interface that you want to export, you don't have to create user-defined interfaces. However, if you don't employ user-defined interfaces, you can't really tap into the power of interface-based designs.

Chapter 2 showed you how to implement user-defined interfaces in a Visual Basic application. When you define an interface in Visual Basic 5 with a *Public-NotCreatable* class and implement it in a class, the resultant IDL code looks something like this:

```
interface IDog {
    HRESULT Name([out, retval] BSTR* Name);
    HRESULT Name([in] BSTR Name);
    HRESULT Bark();
};

interface _CBeagle {
};

coclass CBeagle {
    [default] interface _CBeagle;
    interface IDog;
};
```

Even when your class contains no public members, Visual Basic automatically creates a default interface of the same name preceded by an underscore. You can't change this to make another interface the default. In the next chapter, you will see that on occasion you must put functionality in the default interface. This means that you must put public members in your class. This is always the case when you are creating Visual Basic objects for automation clients.

Visual Basic 6 works differently than Visual Basic 5. When you mark a class module as *PublicNotCreatable*, Visual Basic 6 still creates a coclass and default interfaces. For instance, when you create the interface IDog with a property and a method in a class module marked as *PublicNotCreatable*, the resulting IDL looks like this:

```
[hidden]
interface _IDog : IDispatch {
    HRESULT Name([out, retval] BSTR* Name);
    HRESULT Name([in] BSTR Name);
    HRESULT Bark();
};

[noncreatable]
coclass IDog {
    [default] interface _IDog;
};
```

This means that in Visual Basic 6 you can no longer simply create a COM interface as you could in Visual Basic 5. *PublicNotCreatable* class modules always produce an interface and a *noncreatable* coclass. The *noncreatable* attribute means that the class can't be instantiated from a COM client. However, any code that lives inside the same server can create objects from a *PublicNotCreatable* class. In Visual Basic 6, you should think of these as Public-Not-Externally-Creatable classes.

It turns out that the differences between Visual Basic 5 and Visual Basic 6 are hidden inside the type library. The code you write for Visual Basic 6 is the same way as it is in Visual Basic 5. In the example above, *IDog* is a coclass and *_IDog* is a hidden interface. Whenever you use the type *IDog* with the *Implements* keyword or use it to create object references, Visual Basic silently casts it to *_IDog*.

Distributing Interface Definitions

Your classes can also implement interfaces that are defined in external type libraries. To do this, you must import the type library using the References dialog box (accessed from the Project menu). These type libraries can be built with either Visual Basic or the MIDL compiler. Once your project can see the interface definition, you can use the *Implements* keyword in a class module. In large projects whose designs depend on user-defined interfaces, it often makes sense to distribute the interface definitions in a type library that's independent of any servers that implement them.

You can create a stand-alone type library in Visual Basic. You create an ActiveX DLL or ActiveX EXE project and select the Remote Server Files option on the Components tab of the Project Properties dialog box. (This option is available only in the Enterprise Edition of Visual Basic.) When you build the server, Visual Basic also creates a type library (*.tlb) file that holds only the interface definitions. This file can be distributed to any programmer who needs to compile code against the interface definitions. The type library can be used by developers of both server and client applications.

Writing Visual Basic–Friendly IDL

Some developers prefer to define their interfaces in IDL instead of Visual Basic. This is especially true for projects that also use C++ or Java. Visual Basic type libraries have a reputation for being very messy when used in any environment other than Visual Basic. And it's important to understand that many things expressed in IDL don't work in Visual Basic. Enterprise-level designers should be aware of what works in Visual Basic and what doesn't. If you intend to use Visual Basic in a project, make sure that all the interfaces you create are Visual Basic–friendly.

One way to write Visual Basic–friendly IDL source code is to leverage the Visual Basic IDE. Start by defining your interfaces in a Visual Basic server, and build the DLL or the EXE. Then use *Oleview.exe* to reverse-engineer the IDL text, and use that as a starting point for your IDL source file. If you follow this approach, you'll know that your interfaces can be implemented and used in Visual Basic projects.

Chapter 6 describes how to create type libraries with IDL in greater depth, but for now here's a short list of rules to keep in mind when you're creating Visual Basic–compatible IDL source files:

- Method names can't start with an underscore (_).

- Don't use COM *[out]* parameters unless you also use *[retval]*.

- All methods must return an HRESULT.

- Don't use unsigned long integers or unsigned short integers.

- Don't use parameters that contain pointers.

- Don't derive one custom COM interface from another custom interface. Visual Basic–compatible interfaces must derive from *IUnknown* and *IDispatch*.

EXAMINING THE COM INFRASTRUCTURE

What do you know about COM so far? You know that a client must communicate with an object through an interface, and that a client binds to an object at run time and invokes methods through vTable pointers. You also know that COM clients learn about objects and interfaces by examining type libraries at compile time. These rules are the foundation on which COM is built.

But think about the following questions: How does a client identify a specific coclass or interface? How does a client create a COM object if it can't use the class name? How does a client obtain the first interface reference to an object? The COM infrastructure must address these questions as well.

The COM library is a set of DLLs and EXEs installed on any COM-enabled computer. These components are part of Windows NT 4 and Windows 95, but future versions of COM+ will decouple them from the operating system. Client applications interact with these components through the COM library, an API that is accessible to low-level programmers. Much of the COM library is exposed through OLE32.DLL. C++ programmers must make direct calls to this library, but Visual Basic programmers are shielded from this DLL by the run-time layer. Figure 3-3 shows the differences in the layers between a COM application written in C++ and one written in Visual Basic.

Client applications must call upon the services provided by the COM library to create and connect to objects. The sequence of object creation must be carefully orchestrated because a client must bind to an interface, not to a class. This leads to a catch-22: How can a client create an object when it doesn't know the definition of the creatable class? The following sections describe exactly how COM makes this possible.

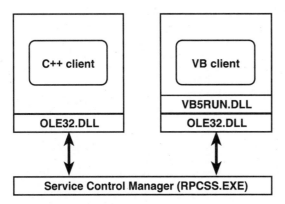

Figure 3-3. *C++ programmers talk to the COM library directly. Visual Basic programmers are shielded from this library by the Visual Basic run-time layer.*

Globally Unique Identifiers (GUIDs)

COM coclasses and interfaces are identified by a *globally unique identifier* (GUID), which is a 128-bit integer. Approximately 3.4×10^{38} values are possible for a 128-bit integer, so it's safe to assume that an unlimited supply of these identifiers is available for use in COM. Most compilers and databases don't support 128-bit integers, so GUIDs are usually stored in other formats. C++ programmers use a data structure that represents a 128-bit value with a set of smaller integral values. A GUID can also be expressed in 32-character hexadecimal form, which makes it somewhat readable. This string format is also used to store GUIDs in the Windows registry. Here is an example of what a GUID looks like in this format:

```
{C46C1BE0-3C52-11D0-9200-848C1D000000}
```

The COM library supplies a function named *CoCreateGUID*, which is used to generate a new GUID. The function relies on an algorithm that uses information such as the unique identifier from the computer's network card and system clock to create a GUID that is guaranteed to be unique across time and space. C++ programmers use a utility named GUIDGen.exe to create GUIDs in the development environment. This allows them to cut and paste GUIDs into IDL and C++ source code. Visual Basic programmers never have to worry about this. The Visual Basic IDE generates GUIDs behind the scenes whenever they're needed.

GUIDs are used in many places in COM, but you should start by examining their use with interfaces and coclasses. Each COM interface has an associated GUID called an interface ID (IID). Each coclass has an associated GUID called a class ID (CLSID). When you examine IDL, you'll notice that each interface and coclass has a Universally Unique Identifier (UUID) attribute. Don't let the UUID attribute confuse you. UUIDs and GUIDs are the same thing.

```
[ uuid(3B46B8A8-CA17-11D1-920B-709024000000) ]
interface _IDog {
    // methods
};

[ uuid(3B46B8AB-CA17-11D1-920B-709024000000) ]
coclass CBeagle {
    // interfaces
};
```

These CLSIDs and IIDs are compiled into a server's type library. A GUID becomes the physical name for an interface or a coclass. When a client application is compiled against the type library, these GUIDs are also compiled into the client's binary image. This enables the client application to ask for a specific coclass and interface whenever it needs to create and bind to an object at run time.

Visual Basic does a pretty good job of hiding GUIDs from programmers. When you reference a type library in a Visual Basic project, you simply use the friendly names of interfaces and coclasses in your code. Visual Basic reads the required GUIDs out of the type library at compile time and builds them into the EXE or DLL when you choose the Make command from the File menu.

When you create a COM server, Visual Basic also hides the GUIDs from you. It automatically generates GUIDs for your interfaces and coclasses on the fly whenever you build a server using the Make command. This is convenient, but it would be nice if Visual Basic offered a little more flexibility. It doesn't allow you to take a specific GUID and associate it with an interface or a coclass. For instance, you might have a cool designer GUID like this:

```
"{DEADBEEF-BADD-BADD-BADD-2BE2DEF4BEDD}"
```

Unfortunately, the Visual Basic IDE won't let you assign this GUID to one of the coclasses in your Visual Basic server. Visual Basic also requires that you build your server projects with an appropriate compatibility mode setting. If you don't, your GUIDs can be changed from build to build. Chapter 5 talks about compatibility in greater depth.

COM Activation

A client application can discover the CLSID of a coclass as well as which interfaces it supports at compile time through the type library. However, COM requires that no other dependencies be built between clients and coclasses. The client application must use a supported interface when it binds to and communicates with an object created from the coclass. This act of loading and binding to an object is called *activation*. A client can activate an object with some help from the COM library if it knows the CLSID and the IID of a supported interface.

Activation support must be built into COM's infrastructure because the client is never allowed to create an object using a visible concrete class definition from the server. If this were the case, the client would be required to see the class definition and know about the object's data layout at compile time. Instead, COM puts the responsibility of creating the object on the server that holds the coclass definition. The infrastructure support supplied by COM plays the role of middleman. It takes an activation request from the client and forwards it to the server.

The COM component that assists activation is the Service Control Manager (SCM), which is affectionately called "the scum" by savvy COM programmers. The SCM is a systemwide service that resides in RPCSS.EXE, as shown in Figure 3-3. (Don't confuse the SCM with the Windows NT Service Control Manager, which is used to start and manage Windows NT Services.)

A client application interacts with the SCM through OLE32.DLL. A C++ programmer can activate an object by calling a function named *CoCreateInstance*. Visual Basic programmers activate objects by using the *New* operator followed by a coclass name. Visual Basic translates a call to the *New* operator into a call to *CoCreateInstance*. In both C++ and Visual Basic, the SCM is passed the CLSID of the desired object and the IID of the interface that the client will use to connect to the object.

When the client passes the CLSID, the SCM uses configuration information in the Windows registry to locate the server's binary image. This is typically a DLL or an EXE. This means that a COM server requires an associated set of registry entries, including a physical path to its location. Each COM server is responsible for adding its configuration information to the registry when asked. Chapter 5 describes the use of the registry in COM in greater depth, but for now just assume that the SCM can always locate the server on the hard disk.

What happens in an activation request? Here's the play-by-play. When a Visual Basic application calls the *New* operator on a coclass that is defined in a COM DLL, the following happens:

1. The Visual Basic run-time library calls *CoCreateInstance* and passes the SCM the requested CLSID and the IID.

2. The SCM locates the server (loading the server if necessary).

3. The SCM calls a well-known entry point in the server and passes it the CLSID and the IID.

4. The server creates the object of the type specified by the CLSID.

5. The server returns an interface reference of the type specified by the IID back to the SCM.

6. The SCM forwards the interface reference back to the client.

7. The client is bound to the object.

8. The SCM is no longer needed and therefore drops out of the picture.

9. The client invokes methods on the object.

As you can see, the SCM is really just a matchmaker. Once it binds a client to an object, it's no longer needed. The client and the object can have a long and fruitful relationship. However, for this architecture to work properly, the SCM must have a predefined way of interacting with the server. Every COM server must therefore provide support for object activation by exposing a well-known entry point through which the SCM can make activation requests.

Class Factories

The rules for server-side activation support are defined in the COM Specification. COM uses a common software technique known as the *factory pattern,* in which the code that actually creates the object is contained in the same binary file. This eliminates the need for the client or the SCM to know about the class definition behind the object being created. The key advantage to this technique is that it allows class authors to revise their code without worrying about client dependencies such as an object's data layout.

When the SCM interacts with a server to activate an object, it must acquire a reference to a special type of object called a *class factory,* which is an agent that creates instances of a class associated with a specific CLSID. A COM server must provide a class factory object for each creatable coclass. When the SCM receives an activation request, it must acquire a reference to the appropriate class factory object. It does this in different ways depending on whether the server code is in an in-process DLL or an out-of-process EXE. Figure 3-4 shows how a single class factory object can be used to create many instances of a particular coclass.

Every COM server, including those built with Visual Basic, must provide class factories for the SCM. When you build an ActiveX DLL or an ActiveX EXE, Visual Basic transparently creates a class factory for each public creatable class. Visual Basic creates class factories in a reasonable and boilerplate fashion. You can't influence how Visual Basic does this. You can't even see the class factories. You have to take it on faith that they are there. Visual Basic also automatically builds the required entry points for the SCM so that it can get at your class factories.

Many C++ programmers have written code for a class factory. Anyone who has done this manually will tell you that it is a tedious undertaking. COM frameworks for C++ programmers such as ATL and MFC provide the boilerplate code for creating these class factories. The Visual Basic team has used a similar technique to hide the code for dealing with class factories from its programmers. You should see this as a good thing. You'll never deal with a class factory in a Visual Basic application. However, this convenience does pose a few limitations.

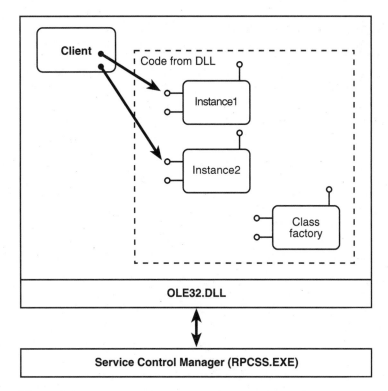

Figure 3-4. *The SCM must interact with a class factory object to create instances of a particular coclass. This design allows the code that is responsible for the creation of objects to remain in the same binary file as the coclass being instantiated.*

C++ programmers who create class factories have more flexibility. A sophisticated class factory can service an activation request by locating an existing object instead of creating a new one. This can allow a DLL to implement an optimized form of object pooling. Visual Basic, on the other hand, doesn't give you any flexibility. Activation requests to your server always result in the creation of a new object.

C++ programmers can also work directly with class factories on the client side of an activation request. They have techniques available for doing things such as optimizing the creation of many objects at once. Unfortunately, no reasonable technique is available to Visual Basic programmers to use a class factory object in a client application. Advanced use of a class factory must be done in C++.

As it turns out, Visual Basic doesn't suffer much from its inability to work directly with class factories. In most cases, a client that calls *New* really wants a new object. Visual Basic does a great job of hiding the requirement of COM activation. What's more, many environments (such as MTS running under Windows NT 4) require a plain vanilla implementation of class factories such as the one provided by Visual Basic. C++ programmers who create fancy class factories will find that they can't run their servers in the MTS environment.

What Happens After Activation?

After the client is bound to an object, the SCM is no longer needed. At this point, the object must provide a certain base level of functionality to the client. In addition to implementing each method in every supported interface, an object must manage its own lifetime and allow clients to move back and forth between the various interfaces it supports.

The next chapter covers these issues and explains some of the other significant responsibilities of COM objects. You'll see how an object can service a less sophisticated group of clients through a mechanism known as *automation*. You'll also see what makes interprocess communication possible between a client and an object.

Chapter 4

Understanding COM Objects

The best thing about a COM object is that it acts in a predictable way. After it's activated, it waits patiently to service your method requests. It knows when you've finished using it, and it politely excuses itself from the application by releasing all its resources back to the system. It can answer intelligently when you ask it what interfaces it supports. What's more, a COM object lets you navigate among all of its interfaces so that you can get at all of the functionality it offers.

This chapter explains how COM objects provide this base level of functionality. It also describes how objects provide access to less sophisticated clients through the use of a COM mechanism called *automation*. The chapter concludes by explaining how a client binds to an object that is running in a remote process. COM does a great job of hooking up the interprocess communication channel between a client and a remote object. What's remarkable is that most of the plumbing details of interprocess communication are completely hidden from most COM programmers.

THE *IUNKNOWN* INTERFACE

COM has one interface from which all other interfaces derive: *IUnknown*. Every interface must derive directly from *IUnknown* or from an interface that has *IUnknown* at the root of its inheritance chain. *IUnknown* is at the top of every COM interface hierarchy. This means that the three methods defined in *IUnknown* are always at the top of any COM-compliant vTable, as shown in Figure 4-1 on the following page. Any connection to an object is made through an *IUnknown*-compatible reference.

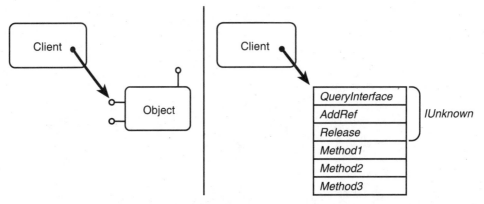

Figure 4-1. *The three methods of the* IUnknown *interface always appear at the top of a COM-compliant vTable. Any connection to an object guarantees a client the ability to call these methods.*

IUnknown expresses the base behavior of a COM object as opposed to a domain-specific behavior that you experience through a user-defined interface. *IUnknown* allows every COM object to manage its own lifetime. It also allows a client to query an object to see whether it supports a given interface and to dynamically cast the object to any of the supported interfaces.

Note that Visual Basic programmers are never exposed to *IUnknown* directly. Visual Basic's mapping layer hides all the code that deals with *IUnknown*. While you can declare variables of type *IUnknown*, you can't invoke its methods because they are marked as [restricted] in the type library *STDOLE2.TLB*. Likewise, on the object side, you never supply implementations for the three methods of *IUnknown*. Visual Basic takes care of all this for you behind the scenes.

In COM, an object is expected to manage its own lifetime. However, an object needs help to make an informed decision about whether to terminate itself or continue running. The client of an object is responsible for calling *AddRef* whenever it duplicates an interface reference and for calling *Release* whenever it drops an existing connection. If all clients live up to their responsibilities, an object can provide a simple implementation of these two methods to properly manage its lifetime. The object maintains a count of connected references and releases itself from memory whenever this count drops to 0.

This model of lifetime management is very different from the way that C and C++ programmers have traditionally dealt with memory allocation. In C and C++, it is common for a client to allocate, use, and then explicitly free memory. The problem with this approach is that it doesn't accommodate multiple clients of a single object. With the reference counting scheme employed by COM, multiple clients can connect to an object. If a client never explicitly deletes an object, it is impossible for one client to delete an object that is currently being used by another client.

C++/COM clients are expected to follow a set of rules for calling *AddRef* and *Release*, which are listed in the COM specification. These rules aren't complicated, but they require a fair amount of discipline to follow when you write COM code by hand. The only time that reference counting is really noticeable in a C++/COM application is when it's done incorrectly.

Visual Basic programmers are never responsible for calling *AddRef* and *Release*. Consequently, they aren't vulnerable to such bugs. COM+ will address this problem with C++ clients by introducing a universal run-time layer that shields all programmers from calling *AddRef* and *Release* explicitly. This will finally give C++ programmers the same benefits that Visual Basic programmers have enjoyed for years.

Visual Basic and Lifetime Management

When you work in Visual Basic, you don't have to worry much about lifetime management. You really need to remember only two rules: Hold the object reference when you want to keep the object alive, and release the reference when you no longer care about the object. Visual Basic handles all calls to *IUnknown* for you. Take a look at the following example:

```
Sub CreateAndUseDog()
    Dim Dog As IDog
    Set Dog = New CBeagle ' AddRef is called.
    Dim Dog2 As IDog
    Set Dog2 = Dog ' AddRef is called.
    Set Dog2 = Nothing ' Release is called.
    ' Release is called on Dog when reference goes out of scope.
End Sub
```

This code results in several calls to *AddRef* and *Release*. When an object is activated, it experiences an *AddRef* call. When you create a second reference to the object, the Visual Basic client calls *AddRef*. If you explicitly set an interface reference to *Nothing*, Visual Basic calls *Release* for you. If you don't explicitly set a reference to *Nothing*, Visual Basic detects when an active reference is going out of scope and calls *Release* on the object just before dropping the connection.

On the object side, Visual Basic automatically implements *AddRef* and *Release* to conduct standard reference counting. A Visual Basic object keeps running as long as active clients remain connected. When the last connection calls *Release*, the Visual Basic object terminates itself. Once again, there's nothing you can do in Visual Basic to influence how an object manages its lifetime, but it's important to understand how your objects will behave.

One of the trickier aspects of lifetime management involves *circular references*, such as when object A holds a reference to object B and object B holds a reference to object A. Even after all interested clients have dropped their connections, the objects remain in memory because of the outstanding references they hold on each other. If your design involves circular references, you must make sure that objects go away when they are no longer needed. One common way to prevent circular references from keeping objects alive forever is to create an explicit method in one of the objects that breaks a connection, causing the composite to start breaking down.

The *QueryInterface* Method

The first and arguably most significant method of *IUnknown* is *QueryInterface*, which allows clients to navigate among the various interfaces supported by an object. This act of dynamically casting different interfaces is known as *type coercion*. A client can also use *QueryInterface* simply to test whether an object supports a particular interface. The capabilities provided by *QueryInterface* are essential to COM. Without *QueryInterface*, COM couldn't achieve polymorphism and run-time type inspection, which are required in an interface-based programming paradigm.

A COM object must implement at least one interface, but it can implement as many as it likes. Objects that implement multiple interfaces must allow clients to navigate among them by calling *QueryInterface*. A client passes a desired IID when it calls *QueryInterface*, and the object responds by returning a reference to the interface. If the client asks for an interface that's not supported, the call to *Query-Interface* will fail. If the call fails, the client can determine that the requested functionality isn't available and thus degrade gracefully.

The Visual Basic run-time layer silently calls *QueryInterface* when you assign an object to a specific reference type. Take a look at the following example:

```
Dim Dog As IDog
Set Dog = New CBeagle
' To get at another interface
Dim WonderDog As IWonderDog
Set WonderDog = Dog ' QueryInterface is called.
WonderDog.FetchSlippers
```

If you have an *IDog* reference to an object and you want to retrieve an *IWonderDog* reference, you can simply use the *Set* statement to cast one interface reference to another. A trappable "Type mismatch" error will occur if the interface is not supported. If the cast is successful, you can use the new interface reference to invoke methods on the object .

Some Visual Basic programmers prefer to blindly cast interface references, as shown in the previous example. If you try to cast to an interface that isn't supported, the Visual Basic run-time layer deals with an unsuccessful call to *QueryInterface* by raising a trappable run-time error in your code. If there's a chance that the cast will fail, you must be prepared to trap and deal with this error. If you would rather avoid dealing with run-time errors, you can query an object for interface support by using Visual Basic's *TypeOf* syntax, like this:

```
Dim Dog As IDog
Set Dog = New CBeagle
' Test for support before using interface.
If TypeOf Dog Is IWonderDog Then ' Call to QueryInterface
    Dim WonderDog As IWonderDog
    Set WonderDog = Dog ' Call to QueryInterface
    WonderDog.FetchSlippers
Else
    ' Degrade gracefully if interface isn't supported.
End If
```

A Visual Basic object automatically implements *QueryInterface*. When you implement one or more user-defined interfaces in a class, Visual Basic provides an implementation of *QueryInterface* that allows clients to move among interface references. As in the case of *AddRef* and *Release*, the Visual Basic implementation of *QueryInterface* is fairly straightforward, but you can never see it. You have to take it on faith that it works perfectly.

AUTOMATION

In the early days, COM was accessible only to C and C++ programmers because of the raw nature of vTable binding. IDL and type libraries then made it possible for development tools such as Visual Basic 4 to build the required vTable bindings at compile time. However, some languages and development environments still can't make sense of a type library. If a client doesn't have the information from a server's type library, it can't build vTable bindings against a user-defined interface. COM addresses this problem with a run-time binding mechanism known as *automation*.

Microsoft was motivated to build automation into the development culture of COM because such an extension would result in many more COM programmers. Automation gives COM greater language independence. The original version of automation (which was called *OLE automation*) shipped at roughly the same time as Visual Basic 3. Previous versions of Visual Basic didn't include any COM support, so automation was the first means by which a Visual Basic programmer could use a COM object created by a C++ programmer.

The COM team and the Visual Basic team worked hard together to make automation work with Visual Basic 3. Version 4 added support for type libraries, so Visual Basic is no longer limited to automation when creating COM clients. However, many languages and tools still rely on automation. For instance, most of Microsoft's Web-based technologies use languages such as VBScript and JavaScript, which cannot build custom vTable bindings. Programmers in these languages rely instead on automation when they need to access a COM object.

The *IDispatch* Interface

Automation relies on an interface named *IDispatch*, which allows clients to discover method bindings at run time in a process known as *late binding*. The vTable that represents *IDispatch* is shown in Figure 4-2. *IDispatch* extends *IUnknown* by adding four methods. Automation clients use *GetIDsOfNames* and *Invoke* to achieve late binding. As in the case of *IUnknown*, Visual Basic programmers never deal with this interface directly. Instead, the Visual Basic mapping layer translates your code and makes the calls to *IDispatch* methods.

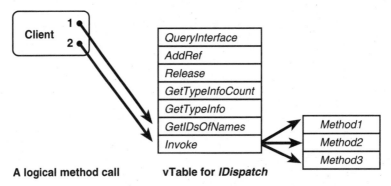

Figure 4-2. *Automation clients bind to a vTable that represents the* IDispatch *interface. An automation client achieves late binding by calling* GetIDsOfNames *and then* Invoke.

Here's how automation works. After a client receives an *IDispatch* reference, it can ask an object whether it supports a particular method by calling *GetIDsOfNames*. The client must pass the name of the method as a string argument in the call. If the object doesn't support the requested method, the call to *GetIDsOfNames* fails. If the method is supported, *GetIDsOfNames* returns a logical identifier for the method called a DISPID. A DISPID is simply an integer that an object provides to identify one of its methods. Positive DISPIDs indicate that a method is user-defined, while negative DISPIDs are reserved for methods with special meanings.

A client armed with a valid DISPID can execute a method through automation by calling *Invoke*. In fact, *Invoke* is the only way to execute a user-defined method through the *IDispatch* interface. As you can see, *IDispatch* is a single physical interface that allows unsophisticated clients to get at any number of logical operations. In essence, *IDispatch* represents a standard vTable with a highly flexible invocation architecture. This arrangement allows clients such as VBScript to access many different types of COM objects while knowing about only a single vTable layout. This effectively eliminates the need for a client to build custom binding code from information in a type library.

While *IDispatch* is very flexible, it isn't very efficient compared to custom vTable binding. Every logical call through *IDispatch* requires two actual calls. The first call to *GetIDsOfNames* requires a string lookup in the object to return the proper DISPID to the client. The call to *Invoke* also requires quite a bit of overhead. This overhead is necessary because of the open-ended nature of this dispatching architecture.

A method can have an arbitrary number of parameters, which can come in all shapes and sizes. Automation deals with this by requiring the client to pass all parameters as an array of variants in the call to *Invoke*. The array allows the method to define any number of parameters, and the variant type allows each parameter to be self-describing. An object responds to a call to *Invoke* by resolving the DISPID and unpacking the variant arguments to their proper types. After the object processes a call to *Invoke*, it must pass the return value to the client as a variant as well.

A client in Visual Basic can go through the *IDispatch* interface by using the *Object* data type. This data type is really an *IDispatch* reference. Here's a Visual Basic example of using *IDispatch*:

```
Dim Dog As Object
Set Dog = CreateObject("DogServer.CBeagle")
Dog.Name = "Fankie"
Dog.Bark
```

When the object is created, an *IDispatch* reference is assigned to the *Object* variable *Dog*. A logical call to a property or a method in Visual Basic code translates to a call to both *GetIDsOfNames* and *Invoke*. Visual Basic could optimize automation by caching the DISPIDs of properties and methods, but it doesn't. Each logical call results in two round-trips between the client and the object. When you add the overhead of a call to *Invoke*, you can see that you don't want to use the *Object* data type if you don't have to.

Another important thing to keep in mind when you use the *Object* data type is that you have no type safety. The Visual Basic environment assumes at compile time that any method call through *IDispatch* will succeed. This means you lose out on wonderful features of the Visual Basic IDE such as compile-time type checking and IntelliSense. You have another reason to avoid using the *Object* data type.

Dual Interfaces

You should note two key facts about late binding and *IDispatch*: Late binding and *IDispatch* are great for clients that can't deal with custom vTable bindings, and they offer slow execution times compared with custom vTables. You can expect a call through a custom vTable binding to be 500 to 1000 times faster than a call using automation for an in-process object.

COM servers that cater to automation clients are often based on *dual interfaces*. A dual interface offers binding through *IDispatch* as well as a custom vTable interface. Figure 4-3 on the following page compares the vTables for the three types of interfaces. A dual interface is simply a hybrid vTable that combines the two others. It offers

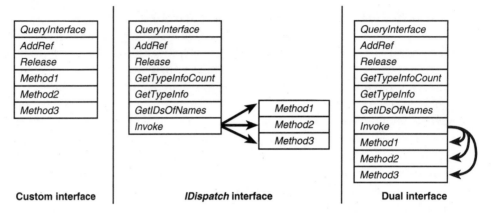

Figure 4-3. *A dual interface is a hybrid of an* IDispatch *interface and a custom interface.*

the speed of custom vTable bindings to sophisticated clients created with tools such as C++ and Visual Basic. It also provides a standard implementation of *IDispatch* for automation clients such as VBScript and JavaScript.

IDispatch restricts interfaces to using variant-compliant data types. This restriction applies to dual interfaces as well because they must expose every method through *IDispatch*. This isn't much of a limitation for Visual Basic developers because all the primitive types supplied by Visual Basic are variant-compliant. C++ programmers, on the other hand, are far more restricted because their language gives them many more types to choose from. A C++ programmer who is building a server exclusively for C++ clients might elect to forgo supporting *IDispatch* or a dual interface in order to use non-variant-compliant data types.

As of version 5, Visual Basic always builds servers using dual interfaces. You don't have to request dual interfaces, and there's nothing you can do to avoid them. When you choose the Make command from the File menu, Visual Basic generates a full-blown dual interface behind every interface in your server. To do this properly, it must also provide a standard implementation of *IDispatch* behind every creatable class. This means that your Visual Basic objects can cater to both custom vTable clients and automation clients.

Binding Techniques

You can experience three types of binding when you create a client with Visual Basic. *Late binding* is used whenever the *Object* data type is used. This is true whether or not you include a type library for the object. Late binding provides the worst performance and no type checking at compile time. Use late binding only when you have no other choice. You can almost always avoid it in Visual Basic code.

Early binding occurs when you have an *IDispatch*-only object but you can use a type library. The client can read the DISPIDs at compile time and embed them in the client executable. This eliminates the need for a call to *GetIDsOfNames*, but the client still goes through *Invoke* to execute the method. Early binding is faster than late binding, but it's still much slower than vTable binding. Early binding also allows the Visual Basic IDE to perform compile-time type checking and to use IntelliSense.

Early binding occurs only if you have a type library for an *IDispatch* object that doesn't provide a dual interface. The consensus among COM programmers is that any object that provides *IDispatch* should also provide a custom interface whenever possible. However, MFC is an example of a C++ framework that creates *IDispatch*-only COM objects. Here's another interesting fact. When you place a control on a form, Visual Basic uses early binding instead of vTable binding because controls must use the *IDispatch* interface to support custom properties.

vTable binding is always best. It is faster than the other two kinds by an order of magnitude. Visual Basic clients always use vTable bindings as long as the following are true:

- The client project contains a reference to the type library.

- The reference is typed to an interface or a creatable class (the default interface).

- The object exposes vTables for dual interfaces or for pure vTable interfaces. (That is, the object isn't *IDispatch*-only.)

Supporting both a User-Defined Interface and Automation

Automation clients can use only an object's default interface. They can't call *Query-Interface*. This makes sense because an automation client can't use a type library and can never ask for a specific IID. When you create objects with Visual Basic, Visual Basic builds the default interface from the public members of a creatable class. You can't change which interface is marked as the default. Consequently, Visual Basic objects can support automation clients only by providing public methods in a creatable class. This means that an automation client can't get at any functionality that you expose through a user-defined interface.

If you are certain that your objects will be used exclusively by automation clients, you can create classes with public methods and avoid user-defined interfaces. This makes the initial design easy. If you are certain that your objects will be used exclusively by clients capable of vTable binding, you can add user-defined interfaces to your designs. Things get tricky when you want to expose functionality through a user-defined interface as well as through automation.

Sometimes a developer needs to expose functionality through both a user-defined interface and automation. In this situation, a Visual Basic programmer must create two sets of entry points into the object. For instance, if the *IDog* interface contains a single method named *Bark*, the *CBeagle* class can provide access to *IDog*-bound clients as well as to automation clients with the following code:

```
'*** vTable client support
Implements IDog

Private Sub IDog_Bark()
    InvokeBark ' Forward call
End Sub

'*** Automation client support
Public Sub Bark()
    InvokeBark ' Forward call
End Sub

'*** Actual implementation
Private Sub InvokeBark()
    ' Your code here
End Sub
```

As you can see, there's nothing terribly complicated about supporting a user-defined interface and automation at the same time. It's just tedious and can easily lead to errors. You must write the code to forward the incoming requests from each entry point to the appropriate implementation. Of course, you have to do this only if you want to cater to both types of clients. If you are certain that you are dealing with either one type or the other, you don't have to worry about maintaining dual entry points into your objects.

TAKING COM OUT OF PROCESS

So far, this book has described the interaction between client and object only in the context of a single process under a single thread of execution. When a client is bound to an in-process object, it can directly invoke methods through the use of function pointers that are stored in a vTable. The interaction is very efficient because the client code and the object code share one thread, one call stack, and one set of memory addresses. Unfortunately, when the object runs in another process, none of those resources can be shared.

The function pointers stored in vTables have no meaning across process boundaries. A client can't use a remote function pointer to access an object in another process. How then can COM remote a method call from the client's process to the object's process? COM makes remote communication possible with a pair of helper objects called the *proxy* and the *stub*.

Figure 4-4 shows how the proxy and the stub are deployed. The proxy runs in the client's process, while the stub runs in the object's process. The proxy and the

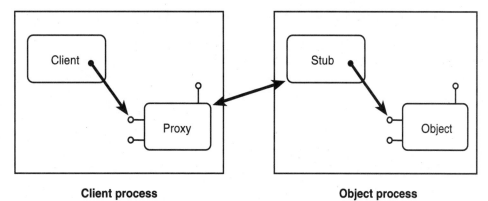

Client process   **Object process**

Figure 4-4. *COM's remoting architecture requires that a proxy/stub layer be introduced between the client and the object. The proxy and the stub establish an RPC channel between them to communicate with each other.*

stub establish a communication channel using remote procedure calls (RPCs) as the interprocess mechanism. The channel passes data back and forth during remote method execution. This act of serializing method parameters for transmission through the proxy/stub architecture is known as *marshaling*.

When the client invokes a method on the proxy, the proxy forwards the request to the stub. To properly transmit this request, the proxy must marshal the method's inbound parameters to the stub. When the stub receives the request, it unmarshals the inbound parameters and locally performs the call on the object. After the object has completed the method, the stub prepares a response packet that includes outbound parameters and a return value. The data is then marshaled back to the proxy. The proxy unmarshals the data in the response packet and returns control back to the client.

The best part about this remoting architecture is that neither the client nor the object can tell that it is being remoted. The client thinks that the proxy is the object. The object thinks that the stub is the client. This allows COM programmers to write code for both clients and objects without regard to whether the objects will be activated from an in-process server or an out-of-process server. This powerful feature is known as *location transparency*.

There is a proxy/stub pair for each connected interface. This allows a client and an object to have two or more proxy/stub pairs connecting them at once. It makes sense that the proxy/stub pair is associated with the interface because the interface describes the methods that need to be remoted. With an interface definition stored in a type library, COM can determine the exact manner in which the data should be marshaled to the object and back. This is why IDL allows you to specify parameters such as *[in]*, *[out]*, and *[in, out]*. Unfortunately, Visual Basic doesn't support COM *[out]* parameters in its current release. Chapter 6 describes these parameter attributes in greater detail and shows you how to efficiently marshal your data among processes.

Responsibilities of the Proxy and the Stub

The proxy and the stub have their work cut out for them. They must work together to give both the client and the object the perception that they're running in a single process on a single thread. They create this illusion by constructing a call stack in the object's process that is identical to the one in the client's process. Any data sitting on the call stack in the client's process must be marshaled to the object's process. What's more, any pointers on the client's call stack require the proxy to marshal the data that the pointer refers to. The stub is responsible for unmarshaling all the data and setting up the call stack, which might include pointers to data that doesn't live on the stack.

As you can imagine, the code that accomplishes the marshaling behind a proxy/stub pair can become quite complicated. Luckily, COM provides a system service called the *universal marshaler* that automatically builds the proxy/stub code at run time. It does this by examining interface definitions in a type library. When an interface reference is exported from the object's process, the universal marshaler builds and loads a stub object. When the interface reference is imported into a client process, the universal marshaler creates a proxy and binds it to the client. The communication channel that is established between the proxy and the stub can thus remote method requests between the client and the object.

Out-of-Process Considerations

You should note two important performance-related points about out-of-process COM. The first is that *out-of-process method calls take much longer than in-process calls*. Generally, you can expect an out-of-process call to take at least 1000 times longer than an in-process call with direct vTable binding. The proxy/stub layer always requires thread switching and marshaling, so it adds a significant amount of overhead.

The second key point is that *objects you create with Visual Basic can be passed only by reference and never by value*. Don't be fooled into thinking that you can simply pass a Visual Basic object from one machine to another. Your methods can define arguments that are object references but not actual objects. The current version of Visual Basic lets you put the *ByVal* keyword in front of object types in argument definitions, but these arguments are still interpreted with pass-by-reference semantics. When you have a reference to an out-of-process object, access to each method or property in the object requires an expensive round-trip.

Out-of-process objects created with Visual Basic are always bound with proxies and stubs built by the universal marshaler. This technique for automatically binding a client to an out-of-process object from the information in a type library is known as *standard marshaling*. Many programmers using languages other than Visual Basic also prefer standard marshaling because it's easy to use and it's part of a service provided by COM's infrastructure.

C and C++ programmers can forgo standard marshaling in favor of *custom marshaling*. Those who are willing to write their own marshaling code can optimize the communication channel in ways that are impossible with standard marshaling. For instance, a programmer can implement pass-by-value semantics with custom marshaling code. The downside to custom marshaling is that it requires using C or C++ on the object side.

Out-of-Process Activation

It's time to revisit object activation and look at how it is accomplished with an out-of-process server as opposed to an in-process server. It's also important to understand how activation differs between a local out-of-process server and a remote out-of-process server.

The Service Control Manager (SCM) must acquire a reference to a class factory object in every activation request, but this occurs in quite a different way when the server runs in its own process. With an in-process server, the SCM connects to a class factory object through a well-known entry point exposed by the DLL. Because an out-of-process server can't expose an entry point the way a DLL can, COM must have another way for the SCM to acquire a class factory object reference.

When an out-of-process server is launched, it must register a class factory object for each of its creatable coclasses with the COM library. The SCM maintains a machinewide internal table called the *class table,* which holds the class factory object references for every registered CLSID. The SCM can scan through this table and retrieve a reference to any local class factory object that has been registered.

When the SCM receives an activation request for a CLSID that is implemented in a local server, it looks through the class table to determine whether the CLSID has already been registered. If it finds the CLSID in the class table, the server is up and running. If the CLSID hasn't been registered, the SCM launches the server process and takes a breath so that the server can register itself. After the server has registered its CLSID, the SCM can revisit the class table and acquire the needed reference to the class factory object. After the SCM connects to a class factory object, it asks the server to create an instance in a manner similar to the in-process scenario.

After the SCM creates the out-of-process object, it must bind the object to the clients using a proxy/stub pair. When the object exports an interface reference to the SCM, the SCM calls on the universal marshaler to create the stub object. Then when the SCM imports the interface reference into the client application, the SCM calls on the universal marshaler to create a proxy object to bind the client and the object together.

Once you come this far, the conceptual differences between activation in a local server and a remote server are not overly complicated. When the local SCM determines that the CLSID in an activation request lives on a different computer, it dials across the network and establishes a connection with a remote SCM.

Interhost communication requires that the activation request be passed through an authentication/authorization layer (which is covered in Chapter 8). What's important to see here is that the remote SCM activates the object in an out-of-process server that is local to itself. The remote SCM goes through the same activation process described above.

The only real change is that the interface reference must be marshaled from one computer to another. The interface reference is exported from the remote server process in the same manner as for a local server. When the interface reference is unmarshaled into the client process, the proxy is populated with enough information to get back to a specific stub for a specific object on a specific host. Once again, none of these details are the concern of either the client or the object.

Note that this binding process requires that the type library holding the interface definition be installed on both machines. It's common practice to produce a stand-alone type library for installation on client machines that must build proxies to remote objects.

The Value of Location Transparency

This process of binding a remote object sounds complicated, but the SCM takes care of it. A client doesn't have to concern itself with the details of in-process activation vs. out-of-process activation. The client requests a specific CLSID and is then bound to the object (or something that feels like the object). After the binding takes place, the client goes about its business by invoking methods and accessing properties. The client perceives that the object is close by, but that doesn't have to be the case.

In the out-of-process scenario, the object also perceives that the client is in the same process. This means that the details of in-process versus out-of-process activation are hidden from object code as well as the client. The ability of programmers to write client code and object code for an in-process relationship and have the code work automatically across process boundaries is one of the most powerful features of COM. Figure 4-5 shows three different ways to deploy a server without changing any code for the client or the object.

COM's ability to seamlessly remote objects is known as *location transparency*. It eliminates the need for programmers to be concerned with the grungy details of interprocess communication. It also means that objects can be redeployed around the network with little impact on code. You can redirect a client that is programmed to activate a certain CLSID from an in-process DLL so that it activates a remote object by making just a few minor modifications to the registry. You don't have to rewrite a single line of code.

You can take code that you have written for a class in a COM DLL and use it in a COM EXE without making any modifications. However, the mere fact that your code compiles and allows you to serve up objects doesn't mean that it's efficient. Code written for in-process objects might not scale when it is deployed in an out-of-process object. Many coding techniques that work well in process can lead to

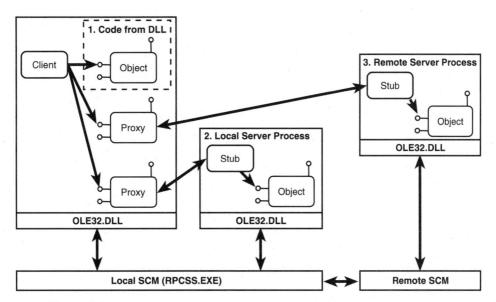

Figure 4-5. *Location transparency eliminates the need for COM programmers to be concerned with the details of interprocess communication.*

unacceptable performance when the proxy/stub layer is introduced. Chapter 6 explains the importance of designing interfaces that work efficiently across the proxy/ stub layer.

OBJECTS AND SERVERS

This chapter has looked at many aspects of COM objects. You have learned how *IUnknown* provides a contract between a COM object and any client that uses it. The *IUnknown* interface allows an object to manage its own lifetime and also allows a client to navigate among the various interfaces supported by the object. You have also seen how automation works, and you are probably happy that Visual Basic hides all the code that deals with *IDispatch*. You don't have to do much to create objects that are accessible to automation clients and to clients that know how to bind to custom vTables.

This chapter also looked at how COM achieves object-oriented interprocess communication. The proxy/stub layer provides the architecture for remoting method calls across processes and across computers while keeping clients and objects ignorant of what's really going on. In this manner, COM achieves location transparency, which hides many of the low-level plumbing details. These details are the responsibility of the SCM and the universal marshaler. The universal marshaler creates the code for remoting method calls by inspecting an interface definition from a type library. You can thus conclude that *interfaces are the key to seamless distribution in COM.*

Now that you know more about objects, it's time to look at the servers in which your coclasses are defined. The next chapter explains how Visual Basic packages classes (you know them now as *coclasses*) in a COM Server. It provides the information you need to decide whether to deploy your components in DLLs or EXEs. It also describes server registration and component versioning. Finally, it explains how to approach error handling in a manner agreeable to Visual Basic programmers and COM programmers alike.

Chapter 5

COM Servers

This chapter begins by explaining how to package your coclasses for distribution. One of the first issues you must address is whether to distribute your classes in an in-process DLL or an out-of-process EXE. You must weigh the pros and cons of each packaging technique. This chapter covers important issues relating to COM and the Registry and explains how to properly register servers on a development workstation and on a user's desktop.

Component versioning is critical in the production environment. To harvest COM's most powerful features, you must be able to revise your servers and replace them in the field without adversely affecting any client applications. This chapter shows you the options that Visual Basic gives you to accomplish this. For many readers, this will prove to be the most valuable topic in the book.

This chapter also delves into a variety of issues relating to server design, such as exposing classes and interfaces, using enumerators and friend methods, and modifying procedure attributes. The chapter concludes by explaining how Visual Basic maps its own internal error handling model onto COM exceptions. This leads to a description of the best techniques for raising errors between servers and clients.

COMPONENT PACKAGING

A COM server must expose one or more coclasses in order to be useful to a client application. The server can be described as a binary file that packages a collection of coclasses. COM supports two kinds of component packaging. COM DLLs are *in-process servers* (also known as *in-proc servers*), and COM EXEs are *out-of-process servers*. You must decide whether to serve up your classes through a DLL or an EXE.

The Visual Basic IDE (integrated development environment) offers three different Project Type settings for building COM servers. You select this setting when you create a new project, and you can change it afterwards in the Project Properties dialog box. You use an ActiveX DLL project to create an in-process server. You use an ActiveX Control project to create a more specialized type of visual in-process server. (This book doesn't cover ActiveX Control projects.) You use an ActiveX EXE project to create an out-of-process server.

In-Process Servers

An in-process server is very efficient. It's loaded into the address space of the client application. An object from an in-process server can usually be directly bound to the client without any need for a proxy/stub layer. This means that the client and the object share the same thread and the same set of memory addresses. Once the object is activated, the communication between the two is as fast as it would be if the class were defined within the client application. Better performance is one of the biggest benefits of using an in-process server.

An in-process server also imposes a few significant limitations. For instance, each client application gets its own private set of the DLLs variables. This makes it impractical to share data among multiple client applications. An in-process server is also not as robust as an out-of-process server because it's tightly coupled to the client application's process in which it's loaded. A defective object can crash the client application, and if the client application crashes on its own, the object also crashes.

An in-process server is also somewhat inflexible when it comes to security. An object from an in-process server (an in-process object) must run under the same security context as the client application. For instance, if two users, Bob and Sally, use your ActiveX DLL, some of your objects will run under Bob's identity while others will run under Sally's identity. This isn't always a problem, but sometimes you'll want all the objects activated from a particular server to run under a single user account. When you load objects into client applications from in-process DLLs, this isn't an option.

Out-of-Process Servers

An out-of-process server is implemented in Visual Basic as an ActiveX EXE. The executable file that Visual Basic builds when you use the Make command can launch and control its own Win32 process. When a client activates an object from an out-of-process server, the Service Control Manager (SCM) finds or loads the server process and negotiates the creation of a new object. The object and the client are then bound together with a proxy/stub layer between them. As you know, this layer adds significant overhead. Calls to out-of-process servers are always much slower than calls to in-process servers.

A local server runs on the same computer as the client application, while a remote server runs on a different computer. In terms of COM packaging, it doesn't really matter whether your ActiveX EXE runs locally or on a computer across the network. An ActiveX EXE is always configured to run as a local server. Once the server has been configured to run as a local server, you can add a few more configuration changes to the Registry to allow remote clients to use it as well. You don't need to do anything special in the Visual Basic IDE to differentiate between these deployment options.

Out-of-process servers are more robust than in-process servers. They're at least as robust as the operating system on which they're running. With an in-process server, either the client or the object can potentially crash the other. An out-of-process relationship has a built-in level of fault tolerance. A client can detect that an object has died by inspecting the HRESULT returned by any method. You'll see how this is done later in the chapter. The infrastructure of Distributed COM can also detect a dead client and notify the object that the connection is no longer valid. With an out-of-process server, either the client or the object can continue to live a productive life after the other has passed on.

So how do you decide between an ActiveX DLL and an ActiveX EXE? You should think about performance first. If your objects can be used exclusively by a single client application, it makes sense to package your coclasses in a DLL. This is the best approach when your code calculates something such as sales tax or an interest rate. You can install your DLL on the user's desktop computer along with the client application. This gives you the best possible performance.

If you need to share a server process among several client applications, you should deploy an ActiveX EXE server on a user's desktop to allow several client applications to connect at once. This means that you can share data among objects owned by different client applications. This also prevents one of the client applications from crashing the server process and all the objects in it.

What if you need to run your objects from across the network? One seemingly intuitive solution is to create an ActiveX EXE project because an ActiveX EXE can serve up objects to remote clients. However, you have another option that will give you far more flexibility. The next section describes another way to serve up distributed objects based on the concept of a *surrogate process*.

Surrogate Processes for DLLs

A surrogate process is a container application that acts as a host for objects served up through a COM-style DLL. Microsoft initially created a generic container application named DllHost.exe for the purpose of deploying out-of-process objects from legacy DLLs. You can modify the Registry entries for a coclass in a DLL in such a way that the SCM activates its objects inside an instance of DllHost.exe. Although deployment using the original version of DllHost.exe is no longer considered strategic, the idea of using a surrogate process is very much alive at Microsoft.

Microsoft Transaction Server (MTS) provides a container application named MTX.EXE. This application provides a surrogate process that can host the objects you create with Visual Basic. This means that you'll usually package your coclasses in an ActiveX DLL when you want to deploy them in an MTS application. Once you build a DLL, you must properly install and configure it on the remote machine running the surrogate process. However, once the DLL is set up properly, clients can activate your objects from across the network.

MTS is made up of much more than just the container application MTX.EXE. A large part of the code behind MTS is maintained in a DLL named MTXEX.DLL. These two components and a few others work together to provide a very sophisticated run-time environment. You can see MTS as an advanced out-of-process server that's capable of running your objects.

There's a significant difference between an out-of-process server that will be used by one or two client applications and an out-of-process server that will run objects for hundreds of client applications. An out-of-process server that will be accessed by a large user base involves more scalability issues, such as connection management, thread pooling, and security. When you build an ActiveX EXE, the code built into your server must address all of these issues.

Over the last few years, several teams at Microsoft have independently built infrastructure support code for scalable out-of-process servers. The Visual Basic team has built this type of infrastructure support into ActiveX EXEs. In a separate effort, the ActiveX Template Library (ATL) team has added code to ATL's framework to help programmers create multithreaded servers. Many other C++ programmers have written code for connection management and thread pooling by hand. As you can see, quite a few people have written redundant code to solve the same problem.

As a result, Microsoft has decided to provide the core of this essential infrastructure support code in a generic run-time environment. MTX.EXE and MTXEX.DLL work together to provide connection management, thread pooling, and security features that are far more sophisticated than those supplied by an ActiveX EXE.

The idea of a generic run-time environment is appealing for a few reasons. First, it makes things easier for developers because it provides most of the infrastructure code required by a high-volume server. Second, it allows Microsoft to maintain all this infrastructure code in a single code base and share it across many different languages. Finally, it allows COM objects to run and behave in a consistent manner, even if they have been created with different languages and tools.

BUILDING A SERVER

Visual Basic makes some things incredibly easy. Even a four-year-old can build an ActiveX DLL or an ActiveX EXE in the Visual Basic IDE using the Make command on the File menu. This command opens a dialog box with various options and an OK button. You simply click OK to build the current project into a binary server.

A few important things happen behind the scenes when you do this. First, Visual Basic automatically publishes information in a type library and bundles it into your server's binary image. The type library is important for marshaling purposes as well as for use by other development tools that need to create vTable bindings for your objects at compile time. Second, Visual Basic adds the code to your server to support self-registration. Finally, Visual Basic adds a class factory for each creatable class and adds support to interact with the SCM during object activation.

When you create a new server, you should open the Project Properties dialog box and change the Project Name and the Project Description, as shown in Figure 5-1. These important pieces of information are written into your type library. The Project Name creates a namespace for the coclasses within it. Clients can refer to coclasses in your server with a fully qualified name such as *DogServer.CBeagle*. The Project Description becomes the description of the type library itself. Other Visual Basic programmers see this when they add your server to their projects using the References dialog box. If you don't include a description, Visual Basic uses the Project Name as the description.

As you know, the type library is bundled into the server's binary image. With an out-of-process server, this information is essential for marshaling purposes. With

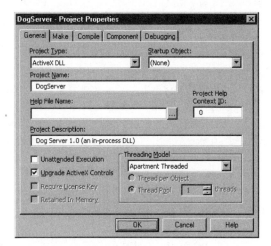

Figure 5-1. *In the Project Properties dialog box, you can assign a Project Name and a Project Description to your server. These settings become top-level attributes of the server's type library.*

a local server, the universal marshaler can simply use the type library bundled into your server file for both the proxy and the stub. Since a remote server lives on a different machine than the client, the client can't take advantage of the server's binary image, which holds the type library. So how does the universal marshaler on the client machine build the proxy? You could copy the server file to each user's desktop machine, but that wouldn't make sense. The server file includes all of the coclass implementations, and the client machines need only the interface definitions.

Visual Basic lets you create a stand-alone type library by selecting the Remote Server Files option on the Component tab of the Project Properties dialog box. When you select this option for an ActiveX EXE or an ActiveX DLL project, the Make command creates a separate type library file with the .tlb extension. This file can be distributed to client desktops in a distributed environment so that the universal marshaler can build proxies as needed.

COM Servers and the Registry

The Registry is a systemwide hierarchical database that is used to bind key names to numeric, string, or binary values. It was originally created to hold information about COM and OLE in the early days of 16-bit Microsoft Windows, but now it is used to store many other types of persistent configuration data. The Registry has top-level keys called *hives*. (A bonus fun fact: The term *hive* was coined as a clever play on words because the Registry uses a "B-tree" structure.) The SCM is entirely dependent on information stored in the Registry.

Every loadable coclass associated with an in-process server or a local server must have a Registry entry that associates it with a physical path to a server's binary image. Every remotable interface must have an associated path to a type library. Even the type library itself must be registered. As you will see, the SCM, the universal marshaler, and development environments such as Visual Basic need this information to do their jobs.

In Windows NT 4, the Registry key HKEY_CLASSES_ROOT\CLSID lists all implementations available to client applications on the machine. Each CLSID key contains one or more subkeys that indicate the location of the coclass, as shown in Figure 5-2. DLLs require an InprocServer32 subkey, while out-of-process servers require a LocalServer32 subkey. These keys hold the physical path to the server; the SCM uses them to find or load the server during object activation.

Any object that will be bound to a client with a proxy/stub pair requires additional Registry entries that allow the universal marshaler to locate the type library at run time. As you will recall from Chapter 3, a proxy/stub pair is specific to an IID. The universal marshaler generates a proxy and a stub by examining interface definitions from a type library. The Registry key HKEY_CLASSES_ROOT\Interfaces lists each interface along with the GUID of the type library where the interface is defined.

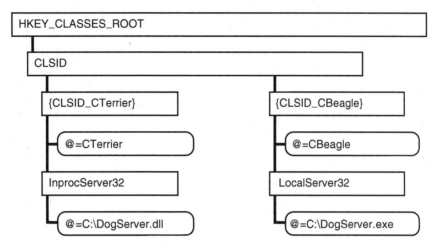

Figure 5-2. *Every creatable coclass must have an associated Registry entry to map the CLSID to the server's location. The SCM uses this mapping information to find and load a server during an activation request.*

The Registry key HKEY_CLASSES_ROOT\TypeLib tracks the physical location of every type library on the local machine. All of this information must also be written to the Registry before the server will work correctly.

All modern COM servers are self-registering. That means that a server, when asked politely, should write all of its required information into the local computer's Registry. In the early days of COM, C++ programmers had to write registration code by hand against the Win32 API. Today C++ frameworks such as ATL and Microsoft Foundation Classes (MFC) can provide boilerplate code that handles these grungy registration details. Fortunately, Visual Basic automatically generates self-registration code when you build a server. A Visual Basic server registers all of the information required for both in-process servers and local servers. Remote servers that are accessed by clients from across the network add more complexity to the registration process and require extra attention. Chapter 8 covers this topic in greater depth.

Registering a Server

When you build a server, the Visual Basic IDE automatically registers it on your development workstation. This makes it easy to build and test a client application after you build the server. Keep in mind that it's one thing to configure a server on a development workstation and another to register it on a user's desktop. Both are equally important for your server to run correctly.

Out-of-process servers register themselves each time they are launched. If you double-click on a server, it launches and registers itself. Once the server process is running, it realizes that it has no client and unloads. However, the polite way to register and unregister an EXE-based server is to use a standard command-line switch, as follows:

```
DogServer.EXE /RegServer
DogServer.EXE /UnregServer
```

DLL-based servers are passive and can't register or unregister themselves. You register and unregister them using the Win32 SDK utility REGSVR32.EXE. You can run this utility from the command line by passing the path to the DLL with the appropriate switch, like this:

```
REGSVR32.EXE DogServer.DLL
REGSVR32.EXE /u DogServer.DLL
```

As you can see, most of the details concerning the Registry and server registration are tedious. As a COM developer, you're expected to loathe all matters concerning component registration. If you're lucky, the responsibility for registering your servers will fall to another individual who's creating the application's setup program. Unfortunately, registration is one of the most painful and expensive aspects of deploying COM-based technologies. Fortunately, Windows NT 5 and COM+ will offer features to make server registration easier and more foolproof.

The SCM and Object Activation (Revisited)

As you read in Chapter 3, typical COM clients create objects by passing a CLSID to the SCM. When you compile a Visual Basic client application against a type library, the CLSIDs are embedded into the client executable. Your calls to the *New* operator are translated into a call to the COM library that passes the CLSID and the desired IID to the SCM:

```
Dim Dog As DogServer.IDog
Set Dog = New DogServer.CBeagle
```

The SCM calls your server and negotiates the creation and activation of a new object. If the object is created in an in-process server, the client is directly bound to the vTable for the requested interface. If the object is created in an out-of-process server, a proxy/stub pair is introduced between the client and the object during the binding process.

In one special case, calling the *New* operator doesn't result in a call to the SCM. When you create an object with the *New* operator using a class name that exists in the same project, Visual Basic can create and bind the object without the assistance of the SCM. This is a subtle but important point. There are times when you want the SCM to be involved in object activation, so using the *New* operator isn't an option.

Visual Basic 3 was the first version of Visual Basic that allowed programmers to activate COM objects using the *CreateObject* function. When you call *Create-*

Object, you must always pass a ProgID. A ProgID is simply a text alias for a CLSID that identifies a coclass by qualifying both the project name and the class name, like this:

```
Dim Dog As Object
Set Dog = CreateObject("DogServer.CBeagle")
```

ProgIDs are used to support clients that can't take advantage of the information in your server's type library. Automation clients such as VBScript and JavaScript must use a ProgID to activate an object. As you know, an automation client is bound to the object's default interface. The physical interface used by these clients is always *IDispatch*.

You don't have to use ProgIDs or the *CreateObject* function in Visual Basic when you compile a client application against a server with a type library. *CreateObject* takes longer than a call to the *New* operator because it requires a call to the SCM just to resolve a ProgID to a CLSID. Once an application has the CLSID, the activation sequence is the same as in a call to *New* that uses the SCM. In the days of Visual Basic 3, *CreateObject* was always used with the *Object* data type. If you ever run across an outdated server that serves up *IDispatch*-only objects and doesn't have a type library, you must resort to using *CreateObject* and the *Object* data type.

Many programmers don't understand that you can use *CreateObject* to bind your client application directly to an interface's vTable. This technique isn't common, but it lets you wait until run time to decide what type of object to create. As long as you don't use references of type *Object*, you get the efficiency of custom vTable binding. You can use this technique in complex designs that exploit the polymorphic nature of COM and interface-based programming. Look at this example:

```
Function GetDog(ByVal Breed As String) As IDog
    Dim ProgID As String
    ProgID = "DogServer." & Breed
    Set GetDog = CreateObject(ProgID)
End Function
```

This example shows an advanced technique for achieving polymorphic behavior. The CLSID information for creating a dog object doesn't even have to exist in the client application. The string value for the breed can be read from the Registry or a database; the client code that uses an *IDog* reference still uses vTable binding.

Such techniques are not essential, but it's good to know that they are available. ProgIDs are used primarily to support automation clients. Today the MTS run-time environment also relies on ProgIDs for object creation. Fortunately, every ProgID in your server will be properly written to the Registry by the self-registration code that is built into your server. Just remember that the value you set for the Project Name on the project's Properties tab is used as the first part of the ProgID.

COMPONENT VERSIONING

One of COM's most powerful features is that it lets you revise a binary component in the production environment without having to touch any of the existing clients. When you revise your DLLs and EXEs, you can replace the previous versions in the field without breaking anything. The client applications in production can benefit from the performance enhancements and bug fixes that you have made to the methods that they are already calling.

In addition to improving the implementations of existing methods, you can extend the behavior of your objects by adding new methods. Existing clients can't take advantage of this new behavior unless you do something exotic such as anticipate support for some future interface with the *TypeOf* operator. However, new clients can fully benefit from any new methods that you have added to a later version of an object.

The question then becomes, "How do you strike a balance between maximum object extensibility and backward compatibility?" Understanding the rules of COM versioning is critical. Clients that use custom vTable binding expect every method in every interface to remain the same from build to build. Every interface is a contract, and if you break the contract, a vTable-bound client might take an action that you don't particularly like. Automation clients are more relaxed about what they expect from your objects, but you still have to meet their expectations.

The best way to approach COM versioning is to think through the expectations that each preexisting client has of your server. A client application expects that the things it knows about will not change across builds. Once you understand what the client knows about the server, you can determine what you can change and what you can't. It's a simple matter of determining what dependencies have been built into the client applications.

Binary Component Versioning

When it comes to versioning components, there are two main classifications of clients: those that use custom vTable binding and those that use *IDispatch*. Versioning against *IDispatch* clients is much easier and will be covered after we tackle the tougher problem of versioning clients that use vTable binding.

What does a vTable-bound client application know about? It knows about each CLSID and IID defined in the type library of your server. It also knows the method signatures defined within each interface. You can revise a COM server used by custom vTable-bound clients if you don't change any of these things.

You should understand all aspects of version control. You must also consider two points of view when it comes to extending an object. The creators of COM promote a specific technique for extending an object: When you want to add a new method to an object, you must create and implement a new user-defined interface. The Visual Basic team has devised a technique that makes it possible to add new methods to a class without creating a new user-defined interface. What's really great is that the Visual Basic team has done this without violating any of the rules of COM versioning at the physical level.

The Visual Basic documentation and the Visual Basic IDE recognize three levels of compatibility when you rebuild a component: *version identical, version compatible,* and *version incompatible.* When a later release of a component serves up its interfaces in a version-identical manner, this means that the physical vTables and the calling syntax for each method remain the same. This is consistent with the vision of the COM architects. If an interface is held constant, a versioning system can be properly maintained. The COM specification reinforces this by stating that *an interface is immutable.* When a client successfully calls *QueryInterface*, an object makes a promise to fulfill a contract.

According to the COM specification, to extend your object by adding new methods, you must create a new interface. Chapter 2 demonstrated this technique in Visual Basic using two interfaces, *IDog* and *IDog2*. The new object is responsible for implementing both the old interface and the new interface. Old clients use the original interface, and new clients use the extended interface. With this versioning scheme, you can continue to extend your objects over time by creating other interfaces such as *IDog3, IDog4,* and *IDog5.*

Unfortunately, the COM purists and the Visual Basic team disagree when it comes to the proper mechanism for extending an object. The Visual Basic team thinks that the rules can be relaxed as long as the server continues to meet the expectations of each client. They believe that it sometimes makes sense to break the most fundamental rule of traditional COM: *Don't ever change an interface once it's in use.* As you will see, you can modify an interface definition in Visual Basic without breaking existing clients if you do it correctly.

Here's how it works. You can safely extend an interface by adding new methods if you don't change the signatures of any existing method. Adding methods to a preexisting interface means extending the physical layout of the vTable by adding new entries at the end. An extended vTable defines the same method signatures as before, and it adds one or more new methods below. This type of vTable is *version compatible.* Old clients are oblivious to the new entries in the vTable. They can use a version-compatible vTable in the same way they use the original. New clients, on the other hand, can take advantage of the new methods added to the second version. This means that you can extend the functionality of an object without explicitly creating a new interface.

This versioning technique is important to Visual Basic programmers who don't use user-defined interfaces. As you know, when a programmer compiles a creatable class with public members, Visual Basic automatically creates a default interface behind the scenes. Visual Basic can thus let programmers participate in COM programming without explicitly dealing with a user-defined interface. Without relaxing the rules of object extensibility in the COM specification, Visual Basic programmers would be forced to deal with user-defined interfaces to extend their objects in later versions. The Visual Basic team managed to find a way to keep the COM purists happy without forcing Visual Basic programmers to work in terms of user-defined interfaces. This was a remarkable achievement.

So what's the problem with a version-compatible interface? Why does the idea make COM purists sick to their stomachs? The problem has to do with a scenario in which a new client comes in contact with an older version of the object. For instance, suppose an object's default interface had 5 methods in the first version and was then extended to contain 10 methods in a subsequent release. If a client that is compiled against a later version of the interface somehow activates an earlier version of the object, it will expect the vTable to be twice as long as it really is. What happens when the client attempts to use the sixth or seventh entry in the vTable? The client will be reading random values from memory when it expects to find a valid function pointer. You can see the problem. When a client tries to invoke a method using an invalid function pointer, bad things happen.

From the COM purist's point of view, an interface (as specified by an IID) is a contract that can never change. Adding methods to the end of the vTable makes the contract invalid. The Visual Basic team believes that it is acceptable to add methods to the end of the vTable as long as you ensure that a new client never activates an older version of the object. If a new client were to activate an older version of the object, it would expect methods that are absent in the original interface. As you will see, Visual Basic generates a trappable run-time error whenever a new client tries to activate an object from an earlier, incompatible, version of the server.

Version-Compatible Interfaces

Visual Basic uses a mechanism known as *IID forwarding* to make interface compatibility work in a production environment. As you'll see in the next section, when you add new public methods to a class between the first and second builds of a server, you can ask Visual Basic to create the new build in a version-compatible manner. This means that clients that were compiled against the first version of the type library will continue to work as before. Newer clients that are compiled against the new version of the type library can take advantage of the new methods.

Whenever a new interface is either explicitly or implicitly created in your server, Visual Basic automatically generates a new IID for it. When you create a version-compatible interface by adding new methods in a subsequent release, Visual Basic generates a second IID for it. (This means that Visual Basic is adhering to the rules of interface immutability at the physical level.) Client applications can activate and communicate with your Visual Basic object through either the old IID or the new IID. The implementation behind *QueryInterface* will know about both IIDs. When a client asks for a reference to either IID, the object simply hands out a reference to the extended interface. A version-compatible interface always satisfies the client.

The old version of the object doesn't know anything about the new IID. When a new client calls *QueryInterface* on the old object and attempts to bind using the new IID, the call fails. And this is the behavior you would expect from any COM object. If an object doesn't support the behavior behind an IID, it should fail the call to *QueryInterface* and put the responsibility on the client to degrade gracefully and decide what to do next.

Visual Basic also builds the self-registration code into the second version of the server to add entries for both the original IID and the new IID. It modifies the original IID by adding a special Forward Registry key, as shown in Figure 5-3. The universal marshaler uses this key to locate the type library for the original IID on the local machine to generate a proxy and a stub. When the universal marshaler tries to find the original interface definition, it is redirected to the newer, version-compatible, IID. As you can see, although this involves a bit of trickery, it does make it fairly easy to extend Visual Basic classes and interfaces in a production environment.

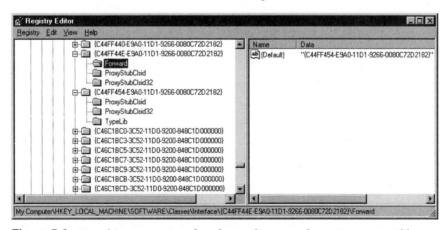

Figure 5-3. *Visual Basic uses interface forwarding to make version-compatible interfaces work in the production environment. The universal marshaler can use the definition of either the original interface or a version-compatible interface when it builds a proxy or a stub.*

Project Compatibility Settings

Figure 5-4 on the following page shows the Component tab of the Project Properties dialog box. When you build or rebuild a server, you must assign to the project one of the three version compatibility modes: No Compatibility, Project Compatibility,

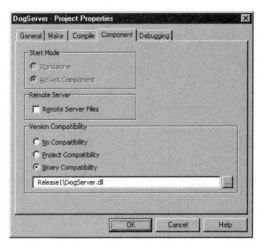

Figure 5-4. *A project's version compatibility setting determines the level of compatibility built into a server when you choose the Make command from the File menu.*

or Binary Compatibility. The default setting for a new project is Project Compatibility, but you should be aware of which compatibility setting is in use when you rebuild your server. If you don't watch out, Visual Basic will change your GUIDs every time you rebuild your server. This can lead to broken compiled client applications and can confuse application developers who work with your server.

No Compatibility mode always generates a new set of GUIDs. A new GUID is created for each IID and CLSID in the server as well as for the server's type library. Precompiled client applications can't use subsequent builds when you select this mode. Also, because the GUID of the type library is changed on every build, application developers who use your server in the Visual Basic IDE will find that your server reference is missing when they try to use your new build. The developer must fix this by rereferencing the type library in the References dialog box (which you open from the Project menu).

You should use Project Compatibility mode when you define the methods in your classes and interfaces. This mode assumes that none of your work is cast in stone and that you don't yet expect client applications to be compiled against your server. When you work in this mode, Visual Basic 5 creates a new set of CLSIDs and IIDs every time you rebuild your project. When you overwrite a server in this mode, Visual Basic unregisters it before it's overwritten. This is important. If Visual Basic didn't unregister your server, your Registry would fill up with invalid IIDs and CLSIDs. Note also that you should always unregister a server before deleting it manually. Using discipline with server registration and unregistration will keep the Registry of your development workstation as clean as possible.

The only GUID that is held constant during a project-compatible build is the GUID for the type library. In the early stages of component prototyping, this is quite useful because other Visual Basic projects for client applications can retain a logical pointer to your server's type library. When you create a new build, any other programmer can use it from within the Visual Basic IDE. Because client application developers always see the newest version of your type library, they see the latest definitions of your coclasses, interfaces, and methods.

The main limitation of project compatibility is that a compiled client application can't use the next build of your server. This is because new CLSIDs and IIDs are generated for each build. Visual Basic 6 improves project compatibility by holding CLSIDs constant across builds. However, both the CLSIDs and IIDs must remain constant to honor dependencies built into compiled client applications. If you want compiled client applications to work properly across builds of your server, you must work exclusively in Binary Compatibility mode once client applications are in production.

You can put your project into Binary Compatibility mode by selecting the appropriate option on the Components tab of the project's Properties dialog box. You must also point to a compiled server file that will serve as a reference. One way to do this is to create an initial build of your server in a subdirectory named \Release1. After you point the Visual Basic IDE to a reference, you can rebuild your server in Binary Compatibility mode. In this mode, you can't overwrite the server that's being used as a reference. You should keep track of each server binary that's released into the production environment. Many developers create a set of directories for this purpose named Release1, Release2, Release3, and so forth.

Binary Compatibility mode does more than just retain your CLSIDs and IIDs. It also compares the server being built against the reference server. Visual Basic conducts a method-by-method check on each interface to make sure that it is identical to or compatible with those defined in the previous version. In Binary Compatibility mode, the Visual Basic IDE warns you when you try to compile an interface that's incompatible. The Visual Basic IDE gives you the option of ignoring the warnings and building an incompatible version of the server. However, to create a server that is compatible with the previous release, you must make the appropriate changes to restore existing methods to their previous form. When you do this correctly, you will be able to rebuild your server without receiving any warning messages. If you choose to build an incompatible version of the server, Visual Basic changes all the GUIDs in the new build to prevent any confusion.

Extending Objects in Binary-Compatible Servers

In Binary Compatibility mode, you can't alter an existing method signature. This means you can't change the name of any method, the type of the return value, or the type of any parameter. You also can't add optional arguments to the end of a method signature. You might think you can add an optional argument because it doesn't require a change in the client's calling syntax, but this requires physical changes to the stack frame during method execution. Therefore, adding an optional parameter to an existing method makes the entire interface incompatible.

You can safely change any existing method implementations in Binary Compatibility mode. When you think about it, this is what COM is all about. You should always be able to change an implementation as long as you don't change the physical nature of the calling syntax. Visual Basic lets you go one step further and add new methods to your classes and interfaces. When you add methods to an interface in a second version of your server, Visual Basic creates a new interface that is version compatible with the original.

When you add new methods to the default interface of a class in a Visual Basic project in Binary Compatibility mode, some interesting things happen when the server is rebuilt. For example, suppose you are working on a server with a class named *CDog* that defines eight public methods. The first time you build the server, Visual Basic automatically creates an interface named _CDog with an IID that defines these eight methods. If you add four new methods to this class and rebuild the server in Binary Compatibility mode, Visual Basic creates a new IID for the new interface that contains all 12 methods. Visual Basic also provides support in the new object and server to deal with clients using either IID.

The implementation of *QueryInterface* behind the *CDog* object hands out a reference for the new IID when a client asks for either the new IID or the old one. Clients built against the original version of the server get a reference to the new IID, but they will know about only the first 8 of the 12 methods defined in the vTable. Because the new interface is version compatible with the old one, it meets the expectations of the client and things work fine. Remember that version-compatible servers also contain registration code. Each server must add a Forward key for each backward-compatible IID. This allows the universal marshaler to locate the type library when it needs to generate a proxy or a stub.

Visual Basic lets you build version upon version of compatible servers. For instance, version 4 can be compatible with version 3, which can be compatible with version 2, which can be compatible with the original version. A client that knows about only the original version of the interface might be forwarded across many compatible IIDs before it reaches one that is supported by a server installed on the host computer.

Starting from Scratch

At some point, you might need to change your server so much that it doesn't make sense to worry about compatibility with clients already in production. This can happen if you have many method signatures that need to be overhauled or if you have a long line of version-compatible servers that are causing havoc. Either situation might lead you to create a server that is version incompatible with the previous version. No existing clients will be able to use the new server. This can be accurately labeled the "start again" approach.

To create a build that is version incompatible, you change your projectwide compatibility setting to No Compatibility. When you rebuild your server in this mode, Visual Basic changes all the GUIDs, including the one for the type library. It also ignores any compatibility support for earlier interfaces defined in earlier versions of the server. After you create a build in No Compatibility mode, you should set the project back to one of the other compatibility modes.

After this build, no existing client can use the new server. Any references to your type library will also be invalid. If you plan to leave earlier client applications in production using an older version of the server, you should change the project name and the project description to avoid confusion. For instance, you should name the new server DogServer2.dll so that all the client applications using DogServer.dll can continue to run in the production environment without encountering a naming conflict.

Version Compatibility for Automation Clients

Compared with vTable clients, automation clients aren't very knowledgeable about your server. They don't know about any GUIDs or the physical layout of any custom vTable. Instead, they know the ProgID and the names of the methods and properties that they will attempt to bind to at run time. They need some knowledge of the parameters that must be passed during method invocation, but automation clients can be more relaxed than vTable-bound clients because everything is passed as a variant. Automation is costly in terms of overhead, but it is certainly flexible and tolerant when it comes to versioning.

When dealing with automation clients, you can use any of the compatibility modes because automation clients use ProgIDs, not CLSIDs and IIDs. Moreover, automation clients don't require any custom vTable binding. The only concern you have is that method signatures must be compatible with any dependencies that automation clients have built. You certainly have a lot more flexibility when method signatures only have to be *compatible* as opposed to *identical*. For instance, you can change an integer parameter to a different type, such as a long or a double. Or you can add optional parameters to the end of a method signature. As you can see, if you can assume that your server will be used only by automation clients, your versioning concerns become far less complex.

SERVER DESIGN ISSUES

The *Instancing* setting of a class module has a profound effect on what is published in your server's type library. It determines what coclasses and interfaces are seen by the outside world. The following are the available settings:

- *Private*: The class can be used only in the local project. It's not exposed through the type library to the outside world.

- *PublicNotCreatable*: The class module generates a noncreatable coclass that can only be instantiated from inside the server. A default dual-style interface is built from the public members.

- *MultiUse*: The class module generates a creatable coclass that allows multiple instances in any process. A default dual-style interface is built from the public members.

- *SingleUse*: (For out-of-process servers only.) The class module generates a creatable coclass that guarantees that each server process contains only one instance. A default dual-style interface is built from the public members.

- *GlobalSingleUse*: Like *SingleUse*, but allow the client access to the object's methods as if the methods were global functions.

- *GlobalMultiUse*: Like *MultiUse*, but allow the client acces to the object's methods as if the methods were global functions.

When you want a creatable class, it's most common to select *MultiUse*. *SingleUse*, however, has some interesting uses. If you create two instances from a coclass that has this setting, each instance is created in a separate server process. If you're running two applications on a user's desktop and they activate the same type of object, you can use a *SingleUse* class to give your objects an extra level of fault protection. Each client will activate its object in a different process. *SingleUse* classes also provide a simple way to achieve multithreading because each process owns its own thread. However, you will learn more efficient techniques for creating multithreaded servers later in this book.

MultiUse and *SingleUse* both allow you to make a coclass "global." This simply makes the class easier for the client to use. If you have a standard *MultiUse* class that calculates a tax rate, for example, you access the object like this:

```
Dim Obj As CTaxCalculator, Tax As Currency
Set Obj = New CTaxCalculator
Tax = Obj.CalculateTax(28600)
```

When you set the instancing property of the class to *GlobalMultiUse*, the client can access the method as if it were a global function, as shown here:

```
Dim Tax As Currency
Tax = CalculateTax(28600)
```

Global classes simply save the client the trouble of instantiating an object before calling a method. They do this by marking the coclass with the *AppObject* attribute in the type library. On the client side, Visual Basic creates an invisible object behind the scenes. Any global call is interpreted as a call to this invisible object. As of this writing, Visual Basic is the only known developer tool that provides the convenience of transparently mapping *AppObject* attributes on the client side. A programmer creating a client application with C++ or Java can't tell the difference between a class marked *GlobalMultiUse* and a class marked *MultiUse*. In this case, global classes just provide a syntactic sugar for other Visual Basic programmers.

Using Enumerations

As a COM developer, you should be aggressive with the use of enumerations. Enumerations let you declare logically related sets of constants in your type library. COM and Visual Basic have borrowed the syntax for enumerations from C. Here's what it looks like:

```
' Dog Server Error Codes
Enum ErrorCodesEnum
    dsDogUnavailable
    dsDogUnagreeable
    dsDogNotFound
End Enum
```

You must declare enumerations in a class module in order to expose them to COM clients. If you don't do this, they will not be published in a type library. Enumerations declared in .bas modules are private to the project.

What's not very intuitive is that the enumerations you declare in a class module are scoped at the type library level, not the class level. Therefore, every enumeration value that you declare in a project must have a unique name. The class instancing property has no effect on this. If you want to create a separate class module just to hold your enumerations, you should mark it as *PublicNotCreatable*. Here's what an enumeration looks like in Interface Definition Language (IDL):

```
typedef[uuid(FFB2C0DE-CD72-11D1-920D-E46FA4000000), version(1.0)]
enum {
    dsDogUnavailable = 0,
    dsDogUnagreeable = 1,
    dsDogNotFound = 2
} ErrorCodesEnum;
```

Here's another thing to think about. If a client application uses several type libraries, each of which defines its own set of enumerations, all of the combined enumerations from every server are visible to the client application in a single projectwide scope. The enumerations from two servers will conflict if they have the same name. You can sometimes prevent this conflict by using a server-specific prefix. The enumerations in the example above have been defined with the prefix *ds* to comply with this convention. However, there's still a potential conflict, which can always be resolved in the client application by preceding the name of the enumeration with the project name, like this:

```
DogServer.dsDogNotAvailable
```

Modifying Procedure Attributes

You can influence how Visual Basic sets attributes for the methods and properties of your classes and interfaces by choosing the Procedure Attributes command from the Tools menu while the class module you want to modify is the active window. Figure 5-5 shows the dialog box that appears.

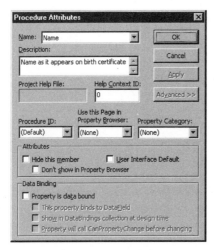

Figure 5-5. *In the Procedure Attributes dialog box, you can modify the definition of the methods and properties in a public class module. All of the settings that you specify in this dialog box are written into the interface definition in the server's type library.*

You use the Description setting to document the semantics of the method or property. Other Visual Basic programmers will see your descriptions when they examine your server's type library with the Object Browser. This is pretty easy to do, and it makes your server seem more polished.

You can also set the Procedure ID to a different value. For instance, if you set the Procedure ID for a property to Default (the value 0), the property will be recognized as the default property of the object. Here's what the resulting IDL looks like:

```
[id(00000000),
   propput,
   helpstring("Name as it appears on birth certificate")
]
HRESULT Name([in] BSTR Name);
```

Now a client can access this property both explicitly and implicitly, like this:

```
Dim Dog1 As IDog, Dog2 As IDog
Set Dog1 = New CBeagle
Set Dog2 = New CBeagle
' Name property is accessible explicitly.
Dog1.Name = "Milli"
' Name property is also accessible implicitly.
Dog2 = "Vanilli"
```

As you can see, you can set many options in the Procedure Attributes dialog box. If you have a help file associated with your server, you can add context sensitivity to your methods so that programmers can jump to a certain part of the help file. You can also hide methods from other programmers. In short, you can make your server far more polished. Note that many of the settings are relevant only to programmers who are building ActiveX controls. Many of the options, such as Don't Show In Property Browser and User Interface Default, aren't useful to programmers who are creating nonvisual servers for the middle tier.

Friend Methods

Marking a method as a friend in a Visual Basic class creates an interesting effect. A friend method is accessible to any code in the server project, but it isn't exposed to the outside world. You could say that it's public on the inside and private on the outside. Or you could say that in a public class, private members provide modulewide access, friend members provide projectwide access, and public members are available to any client inside or outside the server. When you mark a method or a property as a friend, it isn't published in a type library. It has nothing to do with COM.

Use friend members with caution in Visual Basic. C++ has a similar feature, which is often used to remedy problems in the initial class design. Many programmers use this friend syntax without realizing that they are breaking encapsulation. Friend methods can be useful, but you should be sure that you're not unnecessarily exposing implementation details of a class. The encapsulation police might arrive at your door and start asking a lot of questions.

HRESULTs AND COM EXCEPTIONS

HRESULTs indicate the success or failure of method calls in COM. They are particularly important in calls that extend across the network. COM has standardized on this return value so that the remoting infrastructure can inform the client that a problem has occurred when an object can't be reached. Therefore, if an object that is part of an active connection meets an untimely death, the client can discover this fact and respond in the appropriate manner.

All remotable methods return HRESULTs at the physical level to accommodate this requirement, but the Visual Basic compiler and the run-time layer can hide all traces of their existence. However, if you use OleView.exe and inspect your servers, you'll see that every method you have created is defined with an HRESULT as a return value—including Visual Basic methods that are defined as functions. For example, a method defined like this:

```
Function GetTaxRate() As Double
```

results in IDL code that looks like this:

```
HRESULT GetTaxRate([out, retval] double* );
```

Whenever a method needs a logical return value, IDL accommodates this by providing the *[retval]* parameter attribute. There can be only one *[retval]* parameter in a COM method, and it must appear last in the parameter list. Visual Basic and Java are examples of languages that transparently map these special parameters so that programmers can use them as return values instead of as output parameters. This makes calling a function more natural, and it also relieves programmers from manually inspecting HRESULTs. The HRESULT is inspected by Visual Basic's run-time layer, and the client receives an error in the event of a failure.

Sometimes the connection between a client and an object is broken in a distributed application. This can happen when the server crashes or when the server's computer is rebooted by an overzealous administrator. In either case, the client application will have an outstanding reference to an object that no longer exists. It can also happen when network problems make it impossible to route a method request between the client and the object. In all of these cases, a remote method call will fail. The underlying remote procedure call (RPC) layer is responsible for informing the client that the server is unavailable. The HRESULT was created for this purpose.

Visual Basic 6 added support to the run-time layer for catching most of the HRESULTs that indicate that an out-of-process object is dead or unreachable. When the Visual Basic run-time library determines that the RPC layer has reported a dead object, it raises error number 462 along with the description, "The remote server machine doesn't exist or is unavailable." This run-time error assists you in most of the cases in which you need to handle a dead or unreachable object. However, the Visual Basic run-time library doesn't handle certain other situations as elegantly. In these situations, the Visual Basic run-time library raises an error and places the raw HRESULT in Err.Number. Moreover, if you're using Visual Basic 5, you must always deal with HRESULTs in order to determine that an object has died. In times like these, it's very helpful to know exactly what's inside an HRESULT.

An HRESULT is a 32-bit value that contains three distinct pieces of information. Figure 5-6 shows how the physical memory of an HRESULT is segmented to hold a severity level, a facility code, and an application-specific error code. The severity level stored in bit 31 indicates whether the method call was successful. If the bit is left off, the method succeeded. If the bit is turned on, the method did not succeed.

The set of bits in the middle of an HRESULT, known as the *facility code,* informs the client where the error originated. Standard COM error codes use the code FACILITY_NULL. An object, on the other hand, should use FACILITY_ITF when it wants to send an interface-specific error code to the client. The list in Figure 5-6 shows some of the other possible values for the facility code. A number of facility code values aren't shown in this list, but Visual Basic programmers rarely need to deal with them directly.

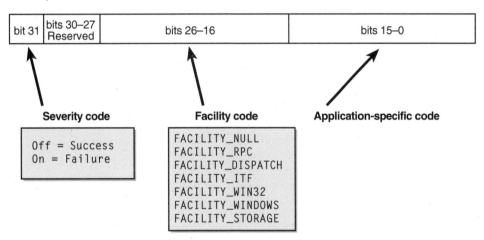

Figure 5-6. *All methods in COM return HRESULTs at the physical level.*

You should be aware of a few important facility codes that inform the client application of a problem in the underlying RPC transport. You can test for these facility codes in a standard Visual Basic error handler to determine whether your call was unable to reach the object. Look at the code on the following page.

```
Enum FacilityCodes
    FACILITY_RPC = 1
    FACILITY_WIN32 = 7
    FACILITY_WINDOWS = 8
End Enum

Private Dog As IDog

Private Sub Form_Load()
    ' Create dog on another computer.
    Set Dog  = New CBeagle
End Sub

' Test for dead object on user command.
Private Sub cmdMakeDogBark()
    On Error GoTo Err_cmdMakeDogBark
    Dog.Bark
Exit Sub
Err_cmdMakeDogBark:
    Const vbDeadObject = 462
    ' First: Test for Visual Basic dead object error.
    If Err.Number = DeadObject Then
        Set Dog = Nothing
        MsgBox "Your dog has unfortunately died."
    ' Second: Test for a bad facility code.
    ElseIf BadFacilityCode(Err.Number) Then
        MsgBox "Your dog might or might not be dead."
    End If
End Sub

Function BadFacilityCode(ByVal HRESULT As Long) As Boolean
    Dim FacilityCode As Integer
    ' Extract facility code from HRESULT.
    FacilityCode = ((HRESULT And &HFFF0000) / 65536)
    If FacilityCode = FACILITY_RPC Or _
        FacilityCode = FACILITY_WIN32 Or _
        FacilityCode = FACILITY_WINDOWS Then
        ' These facility codes signify a failed method call.
        BadFacilityCode = True
    End If
End Function
```

When a Visual Basic client tries to invoke a method on a dead or unreachable object, the RPC layer returns an HRESULT indicating failure. If the Visual Basic run-time library knows about the HRESULT, it raises error number 462. This error is easy to trap and handle. However, if the Visual Basic run-time library doesn't know about the HRESULT, it simply raises an error and places the raw HRESULT in *Err.Number*.

When this happens, you can examine the facility code in an error handler as shown in the utility function *BadFacilityCode*.

By examining the facility code, you can attempt to determine the nature of the problem. Facility codes such as FACILITY_RPC, FACILITY_WIN32, and FACILITY_WINDOWS can mean a dead or unreachable object. Unfortunately, you can't be sure that receiving one of these facility codes really means the object has died. You might receive a facility code when the parameter state of a method call couldn't be marshaled to or from the object. This means that the next call to the object might be successful. When you find that an HRESULT has a bad facility code, you should look at the error code in the lower 16 bits of the HRESULT if you really want to know what has happened. You can find a list of such error codes in the header file *WINERROR.H*, which is part of the Win32 SDK. As you can imagine, working at this level can be very tedious for the average Visual Basic programmer.

When you find that an object has died, you can always attempt to activate another one. If you are successful, you can then reinitialize the object and reexecute the method. Of course, the problem that killed the first object might prevent you from creating a new one. You can add your own fail-over support by attempting to create another object on a different machine. However, you can do this only if more than one remote computer can serve up the same CLSID. Many factors determine what you do next, but at least your client application knows exactly what has occurred and can degrade gracefully.

Throwing COM Exceptions

An HRESULT can convey whether a method has succeeded. It can also contain an application-specific error code. But it can't convey a text-based error message or any information about where the error actually occurred. COM uses COM exceptions for passing elaborate error information between objects and clients. Support for COM exceptions is provided by a handful of functions and interfaces in the COM library.

Before examining the inner workings of COM exceptions, you should note that all these details are hidden from Visual Basic programmers. The Visual Basic team has taken Visual Basic's proprietary error handling model and cleanly mapped it on top of COM exceptions. As a result, Visual Basic programmers don't have to know a thing about COM exceptions. Another, less obvious, benefit is that Visual Basic programmers can throw COM exceptions from their servers and catch COM exceptions in their client applications. This is extremely important when Visual Basic components are used in systems with COM components that were written with other tools and languages. As long as everybody follows the rules outlined by COM's language-independent exception model, everything works out fine.

Here's how COM exceptions work. Any COM object that throws exceptions must advertise this fact by supporting a standard interface named *ISupportErrorInfo*. This interface allows a client to query the object on an interface-by-interface basis to see whether it supports exceptions. This allows the object to tell the client, "Yes, I support COM exceptions for the interface you are using."

When an object wants to throw an exception, it must create an error object by calling a function in the COM library named *CreateErrorInfo*. This function creates the error object and returns an *ICreateErrorInfo* reference. The object then uses this reference to populate the newly created error object with information such as a description and an error source. Next the object must call *SetErrorInfo* to associate the error object with the logical thread of the caller. Finally the object must return an HRESULT that tells the client that something has gone wrong.

When an exception-savvy client inspects an HRESULT and finds that a method call was not successful, it queries the object to see whether it supports the *ISupportErrorInfo* interface. If it does, the client calls a method through this interface to test for support on the IID that is being used. If the object indicates that it supports exceptions on the IID, the client can be sure that an error object exists with contextual information about the nature of the problem. The client can then call *GetErrorInfo* to retrieve an *IErrorInfo* interface reference to the error object. This interface lets the client retrieve all the error information sent by the object. As you can see, COM exceptions require a lot of work on both sides and quite a few round-trips.

Visual Basic's Mapping of COM Exceptions

If you have used Visual Basic's error handling model, you know that it's much easier to use than COM's exception handling model. It is fortunate that the two models work so well together. Visual Basic programmers continue to raise and trap errors in the same way that they have for years, and the details are transparently mapped by the run-time layer to conform to the language-independent model required by COM.

Every coclass in Visual Basic has built-in support for *ISupportErrorInfo*. When you explicitly raise an error from a Visual Basic server with *Err.Raise* syntax, the run-time layer automatically creates and populates a COM error object. It also makes the other necessary calls to properly throw a COM exception. All you really need to do is provide code as demonstrated in the following example:

```
Dim Number As Long
Number = vbObjectError + 2
Dim Source As String
Source = "DogServer.CBeagle.Bark()"
Dim Description As String
Description = "The cat's got the dog's tongue"
Err.Raise Number, Source, Description
```

When you call *Err.Raise*, you must pass a user-defined error code. Visual Basic provides the intrinsic constant *vbObjectError* as the starting point for your user-defined error codes. The previous example also shows how to populate the *Source* and *Description* properties of an error object. The source should tell the client application where the problem occurred. This is most useful during debugging. The description should give the client an indication of what went wrong in a human-readable form. It's common practice to display the description to the user, so keep that in mind. If the error condition has a remedy, it's often valuable to make that known in the description as well.

All of the user-defined errors raised by your servers should have corresponding error codes. The error codes for a server should be published in the type library using enumerations. You can define a set of error codes in the following manner:

```
' Dog Server Error Codes
Enum ErrorCodesEnum
    dsDogUnavailable = vbObjectError
    dsDogUnagreeable
    dsDogNotCapable
    dsDogNotFound
    dsUnexpectedError
End Enum
```

Visual Basic's client-side mapping of COM exceptions is just as transparent as it is on the object side. When a method returns an HRESULT indicating failure, the mapping layer uses the *ISupportErrorInfo* interface to determine whether the object supports COM exceptions. If it does, the mapping layer retrieves the COM error object and uses it to populate a standard Visual Basic Error object. The mapping layer then raises an error to the caller. You can use a *Select Case* statement in a client application to create a handler, like this:

```
Sub MakeDogBark(Dog As IDog)
    On Error GoTo MakeDogBark_Err
    Dog.Bark
' Exit if successful.
Exit Sub
' Enter handler on error.
MakeDogBark_Err:
    Select Case Err.Number
        Case dsDogNotCapable:
            ' Perform necessary handling in client.
            MsgBox Err.Description, vbCritical, "Error: Dog Not Capable"
        Case Else
            ' Always provide a last-chance handler.
            MsgBox Err.Description, vbCritical, "Unexpected Error"
    End Select
End Sub
```

When a Visual Basic client application experiences an error on a COM object that doesn't support COM exceptions, the mapping layer raises an error and places the raw HRESULT into *Err.Number*. You also get a raw HRESULT when a call experiences an error in COM's infrastructure, such as when you attempt a method call on a dead object. When you see an error code that is a large negative number, such as −2147023174, this indicates that you are dealing with a raw HRESULT.

Error-Raising Conventions

When you distribute COM servers, you are expected to follow the rules defined by COM as well as the rules used by Visual Basic programmers. This is especially true if you work in environments in which some components are written with tools and languages other than Visual Basic. This section covers some of the rules that you should keep in mind.

All COM exceptions that leave your server should be explicitly raised by your code. This means that only errors explicitly generated with *Err.Raise* syntax should leave your server. You must prevent any unhandled errors from leaving your server. Most Visual Basic programmers know that an unhandled error in a client application will result in the application's termination. A Visual Basic server, on the other hand, deals with an unhandled error by passing it on to the client. For instance, if a method in your server experiences a division-by-0 error that isn't handled, the run-time layer simply forwards the error on to the client application.

It's considered bad style to let exceptions leave your server that haven't been explicitly raised. Any COM object that implements *ISupportErrorInfo* can pass on its own exceptions only. This means that you must catch any Visual Basic–generated error in your servers. If your server experiences an error that it can't deal with, you should send an application-specific "unexpected error" exception back to the client.

Always include a helpful text description when raising an exception. Try to create informational descriptions at the place where the error occurred. The procedure in which the error occurs usually has the most contextual information. It's easy to propagate this description back to the original caller from anywhere in the call chain. A description such as "Order for $2000.00 could not be accepted. The customer has a credit balance of only $1250.00" is far more valuable than "Order submission failure." The handler in the client application will often display this error message to the user. Remember that error codes are for programmers and error descriptions are for users.

Always use enumerations to define your error codes. This will allow other programmers to see your error codes through the type library. Visual Basic programmers using your server will be able to see these error codes with the Object Browser.

Always define your error codes using **vbObjectError.** The lower error codes are reserved by COM and have special meanings. If you use the *vbObjectError* constant, you can be sure that your codes will not conflict and be misinterpreted as system-defined error codes.

   Try to supply documentation with your servers that describes errors to other programmers. You can convey only so much information with an enumerated value such as *dsDogNotCapable*. If possible, you should include a list of remedies and workarounds for each error condition.

   Never display a message box in your server's error handlers. The decision to interact with the user should always be left to the client application. With an out-of-process server, an error handler that displays a message box will hang the server. You don't want this to happen. Although you can display a message box to the user from an in-process server, this is considered bad style. The client application programmer should ultimately control all interaction with the user.

DESIGNING SERVERS

This chapter covered the basics of creating and distributing COM servers with Visual Basic. You must first decide whether to package your coclasses in an in-process server or an out-of-process server. The way you package your code affects your server's performance, robustness, and security. Many distributed application designs require that your objects be deployed in an out-of-process server. However, many sophisticated run-time environments, such as MTS, provide a surrogate process, which means that you still distribute your code in an ActiveX DLL.

   Visual Basic builds a lot of support into your server automatically. Your job is to concentrate on how to expose things through the type library and how to provide an implementation for the functionality you expose. It is important to understand all the issues surrounding component versioning. As you have seen, you have the choice of two approaches for extending your objects. There is also a huge difference between versioning for automation clients and for clients that use custom vTable binding.

   This chapter also exposed you to the important issues of raising and handling errors. It's comforting that Visual Basic provides a transparent mapping on top of COM exceptions. Visual Basic objects and clients can participate in exception handling with components that are written in other languages.

   The next chapter explores approaches to interface design and describes their effect on maintainability and extensibility. It also takes an in-depth look at designing interfaces for out-of-process servers. You'll see that the overhead of the proxy/stub layer has a profound effect on how you design a remote interface. Many designs that are acceptable in a classic object-oriented programming sense must be adjusted to minimize expensive round-trips to the server.

Chapter 6

Designing
Interfaces

This chapter explains several approaches to designing and managing interfaces in a distributed application. Each approach offers varying degrees of ease of use, extensibility, and scalability. You must understand the costs and benefits of each approach and pick the one that best meets your needs. What's really important is that you commit to one of the approaches before you start your design.

COM has been influenced by many factors to accommodate component-based development and interprocess communication. As a result, many of the designs and methodologies of classic object-oriented programming (OOP) don't work well in the world of COM. In particular, many common OOP interface designs don't scale when they're taken out of process because the proxy/stub layer has such a significant impact on performance. When you design an interface for an out-of-process object, your first priority should be reducing round-trips. This means that your classes and interfaces can become more complex than a simple class design that you would create in a classic OOP paradigm.

This chapter also explains how to implement an object with an outbound interface. It specifies the advantages of bidirectional communication and demonstrates two techniques for creating an outbound interface. One way is to use events, and the other way is to define and implement a custom callback interface. These techniques offer different combinations of ease of use, performance, and flexibility.

MANAGING INTERFACE DESIGN

Before you write any object code or client code for a software project, you must make certain crucial design decisions. Design flaws that you discover midway through the development life cycle can be expensive and can ultimately lead to failure. The most important part of the design phase in a COM application is the creation of the interfaces for client-object communication.

The rules of COM (as defined in the COM Specification) let programmers create extensible objects. If you follow these rules, you can safely refine both object code and client code over time. As you learned in the previous chapter, Visual Basic engages in some trickery behind the scenes to make programmers more productive. Unfortunately, this can cause confusion for those who expect a single set of versioning rules for using Visual Basic by itself or with C++ in an application. There's the original set of rules for extending objects, as defined by the COM purists, and a second set of rules defined by the Visual Basic team.

When you create a large-scale project with Visual Basic, you must make many decisions relating to managing your interface design. In particular, you must decide what role user-defined interfaces will play in your application. If you decide to employ user-defined interfaces in your design, you can take advantage of powerful OOP features such as polymorphism and run-time type information (RTTI). On the other hand, simply using public classes and Visual Basic's transparent mapping of interfaces behind the scenes will result in an application that is far less complex and thus far easier for most Visual Basic programmers to create and maintain.

Complex information systems that will be assembled from a large number of components are good candidates for user-defined interfaces. This is especially true when the components will be owned and versioned by different programming teams. While user-defined interfaces force class authors and client application developers to deal with more complexity, they allow both sets of programmers to revise their work without adversely affecting any other code in the application.

Visual Basic also lets you ignore user-defined interfaces and use *MultiUse* classes instead. Many programmers create successful COM-based applications with Visual Basic without ever explicitly creating a user-defined interface. This can be a reasonable approach for small projects or projects that involve only automation clients. Before you begin a project, you must weigh the costs and benefits of user-defined interfaces and decide whether to use them in your designs.

If you decide to incorporate user-defined interfaces into your designs, you must address some other critical issues. Here are some questions that you should answer:

- Should you publish your interfaces in a separate type library?

- Should you define your interfaces with the Visual Basic IDE or with Interface Definition Language (IDL)?

- Do you want to adhere to COM's original rules for object extensibility?

Publishing Interfaces in Separate Type Libraries

Interface-based programming requires a formal separation of interface from implementation. This means that all interfaces must be defined independently of coclass definitions. You should see this not only as a requirement in COM but also as an opportunity to define the interfaces for your project in a stand-alone type library file. This allows an application's lead designer to create all the interface definitions ahead of time and to distribute them to other programmers in efficient binary packaging.

In a large project, there are several advantages to defining all the interfaces in a type library file that is independent of any implementation code. This approach makes it easy to assign the ownership of interface definitions to a single team or individual. It makes it harder to add or extend interface definitions, but it builds more discipline into the development process. A developer who is creating a server can't casually add or extend an existing interface. Any change to the application's interface design must be made by the developer who owns the one type library that contains all the interface definitions.

Publishing interfaces in a separate type library also makes it easier to use the same interface definition across multiple servers. For instance, what if you want to create two ActiveX DLLs each of which contains a coclass that implements the same interface? When a designer publishes an interface in a separate type library, two independent DLL authors can easily reference this library and implement the interface. This allows several COM servers to serve up objects that are type compatible with one another. This is valuable when a system is designed around the idea of plug-compatible components.

In a smaller project, it might not make sense to publish interface definitions in a separate type library, especially if the project involves only one small team or a lone developer. It's easier to define the interfaces in the same server project as your coclasses. If your project doesn't benefit from maintaining interfaces and coclasses independently, the administrative overhead of building separate files is more trouble than it's worth.

If you decide to publish a type library of interface definitions, you must decide between using the Visual Basic IDE or IDL. Creating a type library of interface definitions with Visual Basic is fairly easy and a bit awkward. You simply create an ActiveX DLL project and define your interfaces in class modules marked as *PublicNotCreatable*. On the Component tab of the Project Properties dialog box, you must select the Remote Server Files option to ensure that a stand-alone type library file (with a .tlb extension) is created when you build the DLL. You can throw away the DLL and distribute the .tlb file to other programmers.

The awkward thing about using the Visual Basic IDE is that you must include at least one creatable class in any ActiveX DLL project. The Visual Basic IDE assumes that you want to create servers only, so you have to trick it into building an "interface-only" type library. You must create one dummy class module with the instancing setting MultiUse. It's a little confusing because anyone who uses your type library must ignore this dummy class. This is somewhat distracting, but it's the only way you can build a .tlb file using the Visual Basic IDE.

Defining Interfaces in IDL

Instead of using the Visual Basic IDE, you can publish your interfaces in a type library by writing IDL code. After you write the interface definitions, you feed the IDL source file to the Microsoft IDL (MIDL) compiler that ships with Visual Studio. You can feed the IDL file to the compiler from the command line as follows:

```
midl DogServer.idl
```

You can also create a workspace in the C++ environment that automates the build process. After you build the .tlb file, you can distribute it to other programmers. A Visual Basic programmer can register the .tlb file by opening the References dialog box from the Project menu and selecting the Browse option. This will open another dialog box that lets you to locate the .tlb file on your hard disk and include it in the current project. This also registers the type library on your development workstation.

Developers who use tools and languages other than Visual Basic like to define interfaces in IDL. For instance, COM-based projects using C++ require the use of IDL, so many developers use this language for publishing their type libraries. IDL gives you much more control over what gets published in your type library than does Visual Basic. For example, IDL lets you create type libraries without a dummy coclass. It also lets you select a specific GUID for an IID in a type library. (Visual Basic doesn't.) As you can see, Visual Basic automatically builds the type library behind the scenes, but it provides little flexibility.

If you use IDL to define your interfaces, you should be aware of Visual Basic's limitations when it comes to implementing COM interfaces. Many interfaces that can be expressed in IDL are usable from C++ but incompatible with Visual Basic. Programmers who are familiar with IDL from COM-based C++ projects must know what works in Visual Basic and what doesn't. If you want your interfaces to be Visual Basic compatible, you must follow these rules:

- Method names can't start with an underscore (_).

- Don't use COM *[out]* parameters unless you also use *[retval]*.

- All methods must return HRESULTs.

- Don't use unsigned long or short integers.

- Don't use parameters that contain pointers.

- Don't use typedefs (UDTs in Visual Basic terms) in earlier versions of COM (prior to Microsoft Windows NT 4 with Service Pack 4).

■ Don't derive one user-defined COM interface from another user-defined interface. Visual Basic–compatible interfaces must derive directly from *IUnknown* or *IDispatch*. (And you should seriously consider deriving interfaces only from *IUnknown*.)

The first six rules above pose a slight inconvenience and can affect your interface's efficiency. For example, designers who are used to C++ must give up such things as unsigned integers and *[out]* parameters. But you must follow these rules if you want to implement your interfaces in Visual Basic classes.

You can quickly create IDL that is compatible with Visual Basic by simply building a server with the Visual Basic IDE that contains the interface definitions you want. You can then examine the server's type library with Ole View. The type library viewer of Ole View reverse-engineers the equivalent IDL from your Visual Basic type library. This lets you copy and paste the resulting interface definitions into a new IDL source file. Anything in a Visual Basic–generated type library is always Visual Basic compatible. Creating IDL in this manner is a great way to learn about the language.

The final rule in the list turns out to be a significant limitation when it comes to designing and refining an application's interface design. This rule states that a user-defined interface can't be derived from another user-defined interface. A Visual Basic class can inherit from an interface, but one interface can't inherit from another. This means that Visual Basic allows only one level of interface inheritance. As you'll see later in this chapter, this limitation changes the way you extend the functionality of objects in an application. An important thing to consider when you're defining interfaces with IDL is whether you should derive your user-defined interfaces from *IUnknown* or *IDispatch*. If you want to create a dual interface, you should derive from *IDispatch* and use the *[dual]* attribute, like this:

```
[
    uuid(079046B1-072F-11d2-B6F2-0080C72D2182)
    object, dual, nonextensible
]
interface IMyDual : IDispatch
{
    HRESULT Bark()
}
```

If you want to create a pure vTable interface, you should derive from *IUnknown* and use the *[oleautomation]* attribute to enable the universal marshaler, like this:

```
[
    uuid(079046B2-072F-11d2-B6F2-0080C72D2182)
    object, oleautomation
]
interface IMyDual : IUnknown
{
    HRESULT Bark()
}
```

Here's why you should derive from *IUnknown* instead of *IDispatch*. The only clients who really need dual interfaces are automation clients such as VBScript. These clients can't call *QueryInterface* either explicitly or implicitly. The only interface they can use is the default interface for a coclass. The only way to create a default interface in Visual Basic is to use public members in a creatable class. This means that any user-defined interface you define in IDL and implement in a Visual Basic class is unreachable by scripting clients.

It's safe to assume that any client that can navigate to a user-defined interface is capable of pure vTable binding. You should therefore derive the user-defined interface you create in IDL from *IUnknown* instead of *IDispatch*. When you use the *Implements* keyword in a creatable class in an ActiveX DLL or an ActiveX EXE, Visual Basic can implement either a pure vTable interface or a dual interface. However, pure vTable interfaces are cleaner than dual interfaces.

Factoring Interfaces with Inheritance

In the world of COM, the term *interface* implies an all-or-nothing contract. When coclass authors implement an interface, they take on the obligation to supply a reasonable implementation for each method in the interface. But what if you want to simply supply an implementation for a subset of the methods in an interface? It seems reasonable to assume that this would violate the rules of COM, but in fact it doesn't need to. COM has a workaround for this. You must supply a response for each method in an interface, but the object can indicate that it has no meaningful implementation for a method by returning a well-known HRESULT, *E_NOTIMPL*.

When several class authors elect to implement the same subset of methods for a specific IID, this is usually a sign of bad interface design. The interface designer should factor out this subset of methods into a smaller interface. Splitting out the subset into its own interface is known as *interface factoring*. If you use this technique properly, an object should never return *E_NOTIMPL*. There should always be a match in the set of methods that a class author wants to implement and in the set of methods you've defined in a user-defined interface.

Most C++ programmers who use IDL factor out interfaces by using interface inheritance. For example, suppose you created an interface named *IWonderDog* that includes both the *Bark* method and the *FetchSlippers* method. After several class authors have implemented your interface, you find that some of them have implemented the *Bark* method, but they raise an *E_NOTIMPL* exception when *FetchSlippers* is called. You can factor out the *Bark* method into the *IDog* interface in IDL using interface inheritance. The *IWonderDog* interface can simply be derived from *IDog*, like this:

```
interface IDog : IUnknown
{
    HRESULT Bark();
}

interface IWonderDog : IDog
{
    HRESULT FetchSlippers();
}
```

Some class authors will implement *IWonderDog* and will therefore supply an implementation of both *Bark* and *FetchSlippers*. Other authors will want to supply only an implementation of *Bark*, so they can implement *IDog* instead. The use of inheritance in interface factoring makes things easy for both the interface designer and coclass authors. An author who implements the *IWonderDog* interface also implicitly implements the *IDog* interface. An object can hand out an *IWonderDog* reference to any client that requests the *IDog* interface because an *IWonderDog* reference "is an" *IDog* reference.

Factoring Interfaces with Visual Basic

Visual Basic can't implement a COM interface that's derived from another user-defined interface; it can only implement interfaces that are derived directly from *IUnknown* or *IDispatch*. If you define the *IWonderDog* interface in IDL by deriving from *IDog*, it will be incompatible with Visual Basic. You can still factor interfaces, but you have to do it in a much more awkward fashion. For instance, you can define the *IWonderDog* interface like this:

```
interface IWonderDog : IUnknown
{
    HRESULT FetchSlippers();
}
```

In this example, the *IWonderDog* interface is unrelated to the *IDog* interface. A client with an *IWonderDog* reference can't invoke the *Bark* method. When you factor interfaces, you typically want one interface to contain a superset of the methods from another. If you want to make the *IWonderDog* interface a superset of *IDog*, you must define it like this:

```
interface IWonderDog : IUnknown
{
    HRESULT Bark();
    HRESULT FetchSlippers();
}
```

If you're creating a class that needs to be compatible with both *IDog* and *IWonderDog*, you must define two sets of entry points for each duplicated method in your class, like this:

```
Implements IDog
Implements IWonderDog

Private Sub IDog_Bark()
    ' Implementation
End Sub

Private Sub IWonderDog_Bark()
    ' Forward to implementation.
    IDog_Bark
End Sub

Private Sub IWonderDog_FetchSlippers()
    ' Implementation
End Sub
```

You can see that interface factoring is possible but awkward with Visual Basic. Visual Basic's inability to make use of interface inheritance is unfortunate. When you create a set of interfaces that you want to implement with both Visual Basic and C++, you can't use interface inheritance; that means C++ class authors suffer along with Visual Basic class authors.

Choosing an Approach to Extending Your Objects

COM purists and the Visual Basic team have starkly contrasting views on how to extend an object. Chapter 5 described the technique promoted by the Visual Basic team. This technique uses the concept of version-compatible interfaces, and the Visual Basic IDE cleverly builds all the code behind the scenes to hook up everything at run time.

You need to remember that Visual Basic creates a new IID each time it makes a new version-compatible interface. This means that Visual Basic is consistent with COM's concept of interface immutability. However, Visual Basic doesn't create a new logical name for the new interface. For example, assume that you have a class named *CDog* in a project marked for binary compatibility. Visual Basic creates a transparent interface for *CDog* named *_CDog* and assigns it an IID in the first build. If you add a few methods to the class and rebuild it, Visual Basic creates a different IID but the interface name remains *_CDog*. What's happening here? Visual Basic automatically changes the physical name of the interface from version to version, but the logical name remains the same.

C++ programmers using IDL, on the other hand, create a new logical name as well as a new physical IID for each new interface. These programmers will look at you strangely when you say that you're going to extend an existing interface (or Visual Basic class) by adding a few new methods. Extending interfaces isn't a part of their culture. When you create an application using both Visual Basic and C++, you should consider taking the concept of interface immutability one step further: When you create a new interface, you should also give it a new logical name (such as *IDog2*). This is difficult or impossible to do without using IDL. If you're working on a large project that involves Visual Basic, C++, and Java developers, it might be best to work strictly with user-defined interfaces defined within IDL source files.

In many situations, using IDL in a Visual Basic project is overkill. With small projects or projects that use only automation clients, IDL is too costly. With projects that use only Visual Basic components, you can trust the versioning and object extensibility model that you get when you build your server in binary-compatibility mode. The Visual Basic team provides you with a scheme that works well. As you can see, you must weigh many factors before you decide how to manage the interfaces for a project.

DESIGNING REMOTE INTERFACES

One of the best things about COM is that it hides the details of interprocess communication. The code you write for an in-process object will automatically work for an out-of-process object. You don't have to change anything in your class module. The client-side code that you write doesn't care whether the object is close by or far away.

The hiding of interprocess communication details from both objects and clients is known as *location transparency*. As you saw in earlier chapters, this powerful feature is made possible by the universal marshaler and its ability to read interface definitions from type libraries at run time. Figure 6-1 on the following page shows how the proxy and the stub are built at run time. When an interface reference is marshaled from one process to another, the universal marshaler builds these helper objects by inspecting the interface definition in a type library.

Code written for an in-process object automatically works in an out-of-process object, but it won't necessarily be efficient. Many techniques that work efficiently for in-process objects yield unacceptable results when taken out of process. The overhead of the proxy/stub layer becomes a significant consideration during the design phase of an application. When you begin to draft a set of remote interfaces, you must consider several factors that aren't part of a classic OOP design methodology.

When a client invokes a method, it passes control to the object for the duration of the call. Every call in which control is passed to the object and then back to the client is called a *round-trip*. When a method is invoked on an object in another process, the round-trip must go across a proxy/stub layer. This means that every out-of-process method call requires a thread switch and the marshaling of data between the client's process and the object's process.

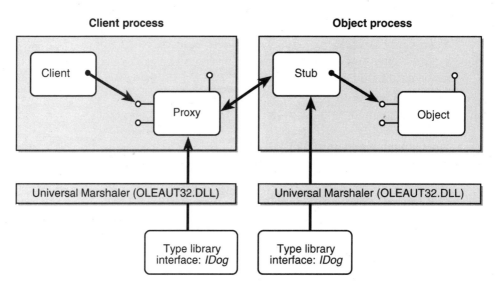

Figure 6-1. *The universal marshaler creates a proxy and a stub when an interface reference is marshaled across processes. If the client and the object are running on different machines, each computer requires a local copy of the type library.*

Figure 6-2 shows a table with benchmarking statistics for method calls in three different scenarios: in-process, out-of-process, and remote. These benchmarks were measured using empty methods to demonstrate differences in the overhead of method invocation. You can see that the round-trip time increases by a factor of about 1000 as you move the object out of process. When you take an out-of-process object and move it onto another machine, you take another significant performance hit.

Benchmark Test	In-Process Calls per Second	Out-of-Process Calls per Second	Remote Calls per Second
Method with a 4-byte *ByVal* parameter	129,041	1765	495
Method with a 100-byte-array *ByRef* parameter	119,240	968	342

Figure 6-2. *Benchmarks for calling empty methods in Visual Basic servers on a 166-MHz Pentium machine.*

If the client machine and the server machine are physically distant, you encounter yet another frustrating obstacle: the speed of light! For example, let's say that a round-trip between a computer in New York and one in Los Angeles is 5000 miles (2500 miles in each direction). If a method call were propagated across the wire at the speed of light, you would experience about 37 calls per second (186,000 miles per second divided by 5000 miles per call). The actual transmission speed of a remote COM method is, of course, less than the speed of light. In reality, you would experience fewer than 37 calls per second between these cities.

The lesson from these benchmarks is that round-trips are inherently evil. Your mission as a COM programmer is to eliminate the need for excessive round-trips. When you design a class or a user-defined interface, you should never expose three public methods or properties when a single method can accomplish the same amount of work. If your class exposes three public properties, a remote client will require three round-trips to access all the data. When a remote interface design isn't very efficient, the client code begins to looks like this:

```
Dim Rectangle As CRectangle
Set Rectangle = New CRectangle
' initialize object
Rectangle.X = 100
Rectangle.Y = 100
Rectangle.Width = 300
Rectangle.Height = 200
```

You can see from Figure 6-2 that marshaling a complete set of data in a single round-trip is much better than marshaling smaller amounts of data in multiple round-trips. If you need to move many bytes across the network to complete an operation, you should try to create a single signature that lets you do it in one shot. How can you improve the interface for the *CRectangle* class from the previous example? If you create a *SetRectangleData* method that takes four input parameters, the client can initialize the object in a single round-trip, like this:

```
Rectangle.SetRectangleData 100, _
                           100, _
                           300, _
                           200
```

Choosing Between *ByRef* and *ByVal*

When you create an interface, you should first think about optimizing round-trips. Then you should tune the parameter declarations in your methods to optimize the packets of data that move across the network. Some parameters must be pushed from the client to the object, and others must be pulled from the object back to the client. Some parameters need to move in both directions. Look at the following three method signatures, and think about how the universal marshaler interprets each one:

```
Sub Sammy(ByVal X As Double)
Sub Frank(ByRef Y As Double)
Sub Dean(Z As Double)
```

The method *Sammy* pushes the *X* parameter from the client's process to the object's process. If you want to marshal your parameters in one direction only, you should declare them *ByVal*. The method *Frank* defines a *ByRef* parameter that pushes the data from the client to the object and then pulls the data from the object back to the client. A *ByRef* parameter always results in the data being marshaled both to and from the object. The method *Dean* does the same thing as *Frank* because Visual Basic's default passing convention is *ByRef*.

Many Visual Basic programmers incorrectly assume that *ByRef* is always more efficient than *ByVal*. In an in-process call, a *ByRef* parameter is simply passed as an address to the data that's being referenced. In an out-of-process call, *ByRef* is always more expensive because the universal marshaler must also transmit the data that is being referenced. This means that *ByVal* is more efficient for parameters in remote interfaces. Use *ByRef* parameters only when you need to, such as when you need to move data from the object's process back to the client's process.

Now you might wonder, "How can I simply pull data from the object back to the client?" Unfortunately, Visual Basic doesn't make it straightforward. COM and IDL define parameters as *[in]*, *[out]*, or *[in, out]*. Visual Basic doesn't know how to deal with the COM *[out]* parameters. The only way to explicitly pull data back from the object is to use a method's return value. The problem with return values is that you can define only one for each round-trip. You're usually better off defining several *ByRef* arguments in a single method. You simply have to tolerate the fact that you're pushing unnecessary data from the client to the object. The following method signature shows the most efficient way to pull several pieces of data back from the object in a single round-trip:

```
' Defined in class CRectangle
Sub GetRectangleData( _
    ByRef X As Long, _
    ByRef Y As Long, _
    ByRef Width As Long, _
    ByRef Height As Long)
```

To call this method from a client, you must create local variables of the correct type and pass them in the call to *GetRectangleData*:

```
Dim X As Long, Y As Long
Dim Width As Long, Height As Long

Rectangle.GetRectangleData X, _
                           Y, _
                           Width, _
                           Height
```

After you call *GetRectangleData*, the local variable is populated with the data sent from the object. If you understand Visual Basic's inability to handle *[out]* parameters, it's simple to choose between *ByVal* and *ByRef*. You simply decide which way you want to move the data. The same rules apply for every primitive data type.

Special Primitive Data Types

With strings, arrays, variants, and UDTs, Visual Basic and the universal marshaler treat complex data types as simple primitive data types. When you declare a method parameter as one of these types, the universal marshaler can figure out how to marshal the required data across the proxy/stub layer. However, this works correctly only if these special data types carry additional metadata that describes their payloads. The universal marshaler reads this metadata at run time to determine how to create the required marshaling packets to send across the network.

The first of the four special primitive types is the Visual Basic for Applications (VBA) string. A VBA string is defined in IDL as a basic string (BSTR). A BSTR is a complex data type that is represented in memory by a cached string length value and a zero-terminated character array. (Characters are stored in Unicode, not ANSI.) The universal marshaler reads the length value of the BSTR to determine how many characters to send across the wire. Whether you declare a string parameter as *ByRef* or *ByVal*, all the data is automatically marshaled across the proxy/stub layer.

The second special primitive type is the VBA array, which is defined in IDL as a SAFEARRAY. A SAFEARRAY keeps track of not only the data for the actual array but also the upper and lower bounds of the array and other metadata that describes the data in the array. The universal marshaler can marshal a complete array in either direction in a single round-trip. You can declare a method signature with a *ByRef* array parameter, like this:

```
Sub SendValues(ByRef Value() As Integer)
```

Using Visual Basic 5, you can pass dynamic arrays if you declare them *ByRef*. This means that you can move an array in either direction. Using Visual Basic 6, you can also use an array type as the return value for a function. When you marshal arrays, you should be careful to pick the most efficient data type. An array of *Doubles* (8 bytes times *n* elements) generates four times the amount of network traffic as an array of *Integers* (2 bytes times *n* elements). Using an *Integer* data type can result in significant savings if you move arrays that have hundreds or thousands of elements.

You must be careful when you declare method parameters based on arrays. All parameters that pass arrays must be declared as *ByRef*. This means that the contents of the array will be marshaled across the network in both directions on every call. The problem is that generally you want to move the array only in a single direction. You want to move the array either from the client to the object or from the object to the client. You should always use dynamic arrays instead of static arrays because then you can pass an empty array in the direction you don't care about. Let's look at the two cases that are possible when you want to move the array in a single direction.

In one case, you want to pass an array from the object back to the client. As long as you use a dynamic array and don't use the *ReDim* statement in the client, you can send an empty array to the object. The object can use the *ReDim* statement to size the array. The object can then populate the array and return it to the client. Remember, with Visual Basic 6 you can use a method's return value to send an array to the client.

In the other case, you want to pass an array from the client to the object. This is where it's easy to make mistakes. You must be careful not to pass the array from the object back to the client when the call returns. Once the array has been marshaled to the object and the object has finished using it, you should use either the *Erase* statement or the *ReDim* statement to remove all the elements from the array before it is returned to the client.

The third special primitive type is the variant, a self-describing data type that is recognized by both VBA and IDL. As you will recall, this data type is the key to making automation and *IDispatch* work. A variant can hold anything—an integer, a double, a string, or even an array. When you marshal a variant, the universal marshaler transmits all the data associated with it, even if the variant references something complex, such as a string or a dynamic array. You can get pretty tricky when you marshal variants. Examine the following method implementation:

```
Sub GetData(ByRef Data As Variant)
    ' (1) Name (2) Age (3) Children
    Dim Temp() As Variant
    ReDim Temp(1 To 3)
    Temp(1) = "John"
    Temp(2) = CLng(34)
    Dim Children() As String
    ReDim Children(1 To 3)
    Children(1) = "Bob"
    Children(2) = "Martha"
    Children(3) = "Wally"
    Temp(3) = Children
    Data = Temp
End Sub
```

This method packs up a fairly complex data structure, which is depicted in Figure 6-3. A top-level variant array holds three elements: a string, a long, and a string array. When you assign the top-level variant array to a *ByRef* parameter, the universal marshaler sends the entire structure across the network and re-creates it on the other side. The client that calls this method must be able to deal with the complexities of the data structure, but you can see that it's still a powerful way to get lots of data across the network in a single round-trip.

The last special primitive type is the VBA user-defined type (UDT). The ability to marshal these custom data types first became available with Visual Basic 6. Not only do you need Visual Basic 6 to marshal these UDTs, you also need a version of the universal marshaler that is available only in later versions of COM, such as

Client process

Object process

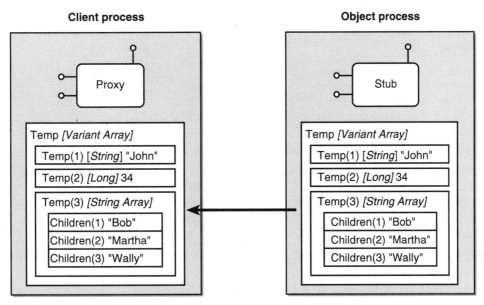

Figure 6-3. *You can marshal this complex data structure in either direction using a single variant parameter or a variant return value. If you use techniques such as this, your code must be able to deal with the complexity on the client side as well as the object side.*

versions included with Microsoft Windows 98, Windows NT 5, and Windows NT 4 with Service Pack 4. Earlier versions of the universal marshaler don't recognize a UDT as variant compliant, so you can't use UDTs in COM method calls in an *IDispatch* interface or a dual interface. You can use UDTs in your methods only if your code will run on computers that have the newer version of the universal marshaler. (The universal marshaler is in the system file OLEAUT32.DLL.)

A UDT is the VBA equivalent of a structure in C. If you define a UDT in a public class module, Visual Basic automatically publishes it in your type library. You can create a UDT in a public class module like this:

```
Type CustomerDataType
    FirstName As String
    LastName As String
    Phone As String
    MailingList As Boolean
    MailingAddress As String
End Type
```

In the equivalent IDL, shown below, you can see that each *typedef* has an associated GUID that identifies its data layout scheme. A UDT can hold any collection of variant-compliant data types.

```
typedef
    [uuid(A2B7676A-EAD1-11D1-98F9-00600807E871)]
    struct tagCustomerDataType {
        BSTR FirstName;
        BSTR LastName;
        BSTR Phone;
        VARIANT_BOOL MailingList;
        BSTR MailingAddress;
    }CustomerDataType;
};
```

After you define the UDT in a public class module, you can use it to define *ByRef* parameters of that type. For instance, you can create methods such as *InitCustomer* and *GetCustomer* that use the UDT to marshal data across the proxy/stub layer. Take a look at the following class definition for the *CCustomer* class:

```
Private FirstName As String
Private LastName As String
Private Phone As String
Private MailingList As Boolean
Private MailingAddress As String

Sub InitCustomer(ByRef Customer As CustomerDataType)
    FirstName = Customer.FirstName
    LastName = Customer.LastName
    Phone = Customer.Phone
    MailingList = Customer.MailingList
    MailingAddress = Customer.MailingAddress
End Sub

Function GetCustomer() As CustomerDataType
    GetCustomer.FirstName = FirstName
    GetCustomer.LastName = LastName
    GetCustomer.Phone = Phone
    GetCustomer.MailingList = MailingList
    GetCustomer.MailingAddress = MailingAddress
End Function
```

As you can see, a UDT lets you move several pieces of related data across the wire using a single parameter. A client application can use the *InitCustomer* method like this:

```
Private Customer As New CCustomer

Private Sub cmdSend_Click()
    Dim Temp As CustomerDataType
    Temp.FirstName = txtFirstName
    Temp.LastName = txtLastName
    Temp.Phone = txtPhone
```

```
      Temp.MailingList = IIf(chkMailingList.Value = vbChecked, _
                             True, False)
      Temp.MailingAddress = txtMailingAddress
      Customer.InitCustomer Temp
End Sub
```

A client can call the *GetCustomer* method like this:

```
Private Sub cmdReceive_Click()
    Dim Temp As CustomerDataType
    Temp = Customer.GetCustomer()
    txtFirstName = Temp.FirstName
    txtLastName = Temp.LastName
    txtPhone = Temp.Phone
    chkMailingList.Value = IIf(Temp.MailingList, _
                               vbChecked, vbUnchecked)
    txtMailingAddress = Temp.MailingAddress
End Sub
```

As you can see, Visual Basic and the universal marshaler do an amazing amount of work for you behind the scenes. The benefit to you as a Visual Basic programmer is that you can use these special data types as if they were simple primitives. You can declare parameters of any of these data types and know that your data will be sent across the wire when the time is right.

C++ programmers, on the other hand, have it much harder. A C++ developer who wants to create components that will be used by Visual Basic programmers must also use BSTRs, SAFEARRAYs, and VARIANT types. These types aren't natural to a C or a C++ programmer. Many macros and convenience functions are available for dealing with these special types, but it takes most C++ programmers some time to get up to speed.

OBJECTS AND THE UNIVERSAL MARSHALER

Location transparency is a wonderful thing. Visual Basic and the universal marshaler work together to move your data magically across the network, and all you have to do is design your method signatures correctly. Without this help, you would have to write the code to move the data between processes. Luckily, the details of moving the data aren't your problem. You can think of every method signature as a sling-shot that you design in order to fling data from the client to the object and back.

There's one frustrating limitation that neither Visual Basic nor the universal marshaler can overcome: The universal marshaler can't move an object across the network. This means that you can pass an object only by reference, not by value. When you declare an object parameter using *ByVal*, the reference is marshaled from the client to the object. When you declare an object parameter using *ByRef*, the reference is marshaled in both directions. However, the COM object (and all the precious data that's inside) never leaves the process in which it was created.

Figure 6-4 illustrates the dilemma. When you pass an object reference to a remote client, the data doesn't move. It remains on the machine where the object was created. The only thing that passes across the network is a COM-savvy pointer that lets the recipient establish a connection back to the object being referenced. When the recipient wants to access a property or a method through the object reference, it must go back across the proxy/stub layer to where the object lives.

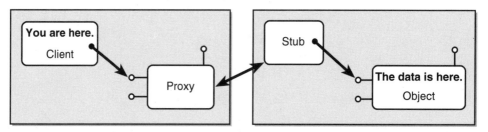

Figure 6-4. *Visual Basic and the universal marshaler don't support pass-by-value parameters with object data types. You can pass an object only by reference.*

What does this mean to the Visual Basic programmer? It means that many straightforward programming techniques that you might use with in-process objects don't work well for out-of-process objects. For example, what if you are using a Visual Basic collection object to manage a set of *CCustomer* objects in a server-side process? How can you get the data for these customer objects over to a client application to fill a grid? One simple technique is to pass a reference to the collection over to the client. The client can then enumerate through the collection with a *For Each* loop and access the customer objects individually. However, this approach creates a big problem. Every loop in the *For Each* construct creates a new connection to an out-of-process customer object, and this connection requires a round-trip to the server to access any single property or method. If each customer object has five properties and the collection has hundreds of objects, the round-trips really start adding up.

It would be wonderful if you could simply marshal an object by value in the same way that you marshal a primitive data type, but this isn't possible. At times, you will want to move all the data associated with an object from one process to another. This is a common undertaking, but the universal marshaler can't help. If you want to simulate pass-by-value semantics, you must write your own code to intelligently move things across the network.

Creating a Pseudo-Custom Marshaler

Programmers using languages other than Visual Basic, such as C++, occasionally resort to writing custom proxy code by hand by implementing a special interface *IMarshal* using a technique known as *custom marshaling*. Custom marshaling doesn't rely on the universal marshaler (Oleaut32.dll). Instead a custom proxy DLL is distributed to client desktops. Custom marshaling can give you complete control over how things are transmitted between the object and the client. It also lets you optimize the connection by simulating pass-by-value at the object level. However, custom marshaling is complicated. It requires in-depth knowledge of the RPC layer under COM, and few programmers are proficient in programming at this level. Another problem with custom marshaling it that it isn't supported by environments such as Microsoft Transaction Server.

A Visual Basic programmer can't participate in "true" custom marshaling but can accomplish something similar by writing intelligent code that optimizes how data is sent across the network. Pseudo-custom marshaling code written in Visual Basic simply leverages the universal marshaler instead of replacing it.

So how can you simulate pass-by-value with an object? One common technique for moving the data for an object uses a *long-winded parameter list*. If an object has 10 properties, you can create a *set* method and a *get* method with 10 parameters apiece. This is a bit tedious for both the class author and the client that calls these methods, but it's a quick-and-dirty way to get the data where it's needed in a single round-trip.

You can use a UDT instead of a long list of parameters to keep a method signature a little saner. This is especially helpful when your classes define a lot of properties. After you define a UDT in a public class module, you can use it to send a complex set of data between the client and the object. You can even create multiple UDTs for each class. For example, if your *CCustomer* class contains 20 properties but you typically need to marshal only 5 of them, you can create two UDTs, such as *CustomerShort* and *CustomerLong*. One UDT can define a common subset of customer properties, and the other can define the complete state of a customer object. UDTs let you dial in what you want to send across the network. They aren't supported in many older versions of COM, however. Before you design with UDTs, you must be sure that all of the computers in your production environment can handle them.

The two techniques described above are used to marshal the data for a single object. However, you will often need to move the data associated with multiple objects in a single round-trip. You can use any combination of variants, arrays, and UDTs to create data structures that are as complex as you like. The only limitation is your imagination. The example below moves the data for multiple customer objects across the network using a single method.

```
Sub GetCustomerData(ByRef arrData As Variant)
    ReDim arrData(1 To 2, 1 To 3) As String
    arrData(1, 1) = "Freddie"
    arrData(1, 2) = "Washington"
    arrData(1, 3) = "(310)594-4929"
```

(continued)

```
        arrData(2, 1) = "Mary"
        arrData(2, 2) = "Contrary"
        arrData(2, 3) = "(310)493-9080"
End Sub
```

Many development teams have discovered that the variant data type is very flexible for marshaling complex data structures. You can change the two-dimensional string arrays in the example above to an array of a different type or a different number of dimensions without changing the method signature. This means you don't have to worry about breaking binary compatibility when you redefine what you're marshaling. However, both the object and the client must agree on how the data structure is built. If you change the way that the object stores the data, you must make sure that the client knows how to use it. Some developers even add metadata to their structures to convey such information as a version number or a schema for the set of columns being marshaled.

Using Smart Proxy Objects

One problem with marshaling a complex data structure is that it requires two complementary pieces of code. One piece constructs the data structure for transmission, and the other piece disassembles the data to use it in a meaningful way. If you are marshaling a complex data structure across the network from an object to a client application, you should probably hide this complexity from other Visual Basic programmers who are creating form-based desktop applications.

You can simplify things by creating a complementary *proxy object* in the client's process that encapsulates the complexity of your data structure. Client application programmers can simply create an instance of the proxy object and use it by calling a simple set of methods and properties. For example, you can create a client-side *CCustomersProxy* class for caching customer data returned from the *GetCustomerData* method. Examine the following class module:

```
' CCustomersProxy class
Private RemoteCustomers As CCustomers
Public LocalCustomers As Collection

Private Sub Class_Initialize()
    Set RemoteCustomers = New CCustomers
    Set LocalCustomers = New Collection
    Dim Temp As Variant
    RemoteCustomers.GetCustomerData Temp
    ' Create a local collection of CCustomer objects.
    Dim Customer As CCustomer, Position As Long
    For Position = LBound(Temp, 1) To UBound(Temp, 1)
        Set Customer = New CCustomer
        Customer.FirstName = Temp(Position, 1)
```

```
        Customer.LastName = Temp(Position, 2)
        Customer.Phone = Temp(Position, 3)
        LocalCustomers.Add Customer
    Next Position
End Sub
```

The diagram in Figure 6-5 shows how things are set up. The proxy object's *Class_Initialize* method takes the two-dimensional string array returned by *GetCustomerData* and uses it to create a set of *CCustomer* objects in the client process. The *CCustomer* objects are added to a local Visual Basic collection object for convenience.

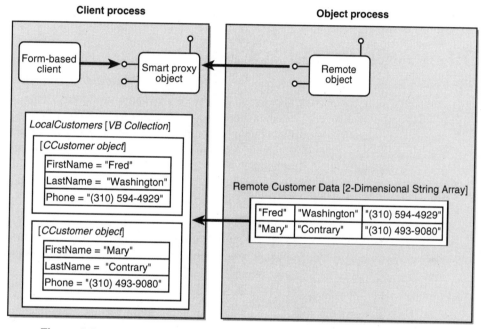

Figure 6-5. *You can use a smart proxy object on the client side to hide the details of marshaling complex data structures. The proxy object can download data and create local objects and collections for fast, convenient client-side access.*

From a high-level design perspective, it makes sense to distribute the *CCustomersProxy* class and the *CCustomer* class in a client-side ActiveX DLL. Visual Basic programmers who create form-based applications on the desktop can simply reference the DLL and use your proxy object. Here is the required code:

```
Private Proxy As CCustomersProxy

Private Sub Form_Load()
    Set Proxy = New CCustomersProxy
End Sub
```

(continued)

```
Private Sub cmdFillListbox_Click()
    Dim Customer As CCustomer
    For Each Customer In Proxy.LocalCustomers
        lstCustomer.AddItem Customer.LastName
    Next Customer
End Sub
```

As you can see, this technique gives you the best of both worlds. It gives you the efficiency of marshaling a complete set of data in a single round-trip, and it allows other programmers to write code in a style that is more natural to the average Visual Basic programmer. You can assume that the proxy object will never be accessed out of process, so you can expose properties and use collections more freely.

OUTBOUND INTERFACES

The typical relationship between a client and an object is based on a simple connection. The client holds an interface reference to the object and uses this reference to access methods and properties. In this type of relationship, only the client can initiate communication. The object can return information to the client in response to a method call using either an output parameter or a return value, but it can't initiate a call back to the client.

Sometimes it's beneficial to establish bidirectional communication between an object and a client. To support bidirectional communication, an object must provide an *outbound interface*. After creating the initial connection to an object, the client can establish a second connection by passing a reference to itself, as shown in Figure 6-6. The object uses this interface reference to invoke methods in the client. You can see that each side in this relationship acts as both a client and an object.

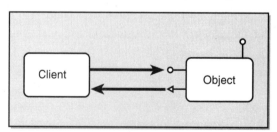

Figure 6-6. *Objects that expose an outbound interface can establish bidirectional communication. An outbound interface allows the object to treat the client as another object. The client provides an implementation for the methods defined in an outbound interface.*

You can establish bidirectional communication using either Visual Basic events or a custom callback interface. Both do the same thing conceptually; they allow the client to pass a reference to the object to set up the second connection. To demonstrate the use of an outbound interface, in the next section we'll look at a simple example in which you create an application with a dog object. The client that creates the dog object is the dog owner. The class behind the dog object provides a *RollOver* method that allows the owner to initiate a command on the dog. However, if the dog's owner requests that the dog roll over an unreasonable number of times, the dog will initiate a command back to the owner. In essence, the dog (object) will call back the owner (client) by invoking the *OnBite* method through an outbound interface.

Using Visual Basic Events

We'll start by implementing the design using Visual Basic events. Events can be hard to use at first because they add a whole new dimension to an object-oriented design. However, once you decide where to use them, they are fairly easy to set up. You define the outbound interface for an object by declaring events in the declaration section of a creatable class module. The other important thing you need to do in the class is to raise your events with the *RaiseEvent* statement in one or more methods. Examine the following code:

```
' CBeagle.cls
Event OnBite()

Sub RollOver(ByVal Rolls As Long)
    If Rolls > 20 Then
        RaiseEvent OnBite
    Else
        ' Be obedient and roll over.
    End If
End Sub
```

The outbound interface for *CBeagle* is defined with a single event, *OnBite*. The *RollOver* method also contains logic for raising the *OnBite* event if the number of requested rolls is greater than 20. As you can see, it's pretty easy to define and use an outbound interface with events. The Visual Basic class defines the events and determines when they are raised. Events can be defined with parameters, just as standard methods are. When you define an event, you define an outbound method signature. However, the actual implementation behind these outbound methods must be defined by the client.

Consider what the client has to do to make everything work properly. It must establish the second connection and supply a response to each event raised by the object. Some tricky stuff goes on behind the scenes to hook up the second connection, but the required Visual Basic code is fairly simple. When the client creates a reference to an event-capable object using the *WithEvents* keyword, Visual

Basic automatically establishes the second connection. Here's what the client looks like:

```
Private WithEvents Beagle As CBeagle

Private Sub Form_Load()
    Set Beagle = New CBeagle
End Sub

Private Sub cmdRollOver_Click()
    Beagle.RollOver txtRolls
End Sub

Private Sub Beagle_OnBite()
    ' React to dog bite.
    MsgBox "Ouch!"
End Sub
```

All you really need to do after you use the *WithEvents* keyword is to supply an implementation for the methods in the object's outbound interface. In the code above, the variable declared with the *WithEvents* keyword is named *Beagle*. You create event handlers by following the convention *Beagle_OnBite*. Visual Basic makes sure that this code is executed whenever the object raises the event. You can even use the wizard bar to quickly generate the skeletons for these handlers after you declare the variable using the *WithEvents* keyword.

When you use the *WithEvents* keyword, you create an *event sink* in the client. This event sink catches event notifications as they're raised by the object. An object that defines events is called an *event source*. So how does Visual Basic hook up the event sink with the event source? The client and the object must negotiate to establish the second connection. Fortunately for Visual Basic programmers, all the work is done behind the scenes. The following paragraph describes the details, but you don't have to care about them. That's one of the best things about using a high-level productivity tool such as Visual Basic.

Event sources are bound to event sinks through the COM interfaces *IConnectionPoint* and *IConnectionPointContainer*. When you use the *WithEvents* keyword, the Visual Basic run-time library silently uses these interfaces to negotiate on your behalf to hook up the client's event sink to the object's outbound interface. An object that defines events publishes a source interface in the type library. Take a look at the following IDL for the *CBeagle* class:

```
interface _CBeagle : IDispatch {
    [id(0x60030000)]
    HRESULT RollOver([in] long Rolls);
};
```

```
dispinterface __CBeagle {
    methods:
        [id(0x00000001)]
        void OnBite();
};

coclass CBeagle {
    [default] interface _CBeagle;
    [default, source] dispinterface __CBeagle;
};
```

You can see that an outbound interface is defined only in terms of automation. (The *dispinterface* keyword in IDL means *IDispatch* only.) You can also see that the outbound interface is marked as the *[default, source]* interface for the *CBeagle* class. A client using the *WithEvents* keyword can use only the default source interface. The only way to create a default source interface in Visual Basic is to define events in a creatable class module. This means that you can't create a user-defined interface with events and implement it in a Visual Basic class module. The way that Visual Basic hooks up events is simple but inflexible. You can't reuse an outbound interface definition across multiple classes, nor can a Visual Basic client hook up to anything but the default source interface.

These events come with a few other significant limitations. First, bidirectional communication requires that the client be a valid COM object. You must use an object created from a Visual Basic form or from a user-defined class to set up an event sink. Thus, you can use the *WithEvents* keyword only in the declaration section of a class module or form module. You can't use it in a local procedure or in a BAS module because there is no object to implement the event sink. Furthermore, when you declare variables using the *WithEvents* keyword, you must use the name of the class in which the events are defined. This means you can't use the *WithEvents* keyword when you declare variables of type *Variant*, *Object*, or *Collection*.

The last thing to consider is that events are implemented in Visual Basic using the *IDispatch* interface. This means that raising an event takes significantly longer than a pure vTable-bound method call. Fortunately, the object already has the DispID for every event, so there's no need for a call to *GetIDsOfNames*; events use early binding as opposed to late binding. An object can raise an event to a client in a single round-trip. However, the call still goes through *Invoke* on the client side, which makes it considerably slower than vTable binding.

Using a Custom Callback Interface

Instead of relying on events, you can establish a custom callback mechanism to get the same effect. You do this by defining a custom callback interface that defines a set of methods that an object can invoke on the client. This approach is more involved than using events, but it offers more flexibility and better performance.

Let's look at how to create an outbound interface for another dog class, *CBoxer*, using a custom callback interface. You start by defining a user-defined interface. We'll use a user-defined interface named *IDogOwner* with a single method, *OnBite*.

You should define this method in a Visual Basic class module with the instancing property set to *PublicNotCreateable* (or better yet, define it using IDL). After you define the outbound interface, you can use it in the *CBoxer* class, like this:

```
Private Owner As IDogOwner

Sub Register(ByVal Callback As IDogOwner)
    Set Owner = Callback
End Sub

Sub Unregister()
    Set Owner = Nothing
End Sub

Sub RollOver(ByVal Rolls As Long)
    If Rolls > 20 Then
        Owner.OnBite
    Else
        ' Be obedient and roll over.
    End If
End Sub
```

The *CBoxer* class does a couple of interesting things. First, it declares an *IDogOwner* variable to hold a reference back to the client. Second, it allows the client to establish the second connection by providing a complementary pair of *Register/Unregister* methods. After the client creates the object, it must call *Register* to pass an *IDogOwner*-compatible reference to the object. Once the client passes a reference to itself or to some other *IDogOwner*-compatible object, the outbound interface has been hooked up. Here's what the code looks like on the client side:

```
Implements IDogOwner
Private Boxer As CBoxer

Private Sub Form_Load()
    Set Boxer = New CBoxer
    Boxer.Register Me
End Sub

Private Sub cmdRollOver_Click()
    Boxer.RollOver txtRolls
End Sub

Private Sub IDogOwner_OnBite()
    ' React to dog bite.
```

```
End Sub

Private Sub Form_Unload(Cancel As Integer)
    Boxer.Unregister
End Sub
```

In this example, the client is a form module that implements the *IDogOwner* interface. The client creates a *CBoxer* object in *Form_Load* and immediately calls *Register* by passing a reference to itself. After the form object registers itself with the *CBoxer* object, either one can invoke a method on the other. You should also note that the form calls *Unregister* in *Form_Unload*. It's important that you break the circular reference when you've finished. When you do this, you ensure that the object doesn't continue to hold a reference to a client that has been unloaded.

Using a custom callback interface is somewhat more complicated than using events because you have to worry about establishing the second connection yourself. It becomes more complicated when you want to connect many clients to a single object. The *Register* method in the *CBoxer* class is written to handle a single client. If you want to connect many clients at once, the *CBoxer* class must be modified to manage a collection of *IDogOwner* references. The *Register* method will also be required to add new client connections to the collection. If you want to make an outbound method call to every connected client, you can create a For Each loop to enumerate through the collection.

Custom callback interfaces do offer quite a few advantages over events. One key advantage is that custom callback interfaces allow an object to determine how many clients are listening. When you use events, the object has no idea how many clients are connected. Every event that is raised is broadcast to each client that has hooked up an event sink. You can't prioritize or filter how events are raised on a client-by-client basis. When you raise an event, the object synchronously broadcasts the outbound calls to all clients, one a time. Writing the code to maintain a collection of callback references isn't a trivial undertaking, but it does give you the flexibility to decide which clients get called first and which clients don't get called at all.

The second advantage of custom callback interfaces is flexibility and speed. Take a look at the IDL from the previous example:

```
interface _IDogOwner : IDispatch {
    HRESULT OnBite();
};

interface _CBoxer : IDispatch {
    HRESULT Register([in] _IDogOwner* Callback);
    HRESULT Unregister();
    HRESULT RollOver([in] long Rolls);
};
```

As you can see, custom callback interfaces defined with Visual Basic class modules use dual interfaces as opposed to events, which use *IDispatch* only. This means that custom callback interfaces use vTable binding; events use early binding. Interfaces based on vTable binding provide better performance and more flexible parameter passing than do events. The methods in custom callback interfaces can use optional parameters and parameter arrays that aren't available to events. You can always elect to define your callback interfaces in IDL instead of Visual Basic class modules.

You should also note that one callback interface can be used by many different clients and objects. This makes callback interfaces far more reusable than events. An outbound interface created using events can be used only by the class module in which the events are defined. If you're using IDL, you can define all your outbound interfaces in the same type library as all your inbound interfaces.

This chapter has described the how of creating an outbound interface, but it hasn't really addressed the when and the why of designing with bidirectional communication. The use of outbound interfaces in the previous examples was limited to making a callback to the client during the execution of a simple method. Outbound interfaces can be used in more sophisticated designs. For instance, if several clients are connected to a single object, you can use an event to inform clients that data in the object has changed. When one client changes some data, the change can be propagated to all the other clients. You can also use events or a custom callback interface to notify a client that an asynchronous method call has been completed. Chapter 7 revisits the idea of creating an asynchronous method.

Designing Distributed Applications

This chapter began by describing ways to design and manage your interfaces in a large application. Each approach has trade-offs in ease of use, extensibility, and scalability. You can design with user-defined interfaces or with simple *MultiUse* classes. You can create type libraries to publish your interfaces using IDL, or you can simply let Visual Basic take care of the details for you. What really matters is that the entire development team agrees on which road to take at the beginning of the project.

We also explored problems with remote interface design and some possible solutions. The overhead of the proxy/stub layer has a significant impact on the way you design your interfaces. You must try to complete every logical operation in a single round-trip. The challenges you face when creating efficient interfaces are compounded by the fact that you can't marshal objects by value. Objects always remain in the process in which they were created.

Most COM interface designs that have been optimized for remote access bear little resemblance to a design that you would see in a book about traditional OOP. Techniques that employ public properties and collections simply can't scale when they are taken out of process. The need to complete every logical operation in a single round-trip adds a necessary and painful layer of complexity to your interface designs. COM programmers learn to live with this. Once you know how the universal marshaler works, you can find the best way to get the data where it needs to be. On the bright side, you can hide complexity from other programmers by creating smart proxy objects.

This chapter also described two techniques that you can use to create an outbound interface. Events are easier to set up and use, but a custom callback interface can provide more flexibility and better performance. It's not hard to learn the mechanics of setting up an outbound interface, but knowing when to use one in your designs is tougher. Mastering outbound interfaces from the design perspective can take months or years.

Chapter 7

Exploring Apartments and Multithreading

Using Microsoft Visual Basic, you can create multithreaded ActiveX DLLs and EXEs. This can be advantageous in a handful of situations, but multithreading also adds a level of complexity to your code that can be highly unpredictable if you don't know exactly what you're doing. You should approach multithreading with extreme caution. You must have a solid understanding of the conceptual issues before you begin to add multithreaded techniques to your production code. Bad things happen to good programmers who approach multithreading with a casual attitude. This chapter shows you what you need to know and encourages you to think long and hard about whether multithreaded applications are really worth the trouble.

Why would you need multiple threads in an application? Many new programmers think that multithreading is done to make things faster. In most cases, however, the purpose of a secondary thread is to improve responsiveness. When a user is editing a document in Microsoft Word, for example, background tasks such as document repagination and print spooling jobs are conducted on secondary threads. This allows the application to be fully responsive to the user at all times.

Can multithreading ever really speed things up? On a computer with a single processor, usually not. Each additional thread creates more administrative overhead for the system's thread scheduler. The overall throughput of the system actually diminishes as more time is spent switching among threads and less time is spent doing real work. The primary situation in which multiple threads significantly increase the throughput and speed of an application is on a computer with two or more processors.

Earlier versions of Visual Basic had few threading capabilities. Since Visual Basic has been used primarily to create forms-based, single-user applications, this limitation hasn't been overly taxing. Many programmers have found that the *DoEvents* statement can simulate multithreading to a degree and provide applications with greater responsiveness.

Recently Visual Basic has become popular for building nonvisual, server-side business objects. In a server-side process with many connected clients, threading becomes a much greater concern. The way that a distributed application deals with threading determines whether it can scale up to accommodate a larger user base. If you're creating server-side objects, you should understand what's going on with threading in both Visual Basic and COM.

You must understand what a COM apartment is if you want to master the multi-threading techniques available in Visual Basic. However, before you can understand apartments, you must understand the principles of threading in the Win32 API. This chapter begins by explaining how threads are created and managed by the Win32 API. Even though you won't directly apply these Win32 techniques and concepts from within Visual Basic, you must understand them. Everything that COM does with apartments is built on top of the Win32 threading model.

A WIN32 THREADING PRIMER

The Win32 programming model is based on two high-level abstractions called *processes* and *threads*. A process is a running instance of an application that owns an address space of virtual memory as well as other various resources. A thread is a schedulable entity that's owned by one and only one process. The operating system recognizes each thread in every process and is responsible for scheduling threads for time in the system's processor(s), as shown in Figure 7-1.

Every thread gets its own call stack. The scheduler allocates processing cycles by giving each thread a time slice. When the time slice is over, the running thread is preempted and another thread is given a turn. A preempted thread can keep enough information on its call stack to remember what it was doing and how far it got before being switched out of the processor. When it gets another time slice, it can pick up where it left off. The abstraction of threads and the scheduler is powerful because it allows a single-processor computer to appear to be doing more than one thing at a time.

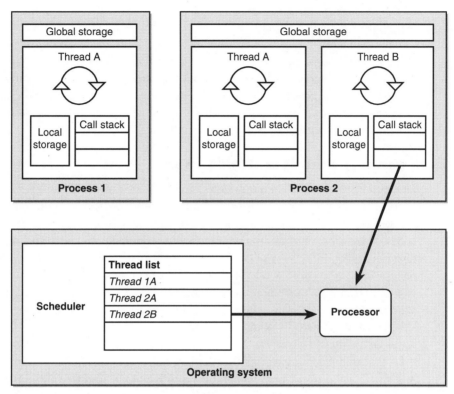

Figure 7-1. *Every Win32 process owns one or more threads. Each thread has an associated call stack and can store data in local storage, which is private to the thread.*

Each process begins its life with a *primary thread*. This system-created thread serves as the entry point into the application. In a typical Microsoft Windows–based application with a user interface, the primary thread is used to create the application's main window and to set up a message loop to monitor incoming messages sent by the operating system. For example, if a user clicks on a main window, the system sends a WM_MOUSEDOWN message to a message queue associated with the window. The primary thread pulls this message off the queue and responds to it. A thread that employs a loop to monitor the incoming messages in this manner is called a *user interface thread*.

When an application with a user interface is written in C or C++, someone must set up a message loop to monitor a message queue. Fortunately, Visual Basic programmers have always been shielded from having to deal with a message queue directly. The Visual Basic run time sets up a message loop in the background. Programming in Visual Basic is simple because the Visual Basic run time translates these system messages into Visual Basic events.

Once an application is up and running, the Win32 API lets you spawn additional threads using a Win32 API function named *CreateThread*. C and C++ programmers typically create secondary threads to carry out lower-priority background tasks. In most cases, the secondary thread doesn't monitor a message queue and therefore doesn't require much overhead. This type of thread is known as a *worker thread*. The obvious benefit of the second thread is that a background task can be run without blocking the responsiveness of the user interface.

Concurrency and Synchronization

Programmers who write multithreaded applications must exercise extreme caution. When two threads run at the same time in a single process, you can encounter problems that don't exist in a single-threaded process. In particular, global data that's accessed by multiple threads is vulnerable to inconsistency and corruption because of a phenomenon known as *concurrency*. In a preemptive multithreading environment such as Microsoft Windows NT, the scheduler switches threads out of the processor arbitrarily. There's no way to guarantee that a thread has completed its work. When another thread is switched into the processor, it can potentially see global data left in an invalid state by some other thread that was preempted in the middle of a series of changes.

For example, imagine that the variables x and y represent the position of a point. Assume that the initial position of the point is (10,10) and that thread A begins to change the position of the point to (20,20). If thread A is preempted after changing the x position but before changing the y position, the logical point is left in an invalid state. This invalid state is the position (20,10). The only two valid positions for the point are (10,10) and (20,20), but thread B might see the point at (20,10). As you can see, concurrency makes an application vulnerable to data inconsistency.

Multithreading also makes an application vulnerable to data corruption. Take a look at another example with a particularly unhappy ending. When thread A inserts a new entry into a linked list, it must modify a set of pointers to accomplish the task. If thread A is preempted in the middle of the operation, thread B can easily get hold of an invalid pointer when it tries to scan the list. When thread B tries to use the invalid pointer, the entire process will probably crash.

Multithreading makes it difficult to write code that is correct and robust. A Win32 programmer who wants to create a multithreaded application must lock and synchronize any global data that is vulnerable to inconsistency or corruption. The Win32 API exposes a set of synchronization primitives for this purpose. Critical sections, mutexes, semaphores, and events are all examples of Win32 synchronization objects. These objects are tricky to work with, but they let experienced programmers write safe, robust code that can benefit from multithreading.

The problems associated with concurrency arise only when two or more threads access the same global memory. You can avoid these problems by using local variables on the call stack. These local variables are private to a particular thread. The Win32 API also allows a thread to store persistent data in a private memory area. This type of memory is called *thread-local storage* (TLS). Using TLS solves many concurrency problems because you don't have to worry about synchronization.

Although TLS solves concurrency problems, it creates a few problems of its own. Data stored in TLS can be accessed only by the owning thread. Objects that store data in TLS generate a dependency on the thread that created them. As we'll see later in this chapter, Visual Basic objects are heavy users of TLS; therefore, every Visual Basic object has a dependency on the thread that created it. A Visual Basic object can never be accessed by any other thread. This condition is known as *thread affinity*. As you'll see later, thread affinity becomes a limiting factor in environments that use thread pooling.

What Is an Apartment?

Many programmers—especially those who write business logic in languages such as Visual Basic—don't think about concurrency and synchronization. They assume that their code will run in an environment with a single thread, or they don't think about threading at all. They never worry about synchronizing their data during method calls. They can't reap the benefits offered by a multithreaded environment, but they are generally much more productive because they never spend time on issues relating to concurrency.

As you can see, there are two very different ways to write code. You can write code that's thread-savvy or you can write code that's thread-oblivious. The creators of COM looked for a way to integrate both types of code into a single application. But they faced a large potential problem. If two components are integrated into a single application, a thread-savvy component might try to access a thread-oblivious component in a way that would make the thread-oblivious component behave unpredictably and crash.

One way to safely integrate these two components is to modify one to accommodate the other. You can make the thread-oblivious component more robust or make the thread-savvy component less dangerous. However, this approach is undesirable because it requires a modification of one of the code bases. COM solves the integration problem with an abstraction known as an *apartment*. Apartments allow a variety of components to interoperate without forcing anyone to change their thread management policy.

An apartment is an execution context that allows any component to assume that all other components are running with the same level of thread awareness. Here's how the model works. Every COM object is created within the context of a COM apartment, as shown in Figure 7-2. A Win32 thread must explicitly enter an apartment before creating and interacting with COM objects. Under strict rules defined by COM, a thread in one apartment cannot touch an object that lives in another apartment. If a method call is made from one apartment to another, the call must be remoted across a proxy/stub pair. The proxy/stub layer for interapartment communication is built the same way as for interprocess communication. As you'll see, an apartment can serialize every incoming method call in a manner that eliminates the possibility of concurrency.

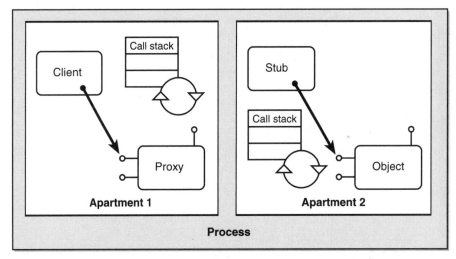

Figure 7-2. *In COM, every object must be created within the context of an apartment. Every COM-aware thread must also run within the context of an apartment.*

COM's Threading Models

COM currently defines two threading models, each based on a different type of apartment. A *multithreaded apartment* (MTA) provides an execution context for components that are thread-savvy. A *single-threaded apartment* (STA) is a safe execution context for running objects that were written without concern for locking and synchronization. STAs are helpful because they eliminate the need for programmer-assisted synchronization, but they're based on an invocation architecture that's less than optimal.

Two different sets of terminology are used to describe COM's threading models. The Win32 SDK documentation uses the terms *multithreaded apartment* and *single-threaded apartment*. Other authors and development tools use the terms *free-threaded* and *apartment-threaded*. A free-threaded component is written to run in an MTA. An apartment-threaded component is written to run in an STA. Whenever you hear the term *apartment*, you can infer that this means an STA. Every COM-aware thread must formally enter a specific apartment, so *MTA* and *STA* are really the more accurate terms.

A process that runs COM objects must have at least one apartment. Figure 7-3 shows three possible layouts for the apartments in a process. A process that runs a single apartment can employ either an STA or an MTA. An application can also run multiple apartments. A process is limited to a single MTA, but it can run many STAs. The MTA can run any number of threads and thread-savvy objects, so there's no need for more than one per process. However, a process can run multiple STAs to provide multithreading in an application that is built using thread-oblivious components.

A thread running in the MTA can directly execute a method on an object that is also running in the MTA. When a method is invoked on an MTA-resident object by a thread running in a different apartment, COM's underlying RPC layer services the call by dispatching a thread from a dynamically managed pool. Figure 7-4 on the following page shows how two incoming calls can be dispatched concurrently on an object. The MTA is a fast and responsive environment, but programmers are expected to write objects that are robust in the face of concurrency.

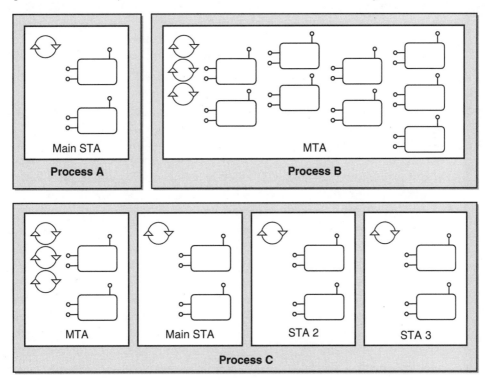

Figure 7-3. *A process that runs COM objects contains one or more apartments. A process is limited to a single MTA, but it can have multiple STAs.*

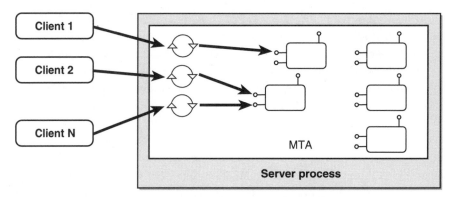

Figure 7-4. *In a multithreaded apartment, when the process receives a method call bound for an object running in the MTA, COM's underlying RPC layer services it by dispatching a thread from a dynamic pool.*

Visual Basic isn't yet capable of creating components that can run in the MTA. You must use some other tool or language (such as C++ or Java) to create a free-threaded component. A C++ programmer writing a free-threaded component must deal with concurrency by using Win32 locking primitives. This style of programming becomes increasingly complex and grungy, but it yields components that are potentially more responsive. Java offers support in both the language and the virtual machine (VM) for synchronization, so Java programmers can write MTA objects in a style that's far simpler than that in C++.

The Visual Basic team had a tough decision to make. They needed to decide whether their programmers should be exposed to synchronization issues. They decided that requiring programmer-assisted synchronization was unacceptable in a tool intended to provide the highest levels of productivity. Their decision means that Visual Basic's multithreaded capabilities derive entirely from running objects in multiple STAs. If you want to make the most of Visual Basic, you must understand how an STA works.

Figure 7-5 shows what life is like inside an STA. The RPC layer and an STA work together to serialize all incoming method calls, with help from a Windows message queue. This is the same kind of message queue used in a typical user interface application. When the COM library creates an STA, it also creates an invisible window that makes it possible for the application to set up a standard message loop. The RPC layer responds to an incoming method call by posting a message to the queue with the Win32 *PostMessage* function. The thread in the STA responds to method requests by servicing these messages on a first-in, first-out basis. When the STA is busy processing a call, incoming requests are queued up and must wait their turn. The STA's thread eventually works its way to the bottom of the queue and goes into idle mode when the queue is empty. While this invocation architecture requires a good deal of overhead, the STA eliminates the need for objects to be concerned about concurrency and synchronization.

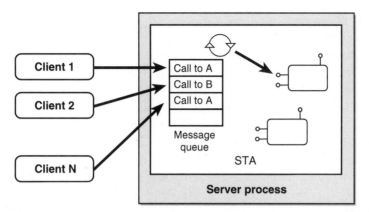

Figure 7-5. *In a single-threaded apartment, an STA serializes all inbound method calls by employing a Windows message queue. The RPC layer posts a message to the queue when a method is invoked.*

An STA has two important limitations. First, it provides a roundabout way of invoking a method call. Posting and reading messages on the queue takes up valuable processing cycles, unlike the way in which calls are dispatched in the MTA. Second, the serialization of all inbound method calls has a significant effect on the application's responsiveness. Not only does an STA prevent multiple calls from executing concurrently on a single object, it also prevents calls from executing concurrently on any two objects in an STA. Unfortunately, when two objects live in the same STA, only one of them can execute a method at a time. It would be better if locking were done at the object level instead of at the apartment level. If you want two Visual Basic objects to run method calls concurrently, you must make sure that each object is created in a separate STA.

Who Manages the Apartments in a Process?

Every application that creates COM objects can control how apartments are created and used. This means that every COM-aware EXE should include code for creating and managing a set of apartments. A C++ programmer who creates an application or an out-of-process server creates apartments by making calls to the COM Library. The functions *CoInitialize* and *CoInitializeEx* are used to associate a running thread with an apartment. A thread can be associated with either an STA or the MTA. If the requested apartment doesn't exist, COM creates it automatically. You can create additional threads and associate them with either the MTA or a new STA. As you can see, the code behind an application has a strong influence on how apartments are laid out within the process.

One situation in which an apartment is created without the assistance of the hosting application occurs when a COM object is activated from an in-process DLL. If the client is running on a thread that's incompatible with the threading model of the object being created, COM transparently finds or creates a compatible apartment in which to create the new object. For example, the components that you distribute in an ActiveX DLL can't run in the MTA. So what happens when an object is activated from your DLL by a thread that is running inside the MTA? COM deals with this situation by silently creating a new STA to host your object. COM also loads the proxy/stub code required to bind the object back to the client.

Every coclass has an associated CLSID key for tracking information for activation in the Windows Registry. The Registry key *CLSID\InprocServer32* can be marked with a *ThreadingModel* attribute to indicate which apartment types can be used to load objects activated from this CLSID. This attribute can be marked as Free, Apartment, or Both. The Free setting means that newly created objects can be loaded only into the MTA. The Apartment setting indicates that a new object must be loaded into an STA. In either case, if the creating thread isn't in a compatible apartment type, COM automatically creates (or finds) a compatible apartment. A setting of Both means that a new object can be loaded into the apartment of the caller regardless of whether it's an MTA or an STA.

In-process components that don't have a *ThreadingModel* attribute are always loaded into the first STA created within a process. This special STA is called the *main STA*. Classes that are configured to run there are often called *single-threaded* or *main-threaded* classes. Many programmers consider a CLSID without an explicit *ThreadingModel* attribute to be an obsolete, legacy component. The problem with such a component is that it can activate objects only inside the main STA. If a client is running in the MTA or any STA other than the main STA, a proxy/stub is introduced between the object and the client. An apartment-threaded component is almost always preferable to a main-threaded component because it allows a client in any STA to bind to an object without the overhead of the proxy/stub layer.

MULTITHREADING WITH VISUAL BASIC

Working directly with Win32 threads and COM apartments is difficult and is far beyond the capabilities of the Visual Basic programming language. However, when Visual Basic 5 first shipped, many unfortunate programmers tried to directly call the *CreateThread* function in the Win32 API by using Visual Basic's new *AddressOf* operator. These programmers found that they could successfully call *CreateThread* but that their applications often died strange and mysterious deaths.

The problem with calling *CreateThread* is that it creates a new Win32 thread that knows nothing about COM or apartments. It's therefore illegal to use this thread to invoke a method on a COM object. This creates quite a problem because all Visual Basic objects, including forms and controls, are also COM objects. One of these objects can be directly accessed only by the thread running in the object's apartment.

When the newly created thread tries to change a value in a text box, the application crashes. This is a pretty good reason for never using *CreateThread* directly from Visual Basic code.

A determined Visual Basic programmer with knowledge of COM's threading models might try to take things to the next level. You can make a thread enter an STA by calling a function in the COM library such as *CoInitializeEx*. However, once you get the thread into an apartment, the complexity increases. For instance, sometimes you must write code to marshal interface references (they're really interface pointers at this level) from one apartment to another. If you pass the interface references through a COM interface, the proxy and the stub are created automatically. However, if you pass them manually, the code requirements increase dramatically. You must make two complicated calls to the COM library. One call is needed to create a stub in the object's apartment, and a second call is needed to create a proxy in the caller's apartment. You also have to know enough about COM to decide when this code is necessary.

As you can see, you shouldn't go down this path unless you know an awful lot about the COM library and the OLE32 DLL. Moreover, anyone who can program at this level would prefer to program in C++ over Visual Basic because C++ is far more powerful when accessing the COM library directly. Now that you know where you shouldn't go, it's time to look at what you *can* do with Visual Basic. The remainder of this chapter will concentrate on what you can do in Visual Basic using reasonable techniques to achieve multithreading.

Apartment-Threaded ActiveX DLLs

The easiest and most reliable way to create multithreaded servers with Visual Basic is to distribute your code as an in-process server. An in-process server doesn't require any code for creating or managing threads or apartments. This means that the application code for managing threads and apartments is handled by somebody else. When you create an ActiveX DLL project or an ActiveX Control project, your objects can take advantage of the threading used by the hosting applications. Sophisticated environments such as Microsoft Internet Explorer and MTS have been optimized to run apartment-threaded objects such as the ones you create with Visual Basic. All you have to do is make sure that your DLL project is marked for apartment threading.

Figure 7-6 on the following page shows the General tab of the Project Properties dialog box. When you create an ActiveX DLL or an ActiveX Control project, you can select the Apartment Threaded or Single Threaded threading model. Apartment Threaded is the default and is almost always the best choice. When you choose this setting, your CLSID's *ThreadingModel* attribute will be marked Apartment. An ActiveX DLL marked as Single Threaded can load objects only into the main STA. Environments such as Internet Explorer and MTS don't work well with components that use

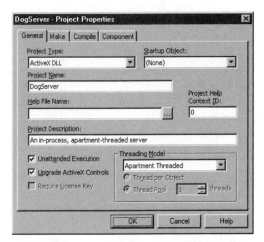

Figure 7-6. *ActiveX DLL and ActiveX Control projects have two possible settings for their threading model. An apartment-threaded server can load its objects into any available STA. A single-threaded server can load objects only into the application's main STA.*

this legacy threading model. You should always mark your DLLs as apartment-threaded unless you have a good reason to do otherwise. Later in this chapter, we'll look at a special technique that involves using a single-threaded DLL.

You should also consider marking your ActiveX DLL project to run with Unattended Execution if you plan to deploy it inside MTS or any other environment that runs nonvisual objects. The Unattended Execution option is for projects that will run without user interaction. Any run-time function such as *MsgBox* that normally results in user interaction is written to the Windows NT event log instead. Using this option guarantees that your code will never hang because of a modal dialog box that has been invoked by mistake.

MTS actually adds a twist to COM threading by adding yet another threading abstraction called an *activity*. (Chapter 9 covers MTS activities.) However, you'll still create DLLs that are marked to run as Apartment Threaded with Unattended Execution.

Creating Multithreaded EXEs

This chapter has made one specific recommendation to Visual Basic programmers: Never create a thread or an apartment on your own. However, you can create an ActiveX EXE project and let Visual Basic create and manage a set of apartments for you. When you build an ActiveX EXE with the appropriate settings, Visual Basic automatically builds the code into your server for creating and managing a set of STAs.

You can build an ActiveX EXE using one of three threading modes. Figure 7-7 shows where to configure these settings in the Project Properties dialog box. It seems

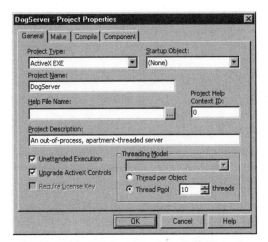

Figure 7-7. *You can set an ActiveX EXE project to one of three threading modes.*

at first that only two options are available, but you can build an ActiveX EXE using any of the following three settings:

■ Thread Pool = 1 (single-threaded)

■ Thread Per Object

■ Thread Pool > 1 (a predefined maximum number of STAs)

A new ActiveX EXE project is single-threaded by default, which means that all objects loaded into the server process will always run in the main STA. It also means that the server can run only one method call at a time. When an object executes a method, all other incoming requests are queued up on a processwide basis. This might be acceptable for an out-of-process server that has a single client, but when an out-of-process server has many connected clients, one client's method calls will block the calls of any other client. If a client invokes a long running method on an object in the server, all other client requests will be blocked until the method call has been completed. In many server designs, this lack of concurrency is unacceptable. You can use a different threading mode to make a server much more responsive in the presence of multiple clients.

If you set the threading mode to Thread Per Object, the server will automatically create a new apartment when an object is activated by a remote client. As you'll recall from Chapter 3, the client calls upon the SCM when it wants to create and connect to a new COM object. The client makes an activation request by calling into the COM library. The request is serviced by the SCM, which locates the server (loading it if necessary) and communicates with it to negotiate the creation of a new object. The Visual Basic team added a hook to create a new thread and apartment based on the project's threading mode. If you select Thread Per Object, the server creates a fresh, new apartment in which to run the new object.

It's important to understand exactly when new apartments are created. It's a bit tricky because the term *thread per object* isn't completely accurate. If an object running in the server process creates a second object with the *New* operator, the second object is loaded into the same apartment as its creator. Only when an external client makes an activation request is a new apartment created. This gives you a reasonable way to manage the apartments in your server process. It allows every connected client to run one or more objects in a private apartment. Each client can invoke methods with the guarantee that its calls won't be blocked by the calls of other clients. Furthermore, this threading mode makes it possible to create a set of objects on behalf of a single user that are all loaded into the same apartment. To do this, the client application should create the first object, and then this object should create all the others using the *New* operator. This is important because these objects can be bound to one another without the overhead of the proxy/stub layer.

Thread Pooling in an ActiveX EXE

One problem with thread-per-object threading is that it consumes a lot of resources when a large number of clients are connected. Remember that an invisible window is created for each STA, so load time and resource overhead are significant when the process has loaded up 50 or more apartments. You also reach a point of diminishing returns when you scale up the number of threads. When you reach this point, your server's actual throughput decreases as the amount of time required by the system to switch between threads increases. The Thread Pool option lets you balance your server's responsiveness with more efficient use of resources.

If you set the threading mode of an ActiveX EXE to a thread pool greater than 1, Visual Basic creates a new STA for each new object request until it reaches the thread pool capacity. If you have a thread pool of size 4, the server creates the first three objects in apartments 2, 3, and 4, respectively. Once the number of apartments is reached, Visual Basic uses a round-robin algorithm that matches new objects with existing apartments. The algorithm is reasonable but somewhat arbitrary. After placing the first three objects in apartments 2, 3 and 4, the server places objects into apartments with the sequence 4, 3, 2, main, 4, 3, 2, main, and so forth. You're better off not taking advantage of this knowledge because the Visual Basic team might decide to change the algorithm in a later version.

Using a thread pool always involves a compromise. You get more efficient use of resources, but you might experience problems with responsiveness. If two clients both activate objects that happen to be loaded into the same apartment, the method calls of one client will block the other. If your method calls are completed quickly, this might not be a problem. Method calls taking more than a second or two to complete might impose an unacceptable concurrency constraint.

Apartments and Global Data

Many veteran Visual Basic programmers get confused the first time they work with multithreaded servers because public variables defined in standard (.bas) modules aren't really global variables. These public variables are scoped at the apartment level. This changes things for programmers who are used to defining global, applicationwide variables in earlier versions of Visual Basic. When your component runs in a multi-threaded environment, two objects see the same public standard-module data only when they are in the same apartment. Objects in separate apartments see different instances of these public variables. This creates random behavior in a server with a thread pool because of the arbitrary way in which objects are matched with apartments.

When the Visual Basic team added support for apartment threading, they had to decide how to handle the data defined in standard modules. If they decided to store this data in global memory, someone would have to be responsible for synchro-nizing access to it in the presence of multiple threads. As in the case of COM objects, the team felt that it was unacceptable to require any type of programmer-assisted synchronization. Instead, they opted to store the data defined in a standard module in thread-local storage (TLS), as shown in Figure 7-8. When the Visual Basic run time creates a new apartment, it also creates a fresh copy of every variable defined in a standard module in TLS. The thread in each new apartment also calls *Sub Main*, which lets you initialize the data in TLS just after it creates the new STA.

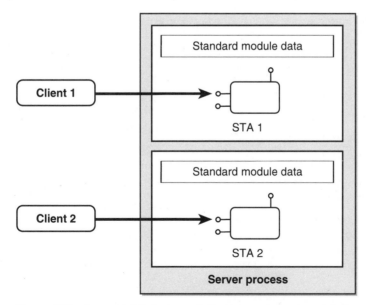

Figure 7-8. *Any variable that you define in a standard module in an ActiveX DLL or an ActiveX EXE project is held in thread-local storage. This means that objects running in different apartments cannot share data.*

The reasoning behind this decision is sound. Visual Basic programmers don't have to deal with the burden of synchronization. It's always taken care of behind the scenes. The cost of this convenience is that you can't use global data in the way that many Visual Basic programmers have in the past. You must either design multi-threaded applications that don't depend on shared data or devise a fairly contrived scheme to share data among objects in different apartments.

One of the simplest ways to simulate global memory in an ActiveX EXE project requires the assistance of a second server project. You must create a single-threaded ActiveX DLL and reference it in the ActiveX EXE project. The trick is to define shared memory in the standard module of the single-threaded DLL project, as shown in Figure 7-9. All objects created from the DLL run in the main STA and therefore see the same copy of data defined in the standard module. Any object in any apartment can create an object from the DLL and call methods to read and write to this shared data. This solution isn't very elegant or efficient and is vulnerable to problems with locking and contention. Chapter 10 will revisit this problem of shared global data and provide a far more satisfying solution.

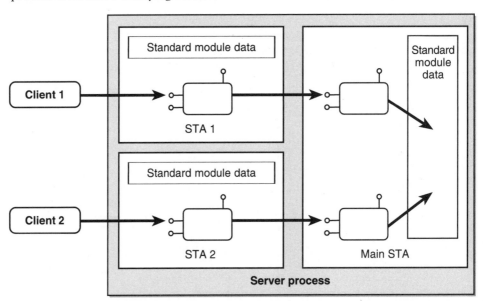

Figure 7-9. *The easiest way to share data among objects in a multithreaded ActiveX EXE is to call upon a single-threaded ActiveX DLL. Any object in any apartment can create an object from the single-threaded DLL.*

MULTITHREADING IN A FORM-BASED APPLICATION

As you have seen, it's fairly simple to create a multithreaded out-of-process server using Visual Basic. All you have to do is set the appropriate threading mode before you build an ActiveX EXE project. You can also create a form-based application that uses multiple threads (although this is far more difficult). Thus you can create a secondary thread in a typical Windows application, which allows you to run a task in the background without freezing the user interface. This can make a huge difference in a desktop application in which running certain tasks on the primary thread would lock down the user interface for an unacceptable period of time.

The technique for running a secondary thread requires using a back door to create a second apartment. Although this requires a little trickery, the results are both safe and predictable. If you create a form-based application with an ActiveX EXE project instead of a Standard EXE project, Visual Basic includes built-in support for creating additional apartments. The trick is to make an internal activation request seem as if it's coming from a remote client. As you'll recall from earlier in this chapter, a thread-per-object ActiveX EXE creates a new apartment when an external client makes an activation request. You can trick the ActiveX EXE into thinking that you're a remote client by using Visual Basic's *CreateObject* function instead of the *New* operator.

When you create an object in an ActiveX EXE project using the *New* operator, the Visual Basic run time will attempt to activate the object directly from the server. If the ActiveX EXE contains a local definition of the CLSID, the object is activated in the same apartment of the client that named *New*. If there's no local implementation for the CLSID, the Visual Basic run time passes the activation request to the SCM. Unlike a call to *New*, however, a call to *CreateObject* always results in a call to the SCM. If you pass the ProgID of a local class to the *CreateObject* function, your server calls the SCM and the SCM responds by calling back into your server's process in the same manner as with any other external activation request. The ActiveX EXE sees an external activation request and creates the object in a new STA.

What happens when you call *CreateObject* from within your thread-per-object ActiveX EXE project? A new STA is created in your process, and the new object is loaded inside it. Next *CreateObject* returns an interface reference to the client, which is bound to the object through a proxy/stub layer. Now you have an object in a separate apartment running on a different thread, as shown in Figure 7-10 on the following page. OK, you've done the easy part. Doing anything meaningful with this new apartment and thread requires significant work.

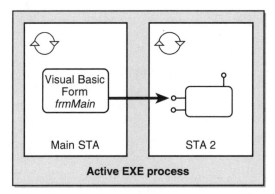

Figure 7-10. *You can create secondary threads in a Visual Basic application with a user interface. You can create a new thread in a thread-per-object ActiveX EXE application by creating an object with the* CreateObject *function instead of the* New *operator.*

A Series of "Gotchas"

The first obstacle that you must face is that you can't run or debug your multithreaded client application in the Visual Basic IDE. The behavior of creating additional STAs can be exhibited only in a compiled EXE. This makes it far more difficult to debug your application. But then again, what could be more reliable in debugging than your old friend the *MsgBox* statement?

When you create an ActiveX EXE instead of a Standard EXE, you must use *Sub Main* instead of a startup form. This means that you must use *Sub Main* to load and show the application's main form. This creates a problem because *Sub Main* executes whenever a new apartment is created. You must use a programming technique to load and show the main form only during your application's first execution of *Sub Main*. You can do this by loading an invisible form on application startup. When *Sub Main* runs, it can search through all loaded windows with a Win32 technique to see whether this form has been loaded. The sample application MTC1.vbp on this book's companion CD demonstrates one way to accomplish this.

The next problem you face is that you can't create additional apartments until the main apartment has been fully initialized. Therefore, you must wait until *Sub Main* completes before you can create any new objects in separate apartments. *Sub Main* won't complete until the form you are loading completes its *Load* method. This means that you can't create objects on separate threads during either of these methods. This isn't overly difficult to overcome, but it's a pain because many of us are used to creating our objects in *Sub Main* or in the *Load* event of our main form.

The first nontrivial problem surfaces when you want to run a task on your secondary thread without blocking the primary thread that's responsible for servicing the user interface. Currently COM lets you run method calls only in a synchronous manner. If you make a simple method call from your main form to an object in a different STA, the primary thread will be blocked until the call has completed. This totally defeats the purpose of creating a second thread.

Getting both threads to run at the same time requires an asynchronous method call. A future version of COM+ will modify the RPC layer to support true asynchronous calls. For now, however, all calls in COM are synchronous. A Visual Basic programmer must handcraft a "logical" asynchronous call by using the *SetTimer* function from the Win32 API. Again, the sample application MTC1.vbp shows how to set up an asynchronous call using this technique.

Finally, after you execute an asynchronous call from the main form to the secondary apartment, you must provide a way for the object to communicate with the main form. The object should notify the form of the task's update status while it's executing and ultimately the success or failure of the task. To do this, you can use either events or callback interfaces, as described in the previous chapter. The steps required for the asynchronous call are shown in Figure 7-11.

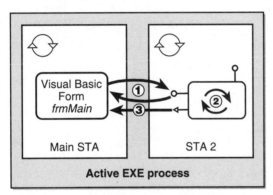

Figure 7-11. *Running an asynchronous task is fairly complicated, even after you've created an object in a secondary apartment.*

THREADING IN THE COM+ ERA

A future version of COM+ will likely address some of the performance limitations of the STA. Currently, if you want COM to serialize access to your objects automatically, you must put them in single-threaded apartments. This has the desired effect of ensuring that all calls to your object are serialized. This practice also has the potentially costly effect of forcing a thread to be dedicated to servicing those calls for the lifetime of the process, rather than simply using an RPC thread borrowed from the RPC thread pool. Microsoft is now working on an enhanced model for concurrency management that has the working name *activity threading,* or *worker threading.* Like today's STA-based objects, activity-threaded objects don't need to worry about concurrent access. However, unlike today's STA-based objects, activity-threaded objects don't require a dedicated thread. Instead, the RPC layer can directly dispatch calls to objects using an arbitrary thread borrowed from the RPC thread pool. The RPC layer will track activitywide locks and block any incoming method requests until all previous calls have completed.

While the locking in the activity-threaded model will still protect your objects from concurrent access, it will provide a faster and more scalable architecture. Today's STA-based model has limited scalability because every new STA requires a dedicated thread in order to service incoming calls. Because COM+ activities won't require dedicated threads, creating hundreds or thousands of activities will be far more acceptable than creating the same number of STAs today. The good news for Visual Basic programmers is that you probably won't have to do anything differently when the activity model becomes available. (Actually, it's available today in MTS, but the current implementation pins activities to STA threads.)

The code you write today for an STA should not behave any differently when COM+'s new activity-threading implementation ships later this century. Your Visual Basic objects will simply run faster and be more responsive. That's the good news. The bad news is that your objects will not be able to take advantage of this new threading implementation until the Visual Basic team modifies both its run-time layer and its compiler to provide support for this new model. As mentioned earlier in this chapter, every component created by Visual Basic today has thread affinity. All Visual Basic objects rely on data that's kept in thread-local storage. This means that a Visual Basic object can be accessed only by the thread that created it. Objects with thread affinity won't be able to take advantage of this new model.

WHEN DO YOU REALLY NEED MULTITHREADING?

An experienced Visual Basic programmer who knows how COM apartments work can use certain techniques to reliably exploit multithreaded behavior. You can use multithreading safely and easily in many situations. In other scenarios, multithreading becomes more difficult and hazardous.

Programmers have always been fascinated by things that are cool and complex. This has compromised their ability to distinguish between necessary features and overpriced luxuries. For inexperienced programmers, threads can fall into the latter category. Think of threads as you think of salt. We need a little bit of it to stay alive, but too much can be harmful. Always consider whether the value that threads add to your application is worth the risk and complexity.

If the costs outweigh the benefits, avoid multithreading altogether. For example, you have seen that creating a secondary thread in a form-based application is extremely difficult. On the other hand, it can be extremely valuable because this technique allows you to run background tasks or execute remote methods without locking down the user interface. However, any programmer who's responsible for writing and maintaining this code has to know exactly how Visual Basic uses apartments. Programming at this level is well beyond the capabilities of all but the most experienced Visual Basic programmers.

The most significant need for multithreading exists in a distributed application that runs as a server-side process. If a distributed application has many connected clients, proper threading support is required to achieve reasonable scalability. To scale up to accommodate hundreds of clients, an application must have very sophisticated threading code. The answer to this problem isn't an ActiveX EXE. Instead, Microsoft provides sophisticated thread management in the MTS run-time environment. You distribute your objects in apartment-threaded DLLs and let MTS manage the thread pooling for you. We'll resume our exploration of this important topic in Chapter 9.

Chapter 8

Examining
Remote Activation

As you saw in Chapter 1, the backbone of COM's distributed infrastructure is based on an interprocess mechanism called the Remote Procedure Call (RPC). This chapter gives you some background on RPC and the process of remote activation. It also covers issues associated with the life cycle of COM objects in a distributed environment.

Security is an important concern in a distributed application. Without a robust security model, COM would be worthless to enterprise developers. This chapter describes how COM creates abstractions on top of the Win32 security model to provide secure access to distributed objects. One of the best things about COM security is that it can be used in either a declarative or a programmatic manner. As a Microsoft Visual Basic programmer, you have minimal control over the programmatic side. However, you can use declarative security to make sure that only authenticated and authorized users can access your distributed application.

This chapter describes how to configure servers and client computers when you deploy an application with Distributed COM. It introduces a new Registry key called the *AppID*, and it shows you how to modify the Registry to track information about the security and server locality of a COM-based application. As you'll see, the AppID plays an important role in both server-side and client-side configuration.

You'll also learn how applications based on Distributed COM worked before the introduction of Microsoft Transaction Server (MTS). You must wait until the next chapter to see how MTS provides a run-time environment for distributed objects.

However, it's important for you to understand that MTS is layered on top of the infrastructure of Distributed COM. Everything that MTS does with regard to remote activation, security, and configuration is based on the capabilities of Distributed COM and the RPC layer. To really understand MTS, you must first appreciate what's going on underneath.

Finally, you'll learn about a few significant limitations associated with the initial release of Distributed COM. Certain problems relating to application security and configuration are tricky and expensive to solve. Fortunately, MTS provides a valuable solution to these problems, which is described in Chapter 9.

RPC AND COM

From the early days of computer networks, some programmers were determined to make code on one computer cause the execution of code on another. At the time, the requirements of interhost communication were amazingly high. Only hardcore systems-level programmers were up to the task. To execute a function on a separate computer typically required code to pass messages between computers. This code was almost always written with a specific network protocol and a specific set of hardware in mind.

In the 1980s, it was generally acceptable to write remote networking code in this fashion. However, porting a distributed application to a different protocol or a different hardware platform was expensive. As distributed programming became more popular, people started looking for ways in which application code could be decoupled from the code that handled the remoting of code execution across computer boundaries. Since companies wanted to shed dependencies on both hardware platforms and network protocols, the need for a more generic solution was great.

A standards group called the Open Software Foundation (OSF) set out to create a specification to solve this problem. The group's goal was to eliminate the need to hardcode platform and network protocol dependencies into distributed application code. The fruit of the group's labors was a specification for RPC and Distributed Computing Environment (DCE). The RPC specification gives programmers a way to write application code that's free of these costly dependencies. The most notable advantage of this specification is that the code written for distributed applications can be used on a variety of platforms and protocols with little or no change to application code.

The RPC specification requires programmers to define remote calls by writing a description in an RPC-specific version of Interface Definition Language (IDL). A set of calls is defined in RPC IDL inside an RPC interface. An RPC interface is simply a group of global functions that defines the calling syntax of each remote procedure call. Each parameter in every procedure is defined with a specific data type and a direction. (This talk of interfaces and IDL should sound familiar to you at this point.)

An RPC client application must establish a connection with the server at run time by negotiating a binding protocol with a server process. Once binding has taken place, the two communicate through the RPC channel. Every procedure call involves moving data back and forth across the channel. An RPC request transmits a procedure call and its inbound parameters from the client application to the server. After the server executes the procedure, the RPC response transmits the procedure's return value and any outbound parameters back to the client application. When a client application makes a synchronous RPC call, it must wait for the response to come back from across the network before it can do anything else.

MS-RPC

As OSF DCE RPC became an industry standard for distributed computing, Microsoft created its own version for Windows platforms. Microsoft's implementation of the OSF specification is called MS-RPC. MS-RPC has been integrated into all 32-bit Windows platforms and promises to provide Windows connectivity to many non-Windows platforms.

Developers use MS-RPC by first creating an IDL source file and feeding it to the Microsoft IDL (MIDL) compiler. The MIDL compiler generates C source code files that have the necessary RPC code stubs for both the client and the server. This code is compiled into client applications and server applications. As a result, the client application can call the functions, which are automatically remoted to the server application. Once again, the big win here is that applications don't require networking code with platform or protocol dependencies.

RPC has one significant problem: It doesn't offer the elegance of object-oriented programming. It's largely based on a procedural paradigm in which clients and servers communicate in terms of global functions. While the RPC specification does provide a few object-oriented extensions, it is fair to say that few of these extensions have made it into mainstream use. RPC needs an object-oriented wrapper in order to achieve the higher levels of productivity that application programmers are accustomed to. What's more, MS-RPC requires low-level programming, so it's difficult to access from higher-level tools such as Visual Basic.

When Microsoft engineers were deciding how to make COM interprocess-capable, they saw that RPC had much to offer. RPC was already ubiquitous in the industry, and MS-RPC had been integrated into every significant Windows platform. The engineers knew that RPC could be valuable to COM because it enables a client application to connect to a server across the network and execute a procedure call. COM desperately needed this functionality to participate in distributed programming. COM also had much to offer RPC. A mapping of COM interfaces gives RPC an object-oriented wrapper and makes writing interprocess code much easier. Figure 8-1 on the following page shows how the connection is set up.

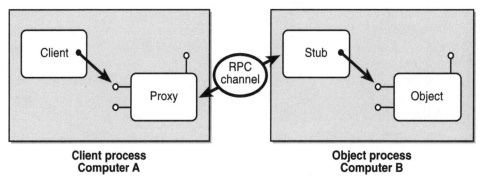

Figure 8-1. *The proxy and the stub are generated with an RPC-IDL compiler. They communicate with one another across an RPC channel.*

Microsoft's version of IDL includes COM extensions that let you map a COM interface to an RPC interface. The MIDL compiler can build proxy/stub code by examining the definition of a COM interface. As you saw earlier, the proxy and the stub can communicate by establishing an RPC channel. The RPC layer allows a client application to establish a connection with an out-of-process COM object. It also supplies the threading support on which COM builds its model of apartments. It turns out that the concurrency model supplied by RPC is very reasonable. As you saw in Chapter 7, the RPC layer is important to both single-threaded apartments and multi-threaded apartments. The threading support provided by RPC allows a server process to service multiple calls concurrently.

The RPC layer is transparent to Visual Basic programmers. This means that when you create an out-of-process COM server with Visual Basic, the COM interface-to-RPC mapping is taken care of behind the scenes. The universal marshaler contains its own IDL compiler. It reads an interface definition from a type library and generates the required proxy/stub code at run time. This allows RPC and COM to work together to provide locality independence. In this respect, you can say that interfaces are the key to seamless distribution in COM. You saw this stated earlier in this book, but I reiterate it here because it's so significant.

Activating Across the Network

Let's take a rest from all this low-level talk about network protocols and the MIDL compiler for a moment and talk about why the interprocess capabilities provided by RPC are so important. They're important because they let you deploy a set of business objects in the middle tier of a distributed application, as shown in Figure 8-2.

In an N-tier architecture, a client application running in the presentation tier activates and uses objects distributed throughout the network. Distributed COM must provide an infrastructure in which two machines can coordinate to load a remote object and bind it back to the client application. Distributed COM must also provide

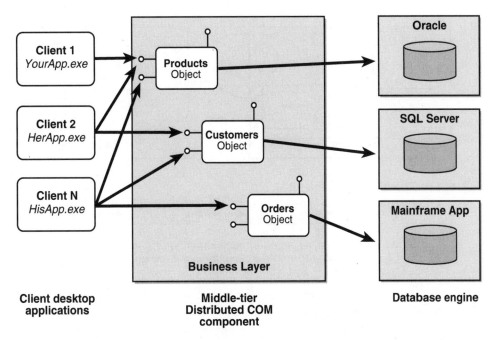

Figure 8-2. *Client applications rely on Distributed COM to communicate with business objects running in the middle tier.*

a security layer so that client applications can use objects only after they have been authenticated and authorized.

Let's examine what happens during remote activation. Recall that in local activation, when an out-of-process object is activated the SCM can launch and/or find the running server process that contains the object. Once it finds the server, it goes through the loading and binding sequence described in Chapter 4. Remote activation is similar to local activation except that it requires two sessions of the SCM running on two different computers. When the SCM running on the client machine determines that the CLSID implementation lives on a separate host, it sends an activation request across the network to the SCM on the server's computer. The client-side SCM passes the requested CLSID and IID as in any other activation request.

The SCM on the server machine can activate the object just as it does when it handles a local activation request. That means that the server-side SCM scans through its Registry looking for a local COM server that serves up objects of the requested CLSID. The SCM launches the server process if this is required. Once the server-side SCM loads the local object, it coordinates with the client-side SCM to move an interface reference across the network. When the interface reference reaches the client machine, the client-side SCM binds it to the client application, as shown in Figure 8-3 on the following page. After the object is bound to the client application, no additional support is required from the SCM on either machine. The client application can invoke remote calls on the object all by itself.

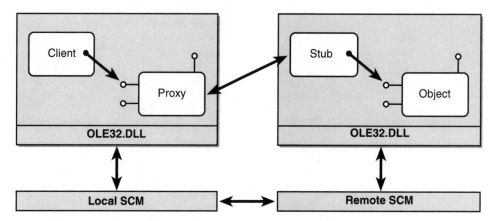

Figure 8-3. *Remote activation is coordinated between two separate sessions of the SCM. If the client application has been authenticated and authorized, the server-side SCM performs a local activation and returns an interface reference.*

What happens if a client application crashes while holding outstanding object references? The object must have a way to determine that its client application has expired. You saw in Chapter 5 that the client can discover that an object has died by inspecting an HRESULT. However, an object needs a little more assistance to determine whether the client has passed away.

COM provides the infrastructure for distributed garbage collection. The system can determine that a client with an outstanding object reference has died. When the system discovers this, it informs the object by calling *Release*. This means that distributed objects can be released from memory when their clients crash. The need for garbage collection is important in a distributed application that will run for months at a time.

COM's mechanism for distributed garbage collection is based on the client machine pinging the server machine with a notification that says, "I'm still alive." The client pings the server every two minutes. If the server doesn't hear from the client for six minutes (that's three missed pings), the server informs the object that the client has died.

The ping algorithm has been optimized to avoid excessive network traffic. Pings aren't sent for individual interface references or for individual objects. Instead, the system transmits a single machinewide ping from the client to the server with information about every connection between the two machines. Note that each ping doesn't transmit all the information about every outstanding interface reference. Instead, it transmits the information about what has changed since the last ping. This "delta" algorithm significantly reduces what needs to be broadcast across the network.

SERVER-SIDE CONFIGURATION

Distributed COM relies on configuration information stored in the Registry of every computer running a distributed application. Each CLSID that can be activated remotely must have a profile in the Registry, which maintains important settings such as the path to the EXE file that's used to launch the server's process. To properly set up a distributed application, you must also configure an applicationwide profile for the server's process. This profile affects the entire out-of-process server, which is known as a COM application. COM uses the AppID key in the Registry to hold important settings associated with a COM application.

The Registry key HKEY_CLASSES_ROOT\AppID contains a list of all the local EXEs that export CLSIDs. Each local server (each a potential remote server) is represented in this list with its own GUID, which serves as its AppID. There's only one AppID for each out-of-process server. If the server contains three or four CLSIDs, all of these coclasses share a common applicationwide profile defined by the server's AppID.

When the SCM attempts to launch an out-of-process server, it uses the settings in the AppID to determine whether an administrator has authorized the client to use the server. This creates a bit of a problem because many servers don't register an AppID as part of the self-registration process. For example, the self-registration code in your Visual Basic server never writes anything to the Registry that has to do with an AppID. Fortunately, the SCM has a way to deal with this situation.

When the SCM launches an out-of-process server during an activation request, it examines the CLSID to see whether it has an associated AppID. If the CLSID has an associated AppID, the Registry settings for the AppID tell the SCM about the server's security profile. If the CLSID doesn't have an AppID, the SCM uses a systemwide default profile. This allows every out-of-process server to be launched under the control of a secure profile.

While you can modify AppIDs in the Registry by hand, it's better to use the configuration utility called Dcomcnfg.exe, which is on all machines that run Distributed COM. You run this utility by choosing the Run command from the system's Start menu. When you run Dcomcnfg.exe, you see a list of all the registered AppIDs on the local machine. (It might take a few seconds to start up Dcomcnfg.exe the first time you launch it because the utility walks through the list of out-of-process CLSIDs and creates an AppID for each one that needs one.)

Dcomcnfg.exe is fairly easy to use. Once you learn how to use it, you can run and test distributed applications in the development environment. You should note that Dcomcnfg.exe is intended for administrators, not programmers. Distributed COM gives more responsibilities to system administrators while taking many responsibilities away from programmers. A programmer can create a component in a generic manner, and the administrator can configure it to run in many possible ways at deployment time. COM security is a good example of how this works.

COM Security

COM offers both *declarative security* and *programmatic security*. Declarative security is beneficial because it makes the system administrator responsible for deciding and enforcing who has access to an application. As the security requirements for the application change, the administrator can address them without having to rewrite any application code.

The administrator configures and adjusts security settings in a Microsoft Windows NT network environment. Often the same individual is responsible for access permissions to resources and services such as Microsoft Exchange, Microsoft SQL Server, and network shares on a file server. The administrator typically knows the physical layout of computers in the network as well as the user and group accounts. Learning how to administer security in a COM-based distributed application is pretty straightforward.

Windows NT security is based on user and group accounts. Each Windows NT account has an associated security ID (SID). When a user logs on to a Windows NT domain, the login process creates a security token that contains the SID of the user's account and the SID of any group account to which the user has been added. The security token is carried by each process that the user runs. When a user attempts to access a resource, the system checks this security token to make sure the user is authorized.

A Windows NT administrator authorizes users by modifying a discretionary access control list (DACL), which is a list of SIDs associated with a resource that tells the system which users have access rights. An administrator manages this list with a DACL editor, as shown in Figure 8-4. Dcomcnfg.exe provides a DACL editor for configuring access rights to a distributed application.

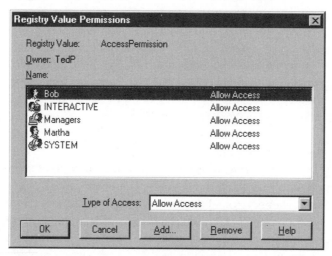

Figure 8-4. *A developer or a system administrator can use a DACL editor to configure permissions for a user or a group.*

Configuring Distributed COM

Figure 8-5 shows the Default Properties tab of Dcomcnfg.exe, which contains the machinewide settings for Distributed COM. The check box that enables or disables Distributed COM is selected by default. If you deselect it, the SCM of the local machine will deny any activation request from a remote client.

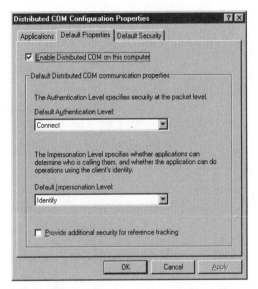

Figure 8-5. *You can use the Default Properties tab of Dcomcnfg.exe to adjust machinewide settings.*

You can also assign a machinewide authentication level on this tab. Authentication is the process of verifying the user's identity. When a user named Bob attempts to activate an object from across the network, the COM security layer on the server examines his credentials to verify that it really is Bob and not another user who is pretending to be Bob.

Authentication is performed by the RPC layer and a loadable security module called a security support provider (SSP). All SSPs are written to a standard API called the Security Support Provider Interface (SSPI). This practice allows third-party vendors to create custom SSPs that can be used in a Windows NT network environment. Windows NT 4 ships with the Windows NTLM SSP, but Windows NT 5 also includes the Kerberos SSP.

Both the client computer and the server computer have their own default authentication levels. The level on each machine should be seen as a low-water mark. When two computers have different authentication levels, the RPC layer uses the higher one. Higher levels of authentication have a negative impact on performance. The levels of authentication are shown in Figure 8-6 on the following page.

Authentication Level	Meaning
(None)	COM calls are never authenticated.
Default	The default authentication level specified by the SSP.
Connect	Authentication occurs only once, when connection is established (the default in Windows NT 4).
Call	Authenticity is guaranteed only for the first RPC packet of each method call. (This level is unsupported and is always promoted to Packet anyway.)
Packet	Authenticity is guaranteed for each packet header in every method call.
Packet Integrity	Packet authentication level plus cryptographic check-sum of payload guarantees detection of tampering.
Packet Privacy	Integrity authentication level plus payload is encrypted for privacy.

Figure 8-6. *The authentication level determines how actively the service provider authenticates messages from clients. Each level is a superset of the previous level and has a greater run-time cost.*

Authentication is part of the infrastructure of Windows NT and RPC. You don't explicitly write application code with Visual Basic that addresses authentication. This is usually beneficial because it makes application code much simpler. A system administrator can also easily change to a new SSP or a different authentication level after an application is in production without having to modify the application code.

In some situations, it's beneficial or necessary to raise or lower the authentication level programmatically. In such situations, the code must been written in a low-level language such as C++ that can talk to COM's security API. The COM library exposes functions that allow you to adjust the authentication level and other security settings on a proxy-by-proxy basis. This might be a good reason to create a shim DLL written in C++ to provide more flexibility to the servers and the client applications that you create with Visual Basic.

While the authentication level allows the object to determine the identity of the caller and provides for privacy on the wire, the impersonation level protects the client. Because authentication allows a client to effectively pass its security credentials across the network, the impersonation level determines how the server process can use the client's token. Higher levels of impersonation allow the server to do more with the client's security credentials. Figure 8-7 shows a list of the available options in Dcomcnfg.exe.

Impersonation Level	Meaning
Anonymous	The server can't see the credentials of the client. This level is unsupported and is transparently promoted to Identify in Windows NT 4 and Windows NT 5.
Identify	The server can see the security credentials and can use them for identification and authorization only (Windows NT 4 default).
Impersonate	The server can use the client's security credentials to access local resources.
Delegate	The server can use the client's security credentials to access local and remote resources. (Not available in Windows NT 4.)

Figure 8-7. *The impersonation level determines what the server can do with the client's security credentials. Each level is a superset of the previous level.*

As with the authentication level, Visual Basic programmers can't easily change the impersonation level at run time. You can use one of three approaches to configure authentication and impersonation. The first and easiest approach is to use the default levels, which are Connect for authentication and Identify for impersonation. The second option is to configure the machinewide levels on each computer for some other level(s). The third approach is to take on the challenge of writing code that changes these levels programmatically. This approach typically requires some help from another language, such as C++.

Configuring the Server's AppID

Each AppID represents a COM application. A COM application is a collection of CLSIDs whose objects are all loaded into a single-server process. When you configure the AppID for a server, you can specify which users can access the application and which Windows NT user account will be used to serve as the identity of the server process. This user account is known as the server's *security principal.*

To configure the settings for an AppID with Dcomcnfg.exe, you must select the AppID on the Applications tab. Each entry in the Applications list box is a local AppID. Remember that Dcomcnfg.exe often creates AppIDs using information from the first CLSID it finds in the Registry. This practice can result in confusion because the application's description looks as if it pertains to the CLSID, not to the server application. When Dcomcnfg.exe creates an AppID, it uses the same GUID that defines the first CLSID. However, once you find the correct COM application in this list, you can select Properties. This opens another dialog box, in which you can modify the attributes for the AppID.

To configure the server's security settings, you can use the Security tab, as shown in Figure 8-8. This tab offers three security configuration choices; you can set and modify each one using a standard Windows NT DACL editor. All access permissions are set in terms of Windows NT user and group accounts. A user must have access permissions to activate and call methods on objects. A user must have these permissions explicitly or through a group in order to use the server. The SYSTEM account must be included in the *Access Control DACL* (at least in Windows NT 4). If you forget this, your application won't function properly.

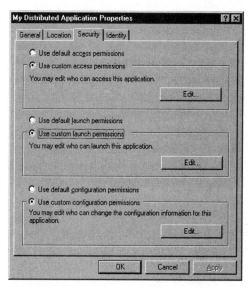

Figure 8-8. *You can use the Security tab of Dcomcnfg.exe to configure access and launch permissions to a COM application.*

A user must have launch permissions to launch the application if the server process isn't already running. This configurable option lets an administrator restrict the times when the application can be used. For example, users who have access rights but not launch rights can't start the server after the administrator has shut it down for the day.

The last set of options on the Security tab allows you to set the configuration permissions. This setting tells the system which users can configure the AppID. Configuration permissions are typically given only to the system administrator and simply set the DACL on the physical Registry key of the AppID, thus preventing unauthorized users from changing the more interesting Access and Launch permission DACLs or other AppID related settings.

Any application that doesn't have a dedicated AppID uses a machinewide default profile. The system retrieves this default profile from the Registry when it fails to find a valid AppID. You can use the Default Security tab in Dcomcnfg.exe to modify these default settings.

Configuring the Server's Identity

Each COM application assumes the identity of one of Windows NT's user accounts when it's launched. This means that objects loaded into the server process run under the identity of this security principal. The setting for a server's identity is stored in the AppID key under the *RunAs* named value. You can modify which user account is used on the Identity tab for a specific AppID in Dcomcnfg.exe, as shown in Figure 8-9. You have three choices when configuring your server's *RunAs* identity. You can select The Interactive User, The Launching User, or a dedicated Windows NT user account.

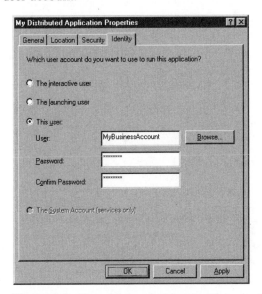

Figure 8-9. *You can use the Identity tab to specify which user account you want a COM application to run as.*

The default setting in Windows NT 4 is The Launching User, but this is almost always the wrong choice for a distributed application. With this setting, the activating client's user account serves as the security principal for the server's process. This can cause multiple instances of the server to be launched on one computer. For example, consider what happens if you use this setting and two remote users, Bob and Martha, both activate objects. This causes two separate instances of the server process to run on the server, since Bob's objects need to run as Bob and Martha's objects need to run as Martha. It's unfortunate that this is the default for Windows NT 4. Future versions of COM will remove this configuration option altogether.

The most common approach is to create a dedicated Windows NT user account that serves as the security principal for distributed applications. Once you create a local or a domain account, you can configure the AppID by selecting This User and entering the user name and password, as shown in Figure 8-7 on page 169. (You must know the password of the user account.) Dcomcnfg.exe does two other important tasks when you select a user in this manner. It grants the *Logon As Batch Job* right to the user account, and it writes the account's password to a special place in the Registry. These two tasks are required to properly assign a user account to the server's identity. Simply adding a *RunAs* named value to an AppID by hand (using Regedit.exe, for example) is insufficient.

Once you configure your application to run using a specific user account, all objects activated from the AppID run in a single-server process. This also makes it easy to configure other areas of security in a distributed application. If your business objects access a file server or use SQL Server's integrated security model, the administrator can grant permissions to a single business object account. There's no need to grant access permissions on a user-by-user basis. The administrator simply has to grant permissions to individual users as they attempt to access the distributed application.

The remaining option you have for server identity is to run the server process as an interactive user. This isn't a good idea for a distributed server application in a production environment. When you configure a server to run as the interactive user, the SCM launches the server's process using the user account of whoever happens to be logged on to the console of the server's computer at the time. If the administrator is logged on, you get one set of permissions. If a tape operator is logged on, you get a different set of permissions. If nobody is logged on, the distributed application can't be launched. As you can see, this choice can be problematic.

There are a few reasons why you might run a server as the interactive user. If the server process will run on the same computer as the client application, you probably want both processes to run under the same account. You can see that the interactive user is the same as the launching user when a user activates an object from a local server. Only the interactive user account can display windows on the desktop of the local machine. When you run objects under a dedicated user account, you can't display windows on the screen. Actually displaying a window will succeed, but the window will be displayed in a "noninteractive window station," which means no human will be there to see it. This situation means that the interactive user account can be useful during debugging, when you want to display a message box from an out-of-process server. This also means that invoking a message box from a business object running under a dedicated user account will hang the object indefinitely, since nobody will ever press any buttons to dismiss it. This is a good reason to create your servers using Visual Basic's Unattended Execution option.

CLIENT-SIDE CONFIGURATION

Setting up client machines in a distributed application is fairly tedious. Each client computer must have the client application's EXE, one or more type libraries, and a significant number of Registry settings. The client-side Registry must contain the same set of keys required for a local out-of-process server, including CLSIDs, IIDs, and the GUID for any type library.

While you can set up client computers by hand, it makes more sense to create a setup program that automates the task. The Visual Basic IDE offers some assistance in configuring the client-side Registry. If you select the Remote Server Files option on your server project's Components tab, Visual Basic creates a remote setup file with a .vbr extension when you choose the Make command from the File menu. A .vbr file contains a list of Registry entries that must be written to the client machine. Visual Basic also ships with a utility named CliReg32.EXE, which accepts a .vbr file as a parameter and writes the appropriate settings to the client's Registry.

A client application that uses remote objects needs a way to redirect activation requests to the target computer running the distributed application. You can accomplish this in a few different ways. One way is to configure the application's CLSIDs on the client computer to use an AppID to point to the target server. Another way is to select the target computer at run time using the *CreateObject* function.

If you want to configure a CLSID to activate remotely, you must provide a custom AppID key with the *RemoteServerName* named value. As long as there isn't a more efficient server type available for the CLSID, the SCM manager will initiate a remote activation request to the target server. This means that the CLSID can't have a valid *InProcServer32* or a *LocalServer32* subkey. The remote server name can be the name of a computer on a Windows NT network, a dotted-decimal TCP/IP address, or a DNS address (for example, *www.microsoft.com*). After you set up the AppID, you must also add an *AppID* named value to each of the application's CLSIDs.

After you configure the AppID, you can easily redirect activation requests to any remote server by using Dcomcnfg.exe, as shown in Figure 8-10 on the following page. If you select a remote server after a local version of the server has been registered, Dcomcnfg.exe temporarily disables the *LocalServer32* subkey for every CLSID associated with the AppID by renaming it *_LocalServer32*. If you then reconfigure the AppID using the Run Application On This Computer option, Dcomcnfg.exe returns the *LocalServer32* subkey to its original state.

It's often advantageous for a client to choose a target computer at run time. This allows applications to provide sophisticated features such as load balancing and failover support. The easiest way to select a remote computer programmatically is to use Visual Basic's *CreateObject* function. Visual Basic 6 has a second optional parameter to *CreateObject* that accepts the name of a remote computer. Note that the client machine still requires a type library and various Registry settings, including the ProgID, which is passed to *CreateObject*.

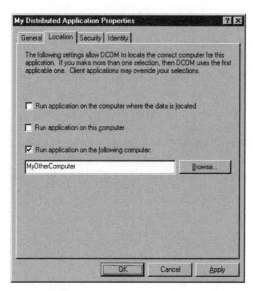

Figure 8-10. *You can use the Location tab to redirect client activation requests to a computer across the network.*

Another approach is to rely on remote activation code written in C++. For teams with C++ expertise, it can be helpful to create thin C++ DLLs that extend the remote capabilities of a Visual Basic application. For example, you can write code in C++ that makes a direct call to a function in the COM Library named *CoCreateInstanceEx*. This function accepts parameters for a CLSID and a remote host name. It also lets the caller pass a Windows NT user account name and password at run time. Note that this technique is the best way to redirect activation programmatically in versions of Visual Basic prior to version 6.

No description of client-side configuration would be complete without our noting an important setting that has stumped many developers and administrators who try to run their applications in a network environment. Any client application that receives events or connects to a callback interface requires access permissions for the security principal of the server application. This means that the client computer must be configured to include access permissions for the user account that represents the server's identity. You can solve this problem by modifying the access permissions for either the correct AppID or the machinewide default security profile.

A more subtle and troublesome problem can occur when the client and the server are in different domains. Often the server's domain controller will trust the client's domain controller to authenticate the client via a one-way trust relationship so that calls from the client to the server succeed without a hitch. However, for authenticated callbacks to succeed, the client's domain controller must trust the server's domain controller to authenticate the server.

USING DISTRIBUTED
COM ACROSS A FIREWALL

Many organizations need to make Distributed COM work across a firewall. I won't dive into all the details in this book, but you should know that you can configure the Registry to enable Distributed COM across many types of firewall software. When the client-side SCM contacts the SCM on the server, the two communicate over port 135. When an object is bound to a client, the system dynamically allocates a different port for the connection from a fairly wide range of available ports.

The trick to making Distributed COM work across a firewall is to configure the firewall software to allow external clients to communicate across all the needed ports. This typically involves modifying the Registry to limit the ports that are dynamically allocated during activation. It also involves configuring the firewall software to make these ports accessible to external clients. If you need more information, you can consult an excellent online resource provided by a benevolent developer named Mike Nelson. Nelson maintains a white paper at *http://www.wam.umd.edu/~mikenel/ dcom/dcomfw.htm* that can give you a head start in configuring your environment.

EVALUATING THE INITIAL
RELEASE OF DISTRIBUTED COM

The current security model of Distributed COM has many good features and a few important limitations. The security model is strong because it leverages the strengths of MS-RPC and loadable SSP packages. This practice gives you a layer that conducts call-level authentication behind the scenes. You can change security providers and authentication levels without having to make any modifications to application code.

The security model is also somewhat limited because access permissions can be applied only with a processwide scope. This means that either you let a user account into the distributed application or you deny the user access. The model can't accommodate a more granular scheme. For example, you can't extend access permissions to one CLSID while denying permissions to another. Note that it *is* possible to write explicit code to provide more granular security: This can be done with a shim DLL written in C++ but not in a declarative fashion via Dcomcnfg.exe.

While Visual Basic provides all the self-registration code for in-process servers and local servers, it doesn't offer any assistance with AppIDs. You can configure an AppID with a utility such as Dcomcnfg.exe or OleView.EXE, but doing so can be frustrating because each utility has a few capabilities that the other doesn't have. To make things worse, certain tasks, such as creating a new AppID, can be accomplished only by hand or by using a script.

The next chapter covers the MTS run-time environment and explains how MTS is based on the RPC infrastructure and COM's security model. As you'll see, MTS builds on the strengths of Distributed COM while offering improved solutions for access-permission granularity and the configuration of servers and clients.

Chapter 9

The MTS Run-Time Environment

Information systems based on an N-tier architecture that run business objects in the middle tier are becoming increasingly popular. Chapter 1 covers many of the issues that have motivated a number of companies to pursue this style of development. However, as these companies have tried to port their existing two-tier applications, they've discovered many new challenges. One of the biggest hurdles for developers of distributed applications is that of creating an infrastructure to accommodate scalability and throughput for a large user base. In the two-tier model, client applications connect directly to a database management system (DBMS). The two-tier system can leverage the scalability features built into a DBMS such as ORACLE or Microsoft SQL Server for managing connections, pooling threads, and monitoring transactions. Each client that connects to a DBMS consumes memory and processing cycles on the server. In the N-tier model, client applications don't connect to a DBMS. Instead, they connect to a distributed application running in the middle tier. In an N-tier system, a distributed application must take on many of the responsibilities for scalability and throughput that were previously handled by a DBMS.

The most significant cost in assembling an N-tier system has been that of building a sophisticated framework to handle the requirements of a distributed application. To reduce this cost, Microsoft created Microsoft Transaction Server (MTS). Companies can now spend more time writing business logic and less time writing complex code to deal with issues such as connection management, thread pooling, and transaction monitoring. MTS 2.0, which was released with the Windows NT 4

Option Pack at the end of 1997, plays two distinct and important roles. First, it is a refinement of the COM run-time environment. It provides a surrogate process that can load and run COM objects on behalf of clients throughout the network, and it offers many valuable run-time services. You can view MTS as an improved version of Distributed COM. Second, MTS acts as a transaction processing monitor for an online transaction processing (OLTP) system. This chapter concentrates on the important aspects of the run-time environment; Chapter 10 explains how to write MTS transactions for an OLTP application.

MTS makes it easier to configure and deploy applications based on Distributed COM. Once administrators and developers learn how to use a tool called the MTS Explorer, they can deploy distributed objects in a straightforward fashion. This chapter shows you how to install ActiveX DLLs created with Visual Basic in the MTS environment. You'll also learn an easy way to configure the computers involved in a distributed application, and you'll be exposed to many of the services offered by the MTS run time.

You must learn how to talk to the system behind MTS if you really want to take advantage of this environment. In particular, you must learn how to interact with an MTS-supplied component known as the MTS Executive. You'll also learn how to communicate with the MTS Executive through the *ObjectContext* interface and how to receive notifications from it by implementing the *ObjectControl* interface when your objects are activated and deactivated. Once you establish the lines of communication with MTS, you can make the most of the MTS threading model and manage the life cycle of your objects.

Finally, this chapter explains the importance of using binary compatibility and how to rebuild and test your DLLs. You'll also learn about options for debugging an MTS application. Debugging components in the MTS environment has always been far more challenging than debugging standard Visual Basic applications. Fortunately, Visual Basic 6 has some new features that make debugging MTS components easier.

DEPLOYING MTS COMPONENTS

MTS provides a distributed run-time environment in which you run business objects. Figure 9-1 shows the relationship between the client applications and the distributed objects running in the MTS environment. As you can see, MTS provides the container application (mtx.exe) that acts as a surrogate process. MTS objects are deployed using COM-style DLLs that are loaded into the MTS environment.

Objects are deployed in the MTS run-time environment using components and packages. Each computer running MTS stores configuration information about its components and packages in a section of the Windows Registry known as the MTS catalog. You can inspect this catalog by locating the following path in the Registry:

HKEY_LOCAL_MACHINE\SOFTWARE\Microsoft\Transaction Server

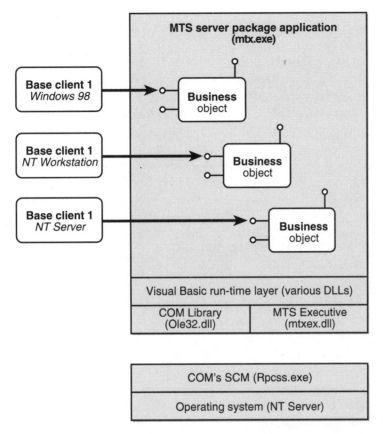

Figure 9-1. *MTS provides a surrogate process for each server package that can load and run distributed business objects on behalf of clients throughout the network.*

MTS uses the term *component* to mean a creatable class, which is the same as a COM *coclass*. To run your Visual Basic objects in the MTS run-time environment, you must create an ActiveX DLL with public *MultiUse* classes. After you install the DLL, each of your classes is recognized as an MTS component.

All MTS components are distributed in packages. A package is a named unit of deployment that contains MTS components. When a package is created, the MTS system assigns it a GUID for identification and creates a profile in the catalog that contains a set of properties. Before you can install a DLL in the MTS environment, you must create a new package or locate an existing one.

MTS supports two types of packages. A *server package* provides a surrogate process for running MTS objects; it represents a distributed application. When a client activates an object from a server package, the MTS system activates and runs the object in a package-specific instance of the MTS container application mtx.exe, as shown in Figure 9-1.

Because a server package runs in its own isolated process, you can see it as both a *security domain* and a *fault isolation domain*. You can partition a distributed application into several server packages to make it more robust and secure. See Chapter 11 for guidance on how to decide whether to run a distributed application in a single process or partition it into multiple server packages.

A *library package,* unlike a server package, doesn't provide its own surrogate process. Instead, objects created from a library package are loaded into the address space of the client application that created them. Library packages provide a way to share component code across several server packages and to run MTS objects in environments other than the MTS container application mtx.exe.

Both server packages and library packages rely on the services of the MTS Executive, which lives in mtxex.dll. This DLL contains most of the logic for the sophisticated run-time services provided by MTS. Because these run-time services are maintained in a DLL, MTS can offer flexibility in deployment.

You'll often use server packages that rely on both mtx.exe and mtxex.dll. However, if a client application creates an object from an MTS library package, the MTS run time is loaded into the client's address space. The Web Server process for Internet Information Server (IIS), Inetinfo.exe, is an example of a client application that exploits the MTS run-time environment by loading mtxex.dll into its address space. While there are deployment scenarios in which library packages are more appropriate than server packages, this chapter focuses on using server packages because it's a better way to start learning about how MTS really works.

Installing an ActiveX DLL

You create MTS components with Visual Basic by adding public *MultiUse* classes to an ActiveX DLL. Be sure you leave the threading model of your ActiveX DLL project set to the default, which is Apartment Threaded. After building your DLL, you can install it in the MTS run-time environment using the MTS Explorer. You can launch the MTS Explorer from the system's Start menu by selecting Programs, then Windows NT 4.0 Option Pack, and then Microsoft Transaction Server. In the Microsoft Transaction Server group, click Transaction Server Explorer.

The MTS Explorer has a tree view control in the left pane, which includes a node named Computers (as shown in Figure 9-2). All of the computers that can be administered from the local machine are listed here. By default, only the local computer is registered under the name My Computer. If you want to add other remote computers, you can right-click on the Computers folder and choose New.

By expanding the tree view under My Computer, you can see a folder named Packages Installed. When you expand this folder, you can see a list of all the packages on your local machine. To create a new package, you click once on the Packages Installed folder. You then right-click on the folder and choose New and then Package.

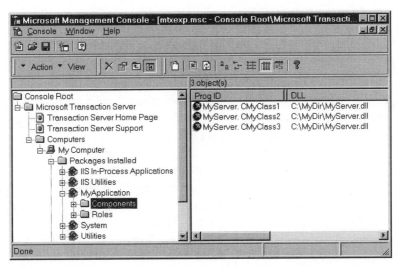

Figure 9-2. *Using the MTS Explorer, you can install in the MTS run-time environment an ActiveX DLL that you created with Visual Basic. Each* MultiUse *class in your DLL becomes an MTS component.*

Let's create a new server package. After you choose the New Package command, you'll see a series of dialog boxes. The first dialog box asks you whether you want to create an empty package or install a prebuilt package from an MTS package script file. Specify that you want to create an empty package. In the next dialog box, enter a name for the new package and then click Next. In the last dialog box, select which user account will serve as the package's identity. You can either select the name of a Windows NT user account or choose to run the package under the identity of the interactive user. Select a user account, and then click Finish to create the package. Carefully consider which user account you pick because it will serve as the package's security principal.

I highly recommend using a dedicated user account in a production environment. When selecting the package's identity, you can select a user account from the local computer or one from a Windows NT domain. In the development environment, however, you might find it quick and convenient to run the package under the identity of the interactive user. Your business objects will run with the same set of permissions as your Windows NT user account, and you can use some of your old development tricks. For example, you can display message boxes while debugging your MTS components.

In Chapter 8, you saw that Distributed COM let you configure an application to run under the identity of the launching user. MTS doesn't allow this option because it would require running separate instances of a server package on one machine for each connected user. MTS allows only a single instance of any package to run on any computer at a time. Running a package under the identity of the launching user doesn't make any sense because only the first client who activates an object can use that server package.

After you click Finish, your new server package will be included in the Packages Installed list. You can examine and modify more of the server package's properties by right-clicking on it in the left pane of MTS Explorer and choosing Properties. This brings up a tabbed dialog box, in which you can perform actions such as configuring security, changing the package's identity, and switching back and forth between a server package and a library package.

Once you create a new package or locate an existing package, you can install your ActiveX DLL. The easiest way to do this is by expanding the package's folder, selecting the Components folder, and then dragging and dropping your ActiveX DLL file onto the right pane of the MTS Explorer. The MTS system will automatically configure all the *MultiUse* classes in the DLL. Each class will be recognized as an MTS component. After your DLL is installed, you'll see your MTS components in the MTS Explorer, as shown earlier in Figure 9-2.

MTS also lets you install a subset of components from a DLL. For example, if a DLL contains three classes, you can install two classes in one package and a third class in another package. You do this by right-clicking on the component folder in the left pane and choosing New. In the dialog box that appears, you can add components individually. While you can install components from one DLL in multiple packages, this makes distributing updates trickier and more error prone. You might consider designing each DLL so that all its classes are targeted for one specific package. This isn't your only option, but it can make things easier in both the development and production environments.

Activation in an MTS Server Package

Each MTS component is based on a coclass and therefore has an associated class ID (CLSID). A client application activates an MTS object by calling in to the Service Control Manager (SCM) and passing a CLSID and an interface ID (IID), just as it does during any other COM activation request. When you install a component in a server package, the MTS system changes the Registry entries of its CLSIDs to redirect activation requests to a package-specific instance of the MTS container application.

Let's examine how activation is accomplished in an MTS application. When a client application running outside the MTS environment activates an MTS object, it's known as a *base client*. A Visual Basic application acting as a base client can activate an MTS object using either the *New* operator or the *CreateObject* function. When the base client attempts to activate a new object, the request is initially sent to the SCM on the client machine. The client-side SCM forwards the client's activation request to the SCM of the computer running the MTS application. The server-side SCM responds by making a local activation request on the CLSID. Up to this point, the activation sequence is just like any other in Distributed COM.

Now here's where MTS begins to get a little tricky behind the scenes. When you installed the DLL in a server package with the MTS Explorer, the MTS system modified the Registry settings for each CLSID to change the routing of every activation request. Each CLSID was given a *[LocalServer32]* subkey with the following path:

```
\System32\mtx.exe /p:{0EAC413A-4696-11D1-B156-0080C72D2182}
```

The GUID that follows mtx.exe in the command line identifies a specific MTS package. If an instance of this server package is already running, the server-side SCM calls in to the process and negotiates the creation of a new MTS object by passing the requested CLSID. If the package doesn't have a process running, the SCM launches a new instance of mtx.exe and then negotiates the activation of a new MTS object. In either case, the new object is created and a connection is established with the base client. As in the case of any other out-of-process connection involving Distributed COM, a proxy/stub layer is introduced between the client and the object.

Exporting MTS Packages

In the short history of COM, one of the most painful and problematic areas of deploying distributed applications has been the configuration of computers in a networked environment. Chapter 8 explained what you must configure on each server-side computer and each client-side computer. The MTS Explorer makes it much easier to handle setup details that system-supplied utilities can't configure. You don't have to rely on Dcomcnfg.exe, nor need you worry about creating your own AppIDs by hand. The MTS system creates a hidden AppID for every server package. You can handle all the administration of security and identity using the MTS Explorer.

MTS also helps automate the configuration of the computers involved in a distributed application. It does this by creating both server-side and client-side setup programs. When you right-click on a package in the MTS Explorer and choose the Export command, MTS generates a server-side setup script file with the .pak extension.

The .pak file contains setup information about the package, such as security details and a list of every component and every DLL. During the export process, MTS copies the .pak file and all the necessary DLLs for deploying the package into the directory of your choice. This makes it convenient to move an application from a development workstation to a production server. It also gives software vendors an easy way to install their MTS applications at a customer site. Note that software vendors can also create setup programs to create packages and install components by programming against a set of catalog objects exposed by MTS.

When you export a package, MTS also generates a client-side setup program in the \clients subdirectory in the directory containing the .pak file. This makes it easy to set up the computers that will run base client applications against your server packages. When you run this setup program from any Windows computer that has Distributed COM, it configures the Registry with an AppID as well as the required

CLSIDs and IIDs. It also installs the required type libraries, which enables the universal marshaler to create proxies at run time.

By default, the client-side setup program directs all base clients to activate MTS objects on the computer on which the Export command has been run. However, by changing the Remote Server Name property, you can direct client applications to activate their objects on any MTS server in the network. You can find the Remote Server Name property for your computer by right-clicking My Computer in MTS Explorer, choosing Properties, and selecting the Options tab.

MTS offers another powerful way to reconfigure a distributed application once it has been put into production. When a network is running several MTS computers, an administrator can push and pull components between computers by dragging and dropping components across machines using the MTS Explorer. You can redirect activation requests throughout the enterprise from a single desktop, and you can balance the processing load between servers and divert activation requests when one system fails. You can push and pull components only if all the machines involved are running MTS. MTS can run on Windows NT Server, Windows NT Workstation, Windows 95, and Windows 98. For more information about reconfiguring remote components from MTS Explorer, see the MTS documentation.

THE MTS EXECUTIVE

As you can see, it's not too difficult to get a simple application up and running using MTS. And you don't have to do anything special to an ordinary ActiveX DLL to deploy it in the MTS run-time environment. However, if you really want your Visual Basic objects to take advantage of MTS, you must understand what's going on inside the MTS environment. You should begin by getting to know the central figure in this environment, the MTS Executive. You can think of the MTS Executive as the MTS run time.

The MTS run time plays the role of quarterback for every MTS application. You can also think of the MTS run time as a control-freak boss who always wants to know what everybody's doing at any given time. Let's look at how the MTS run time micromanages every MTS object starting at activation time.

As you'll recall from Chapter 3, a standard activation request in COM is routed from the SCM to a class factory object that has been loaded by its server. The server must therefore supply a class factory object for each CLSID that it supports. However, when the SCM attempts to activate an object in an MTS application, the MTS run time intercepts the request. It then locates the class factory object for the requested CLSID and calls upon it to create the object.

Here's where the plot thickens. While creating and binding the object, the MTS run time places a wiretap on the connection back to the client. The MTS run time sets up this wiretap by introducing a transparent layer between the client and the object called the *context wrapper,* as shown in Figure 9-3. The context wrapper is situated between the stub and the object. When the context wrapper receives a method call from the client, it forwards the call to the object that it's wrapping. When the object finishes processing the call, the control of execution passes back through the context wrapper before it's returned to the base client. The base client is totally oblivious to what's going on. It can't detect the presence of the context wrapper.

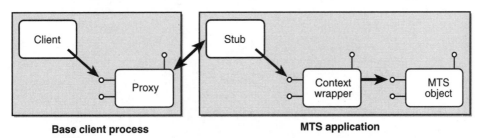

Base client process   **MTS application**

Figure 9-3. *The MTS run time inserts a context wrapper between a base client and an MTS object. This transparent layer allows the MTS run time to monitor the connection and steal away control on a call-by-call basis.*

This is a pretty neat little trick. The context wrapper allows the MTS run time to steal control of every inbound method call just before and just after the object executes its method implementation. This powerful object-oriented technique is known as *interception.* Interception allows the MTS run time to modify the behavior of object code with preprocessing and postprocessing on a call-by-call basis. MTS mixes interception and attribute-based programming to produce a powerful programming model. For example, you can drastically change the behavior of an object by changing its *transaction support* attribute. When you do this, the MTS run time modifies the object's behavior by changing the way it carries out its preprocessing and postprocessing of method calls.

In addition to providing a basis for interception, the context wrapper is used to store state information about the object and the object's creator. The context wrapper holds metadata about the CLSID and the coclass that represent the object's type. It also holds security information about the user who activated the object. The next few chapters explain other essential pieces of information that are stored in the context wrapper.

Programming MTS Objects

When you create an ActiveX DLL that is targeted for the MTS run-time environment, you should include a reference to the Transaction Server type library (mtxas.dll), as shown in Figure 9-4 on the following page. This allows you to communicate directly with the MTS run time and take full advantage of MTS. When you program against

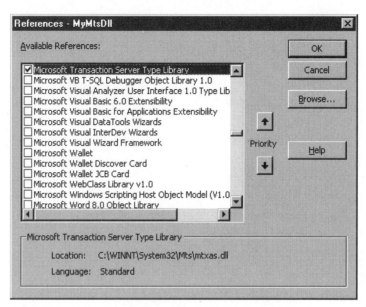

Figure 9-4. *By referencing the MTS type library, you can communicate with the MTS run time.*

the Transaction Server type library, it means that you're writing your ActiveX DLL with the intention of using it exclusively in the MTS run-time environment.

After you reference this type library for the first time, you should examine its contents using the Object Browser. There are two important methods in the class *AppServer* named *SafeRef* and *GetObjectContext*. The *AppServer* class is marked in the type library as an *AppObject*. This means that you can call both *SafeRef* and *GetObjectContext* as global functions. Figure 9-5 shows what these two important methods return.

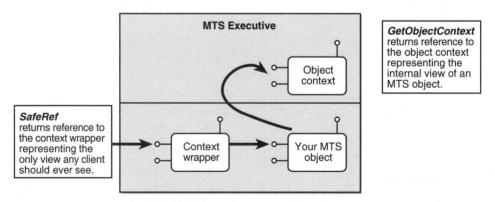

Figure 9-5. *A call to* SafeRef *returns the outside view of the object as the MTS run time intends the object's base clients to see it. A call to* GetObjectContext *returns the inside view of an object as the MTS run time sees it in the context of the current method call.*

SafeRef returns the outside world's view of an MTS object. That is, it returns a reference to the context wrapper instead of a reference to the object itself. Be careful not to pass to a client application a direct reference to an MTS object. If you do, the client application can make a call on the MTS object without going through the context wrapper. This defeats the interception scheme set up by the MTS run time.

Let's say that you're writing a method implementation for an MTS object. In the method, you must create a second object and set up bidirectional communication between the two by registering a callback like that shown in the section entitled "Using a Custom Callback Interface" in Chapter 6. After creating the second object, you must pass it a reference from your object to set up the callback. To do this, you would write the following code:

```
Dim Child As CChildClass
Set Child = New CChildClass
Child.Register Me
```

This code is incorrect under MTS, however. The child object can invoke method calls on your object without going through the context wrapper. You should never bypass the interception scheme set up by the MTS run time. Instead, you should pass a reference to your object as follows:

```
Dim Child As CChildClass
Set Child = New CChildClass
Child.Register SafeRef(Me)
```

By calling *SafeRef*, you allow the child object to establish a connection that passes through the context wrapper. This keeps things in line with what the MTS run time expects. Note that the *Me* keyword is the only valid parameter you can pass when calling *SafeRef* with Visual Basic.

The previous example uses the *New* operator to create objects. As you'll soon see, this can also result in incorrect code under MTS. Later in this chapter, we'll look at the proper techniques for creating objects in the MTS environment in a variety of situations.

While *SafeRef* provides a view of your object to the outside world, *GetObjectContext* provides your object with an internal view to the MTS run time. A call to *GetObjectContext* returns a reference to a new object that the MTS run time creates, as shown earlier in Figure 9-5. The object returned by *GetObjectContext* represents the calling context in which your object is executing. It's important not to confuse the object context and the context wrapper because they're very different. The object context is transient, while the context wrapper lives for the lifetime of the client's connection.

You use the *ObjectContext* interface to communicate with the MTS run time through the object context. The *ObjectContext* interface contains methods and properties that allow you to query different types of state information about the context in which your call is executing. Methods in this interface also allow you to tell the MTS run time to perform specific tasks on your behalf. For example, you can ask for assistance when you want to create additional MTS objects or you want to affect the outcome of the current transaction. Let's start our examination of the *ObjectContext* interface by seeing what kind of information it can give you.

What exactly is the object's context?

The concept *calling context* can be elusive to new programmers. The object behind the *ObjectContext* interface can be seen as an aggregate. First the *ObjectContext* interface can provide information about the state of affairs inside the current application. For example, if you want to find out whether your object has been loaded into a secure MTS server process rather than into the process of a nonsecure client application, you can write the following code:

```
Dim ObjCtx As ObjectContext
Set ObjCtx = GetObjectContext()
Dim IsAppSecure As Boolean
IsAppSecure = ObjCtx.IsSecurityEnabled()
```

You can also use the *ObjectContext* interface to obtain state information about the object that's executing the current call. When the MTS run time creates an object, it stores the user name of the creator inside the context wrapper. You can obtain the name of the creator by using the Security property of *ObjectContext*:

```
Dim ObjCtx As ObjectContext
Set ObjCtx = GetObjectContext()
Dim Creator As String
Creator = ObjCtx.Security.GetOriginalCreator()
```

ObjectContext also provides information that is propagated across the wire with every method call. For example, the user who is initiating a call on the object might be different from the user who originally created the object. Distributed COM transmits the caller's identity across the wire in each method call. The *ObjectContext* interface allows you to retrieve the caller's name like this:

```
Dim ObjCtx As ObjectContext
Set ObjCtx = GetObjectContext()
Dim Caller As String
Caller = ObjCtx.Security.GetOriginalCaller()
```

As you can see, many different bits of information make up the calling context for an object. The MTS run time makes it easy to deal with all this information by grouping it all together in a single easy-to-use object.

ObjectContext lets you do more than just retrieve information. You can also use this interface to tell the MTS run time to do things. Later in this chapter, you'll learn how to create other MTS objects and manage threads using *ObjectContext*. In

Chapter 10, you'll learn how to use the *ObjectContext* interface to affect the outcome of a transaction.

The Life Cycle of an MTS Object

The MTS run time is responsible for managing the life cycle of every MTS object. The life cycle of an MTS object typically includes four stages: creation, activation, deactivation, and destruction. As an MTS programmer, you must be aware of when the transitions between these stages occur so that you can take appropriate action.

A Visual Basic base client can create an object in the MTS environment using either the *New* operator or the *CreateObject* function. When a base client creates an MTS object, the MTS run time does two things. First it locates the class factory and creates the object. Next it binds the client to the context wrapper. However, the object isn't activated inside the context wrapper at this time. The client senses that the object has been activated, but in fact only the context wrapper has been activated. The MTS run time defers activating the object inside the context wrapper until the client invokes the first method call. After the first method call, the object remains in an active state until it's destroyed. An activated object is always deactivated before it's destroyed.

A Visual Basic class module provides an *Initialize* procedure. The code you write in *Initialize* is guaranteed to run when the Visual Basic object is created. However, *Initialize* always runs before the object has been activated. This means that you can't successfully call *GetObjectContext* in *Initialize*. A call to *GetObjectContext* in *Initialize* won't experience a run-time error. It will simply return a null reference. You will get a run-time error, however, when you try to access a property or a method using this null reference.

The *Terminate* procedure in a Visual Basic class is executed prior to the object's destruction and after the object has been deactivated. *Terminate* is similar to *Initialize* in that you can't successfully call *GetObjectContext* in this procedure. These two procedures supplied by Visual Basic don't give you all the control you need to manage your object's life cycle in the MTS environment. Fortunately, the MTS run time can help by notifying your object just after activation and once again just before deactivation.

Here's how it works. The MTS type library includes a definition for an interface named *ObjectControl*. When the MTS run time creates an MTS object, it calls *QueryInterface* to determine whether the object supports this interface. If an MTS object implements *ObjectControl*, the MTS run time calls methods in this interface to notify the object at important transition stages during its life cycle. This means that you should implement *ObjectControl* in every object that you think needs to receive these notifications. The *ObjectControl* interface contains the three methods listed on the following page.

- **_Activate_**   Called by the MTS run time after activation and just before the first method call is executed.

- **_Deactivate_**   Called by the MTS run time just before the object is switched out of the context wrapper.

- **_CanBePooled_**   Called by the MTS run time after deactivation and just before the object is destroyed. This method was included to enable a feature known as object pooling (which isn't supported in MTS 2.0).

To receive these notifications, you should implement the _ObjectControl_ interface in the _MultiUse_ class modules in your ActiveX DLLs. Here's an example of a Visual Basic class module that implements this interface:

```
Implements ObjectControl

Private Sub ObjectControl_Activate()
  ' Your code for initialization after activation
End Sub

Private Sub ObjectControl_Deactivate()
  ' Your code for cleanup before deactivation
End Sub

Private Function ObjectControl_CanBePooled() As Boolean
  ' Object pooling not yet supported in MTS 2.0
  ObjectControl_CanBePooled = False
End Function
```

The MTS run time calls _Activate_ just before the execution of the first method call. This means that the object has been switched into the context wrapper and you can successfully call _GetObjectContext_ from within this method. It's therefore usually best to put your object initialization code inside _Activate_ instead of _Initialize_. Likewise, you should place your cleanup code in _Deactivate_ instead of _Terminate_.

Note that a client must invoke at least one method call to place an object in the active state. If a base client creates an object and then releases it without calling a method, _Activate_ and _Deactivate_ are never called. In some situations, you might need to use _Initialize_ and _Terminate_ in addition to _Activate_ and _Deactivate_.

What about the third method in the _ObjectControl_ interface, _CanBePooled_? Unfortunately, at the time of this writing the method is useless. It was included to support a future feature called _object pooling_. When object pooling becomes available, the MTS run time will be able to recycle objects and thus save some processing cycles associated with object destruction and re-creation. After an object has been deactivated, the MTS run time will call _CanBePooled_ to see whether the object indicates that it wants to be placed in the recycling pool. Objects that return a value of

True from *CanBePooled* will be placed in a pool. Objects that return False will be destroyed. When the MTS run time services a creation request, it will look through the pool for one of the appropriate type.

Although MTS run time calls *CanBePooled* in MTS 2.0, the value returned by your objects is ignored. The MTS run time always destroys your object after calling *CanBePooled*. Many people advocate returning a value of True so that your object will automatically take advantage of object pooling when it becomes available. However, you shouldn't do this casually. Managing the life cycle of pooled objects is far more complex than managing the life cycle of nonpooled objects.

The bottom line is that you should never return True from *CanBePooled* unless you have carefully thought through the semantics of object pooling, including the differences between object construction and object reactivation and the differences between object destruction and object deactivation. In most cases, you will be required to add code to *Initialize*, *Activate*, *Deactivate*, *CanBePooled*, and *Terminate*. If you don't care to think through these issues to accommodate a feature that isn't presently supported, you should simply return False from *CanBePooled* and revisit your code when object pooling becomes available.

THE MTS CONCURRENCY MODEL

MTS provides a new concurrency abstraction called an *activity*. An activity is a logical thread of execution created on behalf of a single base client, as shown in Figure 9-6 on the following page. Each user owns one or more objects in a single activity, which is isolated from the activities and objects of every other user. To support this concept, the MTS run time creates a new activity whenever a base client creates a new MTS object. Activities keep the programming model fairly simple for MTS programmers. However, behind the scenes the MTS run time maintains a fairly complex thread pooling scheme to accommodate application scalability and increased throughput.

In MTS 2.0, a server application maintains a thread pool that can hold up to 100 single-threaded apartments (STAs). The MTS run time creates a new STA for each new activity until the pool reaches this limit. When the number of activities exceeds the number of STAs, the MTS run time begins to assign multiple activities to each STA. When two activities share the same STA, the MTS run time manages multiplexing STAs (physical threads) in and out of activities (logical threads).

When two activities share the same STA, the code executing on behalf of one user can potentially block the call of another user. However, this should not concern you as an MTS programmer. You should think in terms of logical threads and let the MTS run time manage the physical threads as it sees fit. The designers of MTS have tried to make the threading model as simple as possible. The abstraction of the STA relieves you from worrying about synchronization. The abstraction of the activity builds

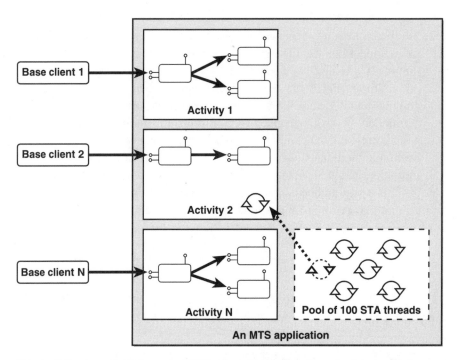

Figure 9-6. *An activity is a set of MTS objects that belong to a single user. Each activity models a logical thread of execution. The MTS run time manages a physical pool of STAs that are multiplexed in and out of activities on an as-needed basis.*

upon the STA by also relieving you from worrying about the complexities of thread pooling. You need only follow a handful of rules to make the most of the MTS threading model.

Remember that each activity should represent a set of objects that belong to a single user. You can draw two conclusions from this. First, no two users should connect to objects inside the same activity. Second, you should avoid creating objects in different activities when they belong to the same user.

It's not hard to ensure that the objects in any given activity are accessed by a single user only. As you know, the MTS run time creates a new activity when a base client creates an object. This means that a client application must pass a reference to another client to connect two users to objects in the same activity. You should therefore avoid designs that pass MTS object references between users. Also note that the MTS threading model discourages the use of singletons or any other application designs in which multiple users connect to the same physical object.

The most important thing you need to learn about threading in MTS is how to propagate a new MTS object into an existing activity. Once the base client creates an MTS object, this object often creates additional MTS objects in the same server process. When you write the code for one MTS object to create another, you must do it properly or your new object might be placed in a different activity.

Let's look at the correct way to propagate new objects inside the MTS environment. When a base client creates an MTS object, the MTS run time creates it in a new activity. This object is known as the *root* of the activity. All MTS objects including the root should create additional MTS objects in the same activity by making activation requests through the MTS run time. You do this by calling the *CreateInstance* method on the object context. *CreateInstance* takes a single parameter for the ProgID of the new object. The following code demonstrates how to create a second MTS object in the same activity as the root:

```
' In a method of the root object
Dim ObjCtx As ObjectContext
Set ObjCtx = GetObjectContext()
Dim Object2 As CMyClass2
Set Object2 = ObjCtx.CreateInstance("MyServer.CMyClass2")
```

When an object in the MTS environment calls *CreateInstance*, it tells the MTS run time to create the requested object in the same activity. The MTS run time creates the new object and places a context wrapper between it and its creator. You should note two important things here. First, since the two objects live in the same STA, there is no need for a proxy/stub layer between them. Second, the context wrapper is inserted between the two objects, so the MTS interception scheme is set up properly.

Problems with *CreateObject* and the *New* Operator

While you should create MTS objects from a Visual Basic base client using the *Create-Object* function and the *New* operator, you should be cautious when using these techniques in the code behind your MTS objects. Using them can result in an undesirable situation.

Let's examine what happens when you try to create one MTS object from another using *CreateObject*. When an MTS object calls *CreateObject*, the activation request bypasses the MTS run time and is sent down to the SCM. The SCM, in turn, calls back to the MTS run time with the same activation request. The MTS run time assumes that another base client is creating the object and therefore places it in a new activity. This means that the new object and its creator will probably run in different STAs. The two objects are bound together with a proxy/stub layer, which significantly degrades performance and consumes another STA from the thread pool unnecessarily.

You'll also get into trouble if you try to create one MTS object from another using the *New* operator. In one scenario, the creator component and the component from which the new object is created live in separate DLLs. In this case, a call to *New* is sent down to the SCM just like a call to *CreateObject*. This causes the new object to be created in a new activity. As you already know, this is undesirable. In the second scenario, in which the two components involved both live in the same ActiveX DLL, the problem is more subtle but can lead to even greater frustration. When a Visual Basic object calls *New* on a class name in the same DLL, the Visual Basic run time creates and binds the object on its own without involving either the MTS run time or the SCM. The new object isn't a valid MTS object because it doesn't have its own context wrapper. Your code won't crash, but it can exhibit unexpected behavior. When this invalid MTS object calls *GetObjectContext*, it's given a reference for the context object of its creator. This can lead to some strange and mysterious results.

As it turns out, sometimes you can and should use the *New* operator in a method implementation behind an MTS object. You can use the *New* operator when you create objects that aren't MTS objects. For example, you should use the *New* operator whenever you want to create ActiveX Data Objects (ADO). ADO components aren't registered with MTS. ADO objects don't need a context wrapper, and they don't use the object context.

You can thus conclude that an MTS application can run a mixture of MTS objects and standard objects. An MTS object requires a context wrapper, but a standard object doesn't. When you create a standard object from an MTS object using the *New* operator, it's created in the same activity, just like a call to *CreateInstance*. However, once a component has been programmed against the MTS type library and uses its object context, it must be registered with the MTS Explorer and properly created as an MTS object. As a rule of thumb, one MTS object must always create another MTS object using *CreateInstance*.

DEVELOPING MTS COMPONENTS

Writing, testing, and debugging MTS components is more difficult than developing a typical Visual Basic application with a user interface. A few tips and pointers will make you more productive and allow you to maintain your sanity.

You should set up your development workstation with either Windows NT Server or Windows NT Workstation. If you're using Windows NT 4, you should install the Windows NT Option Pack, which includes MTS 2.0. If possible, you should also install Windows NT Service Pack 4. This service pack release provides updated components that significantly improve the ability of Visual Basic 6 to debug MTS components. At the time of this writing, the details of installing MTS with Windows NT 5 haven't been finalized. If you're using Windows NT 5, follow the documentation to install MTS and apply the latest service packs.

In addition to Windows NT and MTS, your development workstation also needs an installation of Visual Basic. Visual Basic 6 is best, but you can also work with Visual Basic 5. This workstation configuration allows you to develop and test MTS components and base client applications on a single computer. In later stages of development, you should test your code in a network environment, but working on a single machine can initially make the process go a lot faster.

If you have enough disk space and RAM on your development workstation, you can also install Internet Information Server (IIS), Microsoft Message Queue (MSMQ), and Microsoft SQL Server. You should have 128 MB or more of RAM if you're going to load up your machine like this. With this configuration, you can create advanced distributed applications on your laptop when you're stuck in a hotel room or traveling on a plane.

The MTS Development Environment

When you create and distribute MTS components, keep in mind that everything is based on COM. The MTS catalog tracks information about both CLSIDs and IIDs. You should place your projects in Binary Compatibility mode once you decide to install your ActiveX DLL in the MTS Explorer. You must apply all the principles and guidelines that were covered in Chapter 5 about building compatible servers and managing your versioning.

Once you build an ActiveX DLL, you can install it in a server package in MTS Explorer. One easy way to test your work is to create a simple form-based application that will serve as a base client for your MTS objects. You can create this test client by creating a new Standard EXE project and including the reference to your ActiveX DLL. When you run the test client application, any objects created from the ActiveX DLL will be loaded into the MTS environment. You can run the client from a compiled EXE, or you can run it inside the Visual Basic IDE. In either case, you should be able to look at the MTS Explorer and verify that your objects are being created inside your server package.

You might get some unexpected results if you add the base client project and the ActiveX DLL project to the same Visual Basic project group. When both projects are in the same project group, everything (including the objects from the ActiveX DLL project) will run in the Visual Basic debugging environment and your objects won't be loaded in the MTS environment. This situation has an unfortunate side effect. All of your calls to *GetObjectContext* will return a null reference. This typically results in a series of run-time errors. If you get a bunch of type 91 errors ("Object variable or With block variable not set"), this could be the cause. You can solve this problem by loading the client project and the ActiveX DLL project into two separate sessions of the Visual Basic IDE. Later in this chapter, you'll learn a technique for debugging both the client project and your ActiveX DLL in a single session of the Visual Basic IDE.

You will constantly rebuild your ActiveX DLL as you modify and test your code in the MTS environment. By default, however, a server package is configured to stay loaded in memory for three minutes after all its objects have been released. If you try to rebuild the DLL while the server package is still loaded, you'll receive a "Permission denied" error. You can get around this problem by right-clicking on the server package in the MTS Explorer and choosing the Shut Down command. You can then rebuild your DLL and rerun your test client. You must also close the project of the test client before you can rebuild the server if the project of the test client is referencing the ActiveX DLL.

The MTS Explorer provides a Refresh command for the Components folder of each package. When you invoke this command, the MTS system updates the Registry so that activation will still occur in proper MTS-like fashion. You can also use a Visual Basic add-in that instructs the MTS system to automatically refresh the components every time you rebuild an ActiveX DLL that has already been registered with MTS Explorer.

Even though Visual Basic and MTS provide some assistance with refreshing the Registry after a rebuild, they don't help you when you add new things to your ActiveX DLL. When you rebuild your DLL after adding a new class, interface, or method, the information in the MTS catalog will get out of sync with the information published in the type library of the DLL. In such cases, you can delete your components from the MTS package and then reinstall the DLL. You should be able to verify that the catalog is back in sync by examining your components in the MTS Explorer.

When you delete a component, you lose some security-related configuration information. However, in the early stages of development, you usually haven't done anything with security yet, so this generally isn't a problem. As long as you're working in Binary Compatibility mode, all of your base client applications should continue to work as before.

Debugging an MTS Application

Visual Basic provides a powerful and easy-to-use debugging environment for almost every type of component and application you can create. It's usually pretty easy to debug Standard EXEs, ActiveX DLLs, ActiveX controls, and ActiveX EXEs. However, debugging MTS components with Visual Basic is more difficult and can be frustrating because they must be debugged in the MTS run-time environment. Before version 6, the Visual Basic debugging environment couldn't simulate the MTS run time. And even Visual Basic 6 includes compromises that make debugging less than perfect.

If you don't have Visual Basic 6 and Windows NT with Service Pack 4, you have two choices for debugging. First, you can run your components in the MTS run-time environment and write code in your components to generate debug messages using either the Windows NT event log or the *MsgBox* statement. The second debugging technique involves using the Visual C++ debugging environment.

Let's start by sending debug messages to the Windows NT event log. The Visual Basic *App* object provides a *LogEvent* method. You can easily append a message to the Windows NT event log with the following code:

```
Dim sMsg As String
sMsg = "Your debug message here"
App.LogEvent sMsg, vbLogEventTypeInformation
```

While testing your components, you can use the Windows NT Event Viewer to examine your debug messages. You might also find that logging Windows NT events is useful for more than just debugging. You can use events to audit recurring errors in the production environment. You might consider logging all unexpected errors that are raised in your components.

Another popular technique for generating debug messages in MTS is to call upon your old friend the *MsgBox* statement. You might see the use of *MsgBox* as a trick for novice programmers, but it's a quick-and-dirty way to see the value of your variables and see how your code is branching at run time. When you need to quickly debug some MTS code, this can be the fastest way to get the job done.

To use the *MsgBox* statement, you need to do two things. First, make sure your server package is running under the identity of the interactive user. This allows your objects to access your computer's display console. Second, make sure that you don't have the *Unattended Execution* option selected when you rebuild your server. If you follow these two rules, you can use a message box to send a debug message, as follows:

```
Dim sMsg As String
sMsg = "Your debug message here"
MsgBox sMsg, vbInformation + vbMsgBoxSetForeground
```

The painful thing about this style of debugging is that you have to remove these statements before you distribute your code. If you don't, one of these calls will hang your application. You might consider using a conditional compilation argument so that you can easily switch between builds that generate debug messages and those that don't.

You can employ a more advanced debugging technique using the Visual C++ IDE. This technique lets you set break points inside the class modules from your ActiveX DLL project and single-step through your Visual Basic code. To use the Visual C++ debugger, you must build your ActiveX DLL with symbolic debug info (accessible in the Compile tab of the Project Properties dialog box) and register it with the MTS Explorer. The documentation for MTS 2.0 has the full step-by-step instructions for how to get up and running in the Visual C++ IDE.

Using the Visual C++ debugger can be pretty tricky, but it does provide the best simulation of the actual MTS run-time environment. All of the MTS debugging techniques using the Visual Basic run-time environment involve compromises regarding threading and security.

Visual Basic 6 provides a few new features that let you debug your MTS components in the Visual Basic IDE. The first feature is the new Debugging tab of the Project Properties dialog box. This tab provides a Start Program property that allows you to enter a host application when debugging an ActiveX DLL. This provides some of the debugging capabilities that you have with the Visual C++ debugger. Once you install an ActiveX DLL in the MTS Explorer, you can add the following line as the Start Program setting for the project:

```
C:\WINNT\System32\mtx.exe /p:{5E440C1C-0AA2-11D2-B6FA-0080C72D2182}
```

Note that this Start Program setting is the same one you use to activate an MTS component inside the Visual C++ debugger. The GUID after the */p:* switch identifies the server package. You can optionally include the name of the package instead of the GUID. Once you enter the Start Program setting and set the appropriate break points in your class modules, you can run the project in debug mode by choosing Run With Full Compile from the Start menu. This launches a special debug version of your server package. When you run your test client application, you can single-step through your code. Remember that you must be working in Binary Compatibility mode.

One other MTS debugging feature has been added to Visual Basic 6. This feature allows you to use a technique that lets you debug MTS components without having to register them first with the MTS Explorer. This makes it much faster and easier to debug your MTS code. You must be running Windows NT with Service Pack 4 to use this technique, and you should note that it too has a few shortcomings when it comes to simulating the MTS run-time environment. However, this technique is definitely the fastest and easiest to use.

Let's examine how to create the setup to use this technique. Visual Basic 6 simulates the MTS run-time environment by temporarily registering your components in an MTS library package. When you run your project, mtxex.dll is loaded into the Visual Basic debugging environment. In Visual Basic 6, each *MultiUse* class module in an ActiveX DLL project has a new *MTSTransactionMode* property setting. If you set this property to a value other than *NotAnMTSObject*, you can debug your MTS code in the Visual Basic IDE.

For example, you can set the *MTSTransactionMode* property to *NoTransactions* for your class modules, and Visual Basic will run your objects under the control of the MTS run time. This technique is convenient because you can add the test client project and your ActiveX DLL projects to a single project group. When you run the test project, the objects created from your ActiveX DLLs are created with context wrappers. You can thus safely call *GetObjectContext* and make method calls on the object context.

You shouldn't register your ActiveX DLLs with the MTS Explorer before using this technique. You'll also encounter some limitations when it comes to testing multithreading and security-related code. Consult the Visual Basic 6 documentation to find out what these limitations are.

Despite a few limitations with this last technique, it significantly improves the debugging facilities over what is possible in Visual Basic 5. For example, when you debug ADO code in an MTS component, single-stepping through your code and examining your variables is just as easy as in other areas of Visual Basic development.

However, each debugging technique has its strengths and weaknesses. If you spend a lot of time creating MTS components with Visual Basic, you might use each of the various debugging techniques covered in this chapter from time to time.

Moving On to More Advanced MTS Topics

This chapter has covered the basics of writing components for use inside the MTS run-time environment, including the fundamental architecture of the MTS run time and the purpose of context wrappers. You've learned how to communicate with MTS through the *ObjectContext* and *ObjectControl* interfaces and how to propagate new objects in the current activity.

Chapter 10 builds on this knowledge and shows you how to program transactions with an MTS application. As you'll see, MTS provides a powerful transaction processing monitor. The skills you learned in this chapter will be important as you begin to create components that are transactional. Chapter 11 explores other issues related to designing and creating MTS applications with Visual Basic, such as security and application partitioning.

Chapter 10

Programming Transactions

Just about every business application uses data in one form or another. Some applications are concerned only with querying and analyzing data, while others are primarily concerned with modifying data. Applications that modify data and have a large number of concurrent users are commonly referred to as *online transaction processing* (OLTP) systems. This chapter covers this type of application.

You should understand certain things about OLTP systems before you write transactions for Microsoft Transaction Server (MTS). This chapter covers the ABCs of transaction processing. It also explains why a transaction must meet the "ACID rules" and what is meant by a transaction's isolation level.

The chapter looks at a common OLTP architecture for distributed systems that many vendors use. It explains how to assemble a reliable OLTP system using a transactional application and transaction managers when the data is spread across many servers. Special attention is given to Microsoft's version of the transaction manager, the Distributed Transaction Coordinator (DTC).

You'll also learn how MTS transactions are used to run distributed transactions in OLTP applications. MTS uses a model based on declarative transactions to leverage the facilities of the DTC while hiding many of the tedious low-level details.

Finally, you'll learn how to write transactional MTS components with Visual Basic and how to use four basic methods of the context object—*DisableCommit, EnableCommit, SetComplete*, and *SetAbort*—to control the outcome of your transactions. The chapter also delves into a variety of transaction-related topics such as deadlocks and stateless programming.

FUNDAMENTALS OF TRANSACTION PROCESSING

A typical command in an OLTP application often must modify several items of data to complete its work. Suppose you're building an application that lets users submit orders to purchase products. To keep things simple, let's say that each order is submitted on behalf of a single customer for a specific quantity of one type of product. The application must make three modifications to a database to properly record the purchase:

■ Subtract the purchased quantity from the product's inventory level in the Products table.

■ Add the purchase price to the customer's account balance in the Customers table.

■ Add a new order record to the Orders table.

These three modifications make up a single unit of work. In essence, they make up a single transaction. A transaction can be defined as a related set of operations that read and modify data. As you'll see, quite a few requirements must be met when transactions are run in a high-volume multiuser environment.

Many OLTP systems are written against relational database management systems (DBMSs) such as SQL Server and Oracle, but this isn't a requirement. You can build an OLTP system using many other types of data sources, including mainframe applications, message queues, and the file system. However, the examples in this chapter primarily use SQL Server as the data source.

Every transaction must meet four essential requirements. It must be *atomic, consistent, isolated,* and *durable.* These requirements are known as the *ACID rules.* When you write a transaction for an OLTP system, all participants must follow these rules. Let's look at what these requirements mean:

■ *Atomic* A transaction must be an all-or-nothing proposition. Everything must be successfully updated or nothing should be updated.

■ *Consistent* Individual operations within a transaction may leave data in such a state that the data is in violation of the system's integrity constraints. However, when an OLTP system completes a transaction, the data as a whole must be left in a valid state.

■ *Isolated* One transaction can't view the uncommitted changes of another transaction. This means that the uncommitted changes of a transaction must be isolated from all other transactions.

■ *Durable* When a transaction is committed, the data sources involved must store all changes in stable storage and these changes must be recoverable in the event of a system failure.

When an application successfully completes all the modifications associated with a transaction, it commits the transaction. This is obviously the most desirable outcome. After a transaction has been committed, the data source must be able to account for all changes, even in the face of a system failure. This makes the transaction durable.

If an application can't complete all of its work, it must abort the transaction. When an application aborts a transaction, it tells the data source to roll back any work that has been completed. This means that the data source must provide the ability to roll back uncommitted changes. Most data sources do this through the use of a logging mechanism. For example, some DBMSs undo changes made by a transaction by playing the logged updates in reverse. However, many data sources use rollback mechanisms that are completely different. All that's required is that the data source be able to undo any changes that haven't been committed. This makes the transaction atomic.

Now let's look at what it takes to meet the requirement of consistency. The data in a system typically has a set of integrity constraints. These constraints are defined so as to keep the data for the entire system in a valid state. For example, one constraint could be that no two customers in a Customers table can have the same primary key. Another constraint could be that a customer record can never have an account balance that exceeds the credit limit. These are just two of the many types of constraints that can be used.

It's sometimes permissible to make changes while a transaction is running that violate the data integrity constraints of the system as a whole. However, when the system completes the transaction, it must make sure that all the data integrity constraints are met. Much of this burden falls on the programmer who's writing the transaction. When you're writing business logic and data access code for a transaction, you must have an understanding of what the constraints are. You should never commit the changes for a transaction unless you're sure that you're returning the database to a consistent state.

As you can see, you're required to write a transaction so that when it ends it leaves the data in a consistent state. However, your code needs additional help to maintain consistency when multiple users are involved. A change made by one transaction isn't real (stable) until it has been committed. Therefore, one transaction shouldn't be able to see the uncommitted changes of another transaction. If this isn't the case, the system's data can easily get into an inconsistent state.

Imagine two transactions, one running for user A and one running for user B. If transaction B can see uncommitted changes made by transaction A, transaction B might use values from these uncommitted changes when making its own changes to the database. If transaction A is rolled back, a problem occurs: Transaction B has used one or more values that never really existed. As you can see, a transaction can't read uncommitted data if it is to remain consistent.

A transaction must be isolated from the uncommitted changes of every other transaction. The application therefore needs some locking help from the data source. Locks allow transactions to run without compromising consistency. Each data source that supports transactions in a multiuser environment must provide some type of lock management. A data source's *lock manager* acts as blocking agent to make sure that transactions wait while other transactions use shared resources such as a record in a database.

A lock manager places locks on different types of data items. A data item can be a table, a page, a record, or a file. Each type of data item provides a different level of granularity. Some levels of locking granularity provide better performance, while others provide higher levels of concurrency.

Most data sources provide locking at more than one level of granularity. Microsoft SQL Server 6.5 provides locking at the page level and at the table level. Locking at the page level is better for concurrency—many users can access the data in a table at the same time. On the other hand, what if a transaction must lock every page in a table? Concurrency isn't an issue because the entire table must be locked. However, a single table lock can be acquired much faster than hundreds or thousands of page locks. SQL Server automatically determines which types of locks to use and escalates page locks to a table lock when a certain threshold is met.

SQL Server 7 and many other relational DBMSs, such as Oracle, provide row-level locking, in which two different transactions can independently lock individual rows on the same physical page. Row-level locking can provide greater concurrency than page-level locking in an OLTP system.

From here on, I won't differentiate among these levels of granularity. While each level offers trade-offs in performance and concurrency, all of the levels work the same way in terms of lock management. I'll use the generic term *data item,* which can mean any level of granularity.

When a transaction accesses a data item, the lock manager places a lock on it. However, if a conflicting lock has been placed on the data item by another transaction, the lock manager blocks the transaction until the conflicting lock is removed. The transaction must wait its turn until the other transaction has ended. Most of the time transactions simply wait their turn and then complete their work. In some rare cases, transactions are aborted when the system detects a deadlock. We'll revisit deadlocks later in this chapter.

Write Locks and Read Locks

Lock managers use two primary lock types: write locks and read locks. The data source places a write lock (also called an *exclusive lock*) on a data item when it's modified by a transaction. Write locks isolate uncommitted changes from other transactions. A read lock (also called a *shared lock*) is placed on a data item while it's being read by a transaction.

A write lock conflicts with other write locks and with read locks. A transaction that has a write lock blocks all other transactions from reading from or writing to the data item in question. The data item remains locked until the transaction is committed or rolled back. This makes sense because the system must isolate uncommitted changes to ensure data consistency. However, this isolation has a price: The blocking reduces overall system concurrency and throughput.

Read locks don't conflict with read locks. Many transactions can obtain a read lock on the same data item concurrently. However, a transaction can't obtain a write lock on a data item that has outstanding read locks. This ensures that a transaction doesn't overwrite a data item while another transaction is reading it. The following table summarizes how the lock manager handles lock requests when locks are already in place.

	No Lock Held	**Read Lock Held**	**Write Lock Held**
Read Lock Requested	Lock acquired	Lock acquired	Request blocked
Write Lock Requested	Lock acquired	Request blocked	Request blocked

Finding the Correct Isolation Level

While locks help enforce data consistency and transaction isolation, they also can degrade concurrency and throughput. You can increase or decrease the level of blocking by adjusting the transaction's isolation level. The lock manager uses the isolation level of a transaction when determining how to handle locking. The four commonly supported isolation levels are the following:

■ ***Read Uncommitted*** The transaction can read any data items regardless of whether they have outstanding write locks. Additionally, the transaction will not acquire read locks. This isolation level provides the fastest access but is highly vulnerable to data inconsistency.

■ ***Read Committed*** Only data items that have been committed can be read. A transaction running at this isolation level must wait until a write lock is released before accessing a data item. Read locks are acquired while the transaction reads a data item, but they aren't held for the transaction's lifetime. A read lock is released once the data item has been read. This is the default isolation level used by both SQL Server and ADO when you run a transaction without MTS.

■ ***Repeatable Read*** This level is like Read Committed except that all read locks are held for the lifetime of the transaction. Any data item that's read in any stage of a transaction can be read later without any change. That is, all data read by the transaction remains in the same state until the transaction is committed or rolled back. This level isn't supported by SQL Server 6.5, which automatically escalates it to Serializable.

■ ***Serializable***   This level is like Repeatable Read with one extra qualification: A query that runs multiple times in a serializable transaction should always have the same results. Phantom data items can't be inserted by other transactions until the OLTP system has completed the transaction. For example, if a transaction running at this level runs a query to determine the number of records in a table, no other transaction can insert a row in the table until the transaction is completed. This is the default *(and only)* isolation level used by SQL Server when called by an MTS transactional object.

Every level except Serializable compromises isolation in order to improve concurrency and throughput. When you run transactions with an isolation level of Serializable, the data source attempts to provide the best level of concurrency and throughput without compromising consistency and isolation. A transaction is said to be serializable if it isn't affected by other transactions. When every transaction is serializable, it has the same effect on an application as running the transactions one at a time.

Programming Simple Transactions

It's not complicated to write a transaction against a single data source. Let's say you're creating a two-tier application using a SQL Server database. You can control a transaction programmatically using Transact-SQL. For example, you can write the following code to run a transaction:

```
-- Set isolation level to Serializable.
SET TRANSACTION ISOLATION LEVEL SERIALIZABLE
-- Run transaction to purchase a dog for $20.
BEGIN TRANSACTION
    -- Decrement product quantity from inventory.
    UPDATE Products
    SET Quantity = Quantity - 1
    WHERE Product = 'Dog'
    -- Charge price to customer account.
    UPDATE Customers SET AccountBalance = AccountBalance + 20
    WHERE Customer = 'Bob'
    -- Add order record.
    INSERT Orders(Customer, Product, Quantity, Price)
        VALUES('Bob', 'Dog', 1, 20)
COMMIT TRANSACTION
```

This example doesn't include any code to deal with problems and transaction rollback, but it illustrates how to execute a series of SQL statements as a single transaction. When you execute this code, SQL Server uses its own internal transaction manager to enforce the ACID rules. All of the changes are committed or no changes are committed. Because the transaction's isolation level is set to Serializable, SQL Server also makes sure that the uncommitted changes of one transaction don't affect any other transactions.

You can also manage transactions from a database API such as ADO, RDO, ODBC, or OLE-DB. These APIs let you create and manage a transaction within the scope of an open connection. For example, here's how to run a transaction against SQL Server using ADO:

```
Dim conn As Connection
Set conn = New Connection
conn.Open "DSN=Market;UID=sa;PWD="
conn.IsolationLevel = adXactSerializable
conn.BeginTrans
    ' Assume the same SQL statements from the Transact-SQL example.
    conn.Execute SQL_DecrementInventory
    conn.Execute SQL_ChargeCustomer
    conn.Execute SQL_AddOrder
conn.CommitTrans
```

As you can see, it's not difficult to program a transaction with either Transact-SQL or ADO. All you do is set the appropriate isolation level and then use three commands to begin, commit, and roll back the transaction. The DBMS does its part to enforce the ACID rules. As long as you understand isolation levels and locking, you can find opportunities to optimize concurrency without sacrificing data consistency. If you are programming a two-tier OLTP application against a single DBMS, this might be all you need.

DISTRIBUTED TRANSACTIONS

As you've seen, a single DBMS can enforce the ACID rules when it holds all the data involved in a transaction. For example, SQL Server supplies its own internal transaction manager and can provide commit and rollback behavior as well as recover committed data in the event of a system failure. However, OLTP systems that require distributed transactions are far more challenging. Commit and abort behavior as well as recovery must be coordinated across several data sources for each transaction.

Quite a few products use a similar high-level architecture to solve the problems of coordinating distributed transactions. For example, CICS from IBM, TUXEDO from BEA Systems, and MTS from Microsoft all use a high-level abstraction called a *transaction manager* (TM) and a special protocol called *two-phase commit*. Figure 10-1 on the following page shows how the TM is used in this distributed architecture. The application that controls the transaction serves as a *transactional application*. Each data source is known as a *resource manager* (RM). Each node (computer) in the system typically runs its own session of a TM. Let's examine the usual sequence of actions that occur when an application runs a distributed transaction.

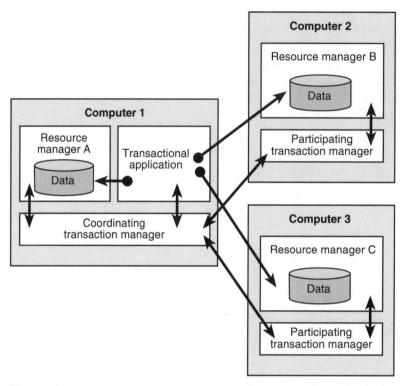

Figure 10-1. *A transactional application and transaction managers work together to monitor a distributed transaction and to execute the two-phase commit protocol across multiple resource managers.*

A transactional application calls to its local TM to begin a transaction. This TM is known as the *coordinating transaction manager* (CTM). The CTM creates a unique ID for the transaction and initializes various state variables to manage the transaction. As the application establishes connections with various RMs, it must enlist these connections in the transaction. When the connection is enlisted, the RM establishes a connection with its local TM. There are two common enlistment cases that you should understand.

When the RM is running on the same node as the transactional application, the RM enlists with the CTM. When the RM is running on a different node, the RM enlists with its local TM, which is known as a *participating transaction manager* (PTM). During the enlistment of a remote RM, the CTM must also establish a connection with the PTM unless a connection has already been established. Once each connection has been enlisted, the lines of communication are set up as shown in Figure 10-1. The CTM can now coordinate the transaction across one group of *participants*. The participants group is made up of the local RMs and PTMs.

The CTM enforces the ACID rules in a distributed transaction by running the two-phase commit protocol. After the transactional application indicates that it wants to commit the transaction, the CTM runs phase 1 to prepare the transaction. In this phase, the CTM sends an "are you prepared" message to each participant. If everything goes according to plan, each participant responds with an "I'm prepared" message. When every participant has responded with an "I'm prepared" message, the CTM knows that the changes can be committed. You should note that at this point the locks that have been acquired by the transaction are still being held.

After receiving an "I'm prepared" message from each participant, the CTM begins phase 2. The CTM writes to its log that the transaction has been committed and sends a "time to commit" message to each participant. When a local RM receives this message, the RM commits its changes and releases its locks. When a PTM receives this message, it tells its enlisted RM to commit its changes and release its locks. After a participant has committed its changes, it sends an "I'm done" message back to the CTM. Once the CTM receives this message from every participant, it assumes that all of the work has been successfully completed.

I have just given you a brief overview of the two-phase protocol. As a programmer, you don't have to be overly concerned with its inner workings. The two-phase commit protocol is really just an implementation detail. When you commit a distributed transaction in MTS, you should assume that the system will enforce the ACID rules. There is nothing in the MTS programming model that requires you to think about the two-phase commit protocol. However, if you want to read more on the subject, pick up a copy of *Principles of Transaction Processing,* by Bernstein and Newcomer. This book covers many aspects of the two-phase commit protocol that are important to system implementers and administrators.

Distributed Transaction Coordinator

Microsoft's transaction manager is the Distributed Transaction Coordinator (DTC). This product initially shipped with SQL Server 6.5, but it's now heavily used by other products such as MTS and Microsoft Message Queue (MSMQ). The DTC runs on Windows NT as a system service. Figure 10-2 on the following page shows that the DTC can act as a coordinating TM and also as a participating TM.

The DTC uses a protocol called *OLE Transactions,* which defines a set of COM interfaces through which applications and RMs communicate with the DTC. X/Open is another popular standard used by products such as TUXEDO, Encina, and TOP END. X/Open, like OLE Transactions, standardizes the way in which applications and RMs communicate with the transaction manager. These standards have a few differences. OLE Transactions is object based, while X/Open is not; OLE Transactions supports multithreaded applications, while X/Open supports a single thread of control. For details about interoperability between these standards, see the MTS SDK.

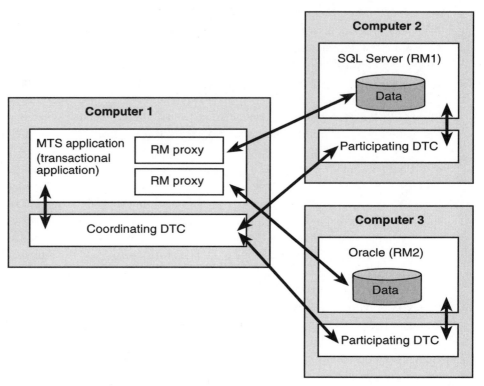

Figure 10-2. *The DTC, Microsoft's transaction manager, is used by products such as MTS, MSMQ, and SQL Server.*

If you want to execute distributed transactions using the DTC, you have two choices. The easy way is to use MTS and let the MTS run time make all the complicated calls to the DTC for you. Another option is to create an application that communicates directly with the DTC. If you choose the second option, you should write your code in C or C++.

Let's look at what it takes to write code directly against the DTC. As a Visual Basic programmer, you will never have to code at this level, but if you look behind the scenes you'll gain an appreciation for what MTS does on your behalf.

The transactional application must first establish a connection with the DTC by calling *DtcGetTransactionManager* to obtain an *ITransactionDispenser* reference to the DTC Proxy Core Object. The *ITransactionDispenser* interface contains a method named *BeginTransaction*. When you invoke this method, the DTC creates a new transaction object and returns a reference to your application. This transaction object exposes a *Commit* method and an *Abort* method through the *ITransaction* interface. When you create a transaction, you can specify both the isolation level and a timeout interval.

Next you must establish a connection to one or more resource managers. For example, you can connect to a DBMS such as SQL Server or Oracle using an ODBC driver. The ODBC driver acts as the RM proxy. After establishing an ODBC connection, you must propagate the transaction to the resource manager using the ODBC *SQLSetConnectAttr* function. When you make this call, the RM proxy tells the resource manager to enlist with its local DTC so that the resource manager can participate in the two-phase commit. At this point, you can use the ODBC connection to execute SQL operations such as INSERT, UPDATE, and DELETE. All of your operations will be charged against your transaction.

If the transactional application calls *Abort*, the local DTC tells all the participants to roll back their changes and release their locks. If the transactional application successfully completes its work on all RMs, it calls *Commit* to tell the local DTC to start executing the two-phase commit protocol. The local DTC calls in parallel to each participant, telling it to prepare its work. The fact that these calls are made in parallel means that the local DTC doesn't have to wait for the first participant to respond before sending the prepare request to the second participant. This parallelism improves performance significantly.

After the local DTC receives an "I'm prepared" response from each enlisted participant, it begins phase 2. First the local DTC writes to its log to record the fact that the transaction has been committed. Next it sends a commit message to each participant in parallel. Each participant commits its changes, releases its locks, and sends an "I'm done" message back to the coordinating DTC. Once the coordinating DTC receives all the "I'm done" messages, it can forget about the transaction because there's no longer any need to recover the transaction in case of a system failure.

Note that the DTC can perform an optimization if the two-phase protocol isn't required. Commit coordinator delegation occurs when the coordinating DTC detects that only one participating DTC is enlisted in the transaction. This is the case if you create a DTC-based transaction using only one RM. The coordinating DTC sends a "delegated commit" message instead of an "are you prepared" message. The "delegated commit" message transfers commit coordinator responsibility from the coordinating DTC to the participating DTC. This simply reduces the number of round-trips required to commit a transaction. This is useful to know because many transactions involve only a single SQL Server database, and those transactions must be optimized to run as fast as possible.

As you can see, the requirements for writing an application directly against the DTC are pretty strict. Fortunately, MTS provides a much easier programming model. Your MTS application is just another client to the DTC. Behind the scenes in your MTS application, things happen as described here but MTS hides the details of interacting with the DTC and enlisting RMs.

MTS AND DECLARATIVE TRANSACTIONS

MTS lets you create distributed transactions with the DTC while hiding many of the low-level details. It does this by proving a programming model based on declarative transactions. You are responsible for creating objects inside the scope of an MTS transaction. When you do this, MTS creates the distributed transaction with the DTC and silently enlists all your RM connections for you.

After you create your objects inside a transaction, you use a handful of methods supplied by the *ObjectContext* interface to control the flow of the transaction and to make sure the transaction is released as soon as possible. Let's examine how you create one or more objects inside an MTS transaction.

Every MTS component has a transaction support attribute. Figure 10-3 shows the Transaction tab of the component's Properties dialog box in the MTS Explorer. This dialog box lets you see and modify the transaction support attribute for each component in an MTS package. If you're using Visual Basic 5, you must install your components first and then adjust the transaction support attribute setting by hand.

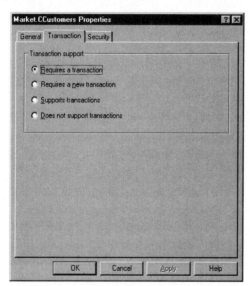

Figure 10-3. *Each MTS component has a transaction support attribute. When the MTS run time creates an object from a component, it looks at this attribute to determine whether the object should be created in a new or in an existing transaction.*

Visual Basic 6 added the *MTSTransactionMode* setting to the property sheet of each public class module inside an ActiveX DLL project. When you set this property, as shown in Figure 10-4, Visual Basic publishes the corresponding MTS transaction support attribute in your server's type library. When you install your DLL with the MTS Explorer, MTS automatically configures your components with the appropriate transaction support attributes. The person installing a DLL created with Visual Basic 6 in an MTS package doesn't have to set these attributes by hand, as is the case with DLLs created with Visual Basic 5.

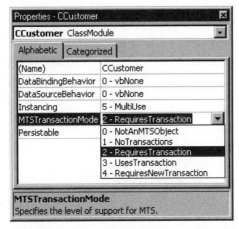

Figure 10-4. *The* MTSTransactionMode *setting is published in the server's type library. When you install your DLL with the MTS Explorer, each component is configured with the transaction support attribute that corresponds to its* MTSTransactionMode *setting.*

Notice the difference between the transaction support setting in MTS and the *MTSTransactionMode* setting for a Visual Basic class module. Don't let this bother you; it is just a slight inconsistency in the wording used by MTS and Visual Basic. Every transaction support property has a corresponding *MTSTransactionMode* setting. Here's how they map to one another:

MTSTransactionMode *Setting*	***Equivalent MTS Transaction Support Setting***
RequiresTransaction	Requires a transaction
RequiresNewTransaction	Requires a new transaction
UsesTransaction	Supports transactions
NoTransactions	Doesn't support transactions
NotAnMTSObject	N/A

Creating Objects Inside a Transaction

There's only one way to place an object inside a transaction. You must ask the MTS run time to place the object inside the transaction when the object is created. When the MTS run time creates a new object, it examines the component's setting to see whether the new object should be created inside a transaction. You use the transaction support setting to tell the MTS run time what to do.

You can't add an object to a transaction after the object has been created. Likewise, you can never disassociate an object from the transaction in which it was created. Once an object is created inside a transaction, it spends its entire lifetime there. When the transaction is committed or aborted, the MTS run time destroys all the objects inside it. As you'll see, this cleanup activity is essential to achieving the proper semantics of a transaction. The objects must be destroyed to enforce the consistency requirement of the ACID rules.

Both base clients and MTS objects can create new MTS objects. When the MTS run time receives an activation request to create a new object, it determines whether the object's creator is running inside an existing transaction. The MTS run time also inspects the transaction support attribute of the component. From these two pieces of information, it can determine how to proceed. A component can have one of the following transaction support settings:

- ■ **Requires A Transaction**   The object is created within the context of a transaction. The object is placed inside the transaction of its creator if one exists. If the creator isn't running in a transaction, the MTS run time creates a new transaction for the object.

- ■ **Requires A New Transaction**   The MTS run time creates a new transaction for the object.

- ■ **Supports Transactions**   The object is placed inside the transaction of its creator if one exists. If the creator isn't running in a transaction, the object is created without a transaction.

- ■ **Doesn't Support Transactions**   The object isn't created within the context of a transaction.

A base client can initiate a transaction by activating an MTS object from a component marked as Requires or Requires New. The MTS run time determines that the new object must run inside a transaction and that the creator isn't running inside a transaction. The MTS run time therefore creates a new MTS transaction and then creates the new object inside it. The first object created inside a transaction is known as the *root* of the transaction.

The root object can create additional objects inside its transaction. If you're writing a method for an MTS object and you want to propagate another object inside that transaction, you must follow two rules. First, you must create the object from components marked as either Requires or Supports. The MTS run time will create the new object in the same transaction as its creator with either setting. Second, you must create additional objects with *CreateInstance*. The scope of every transaction is always contained within the scope of a single activity. As you'll recall from Chapter 9, *CreateInstance* always creates the new object inside the same activity and gives the new object its own context wrapper.

A Tale of Two Transactions

In most cases, you create several objects inside an MTS transaction. However, let's look at a transaction that involves only the root object. Once you understand how the root object works, you'll be ready to examine what happens when you have several objects running inside a transaction.

When a base client creates an MTS object from a component marked as Requires, the MTS run time creates a new MTS transaction in which to place the new object. The MTS run time also calls down to the DTC to create a new distributed transaction on your behalf. You should think of the MTS transaction as the *logical transaction* and the DTC transaction as the *physical transaction*. Note that the MTS run time doesn't create the physical transaction when it creates the logical transaction.

The MTS run time creates the logical transaction when it creates the root object, but it defers creating the physical transaction until the root object is activated. As Chapter 9 explained, an MTS object isn't activated until the client invokes the first method call. Thus there can be a short or a long delay between the creation of these two transactions. The MTS run time delays creating the physical transaction as long as possible.

When the root object is activated, the MTS run time calls down to the DTC to begin the transaction by obtaining an *ITransactionDispenser* reference and calling *BeginTransaction*. The MTS run time creates the physical transaction with an isolation level of Serializable and a timeout interval of 60 seconds. This means that you work with the highest level of isolation and have one minute to complete your work. (The timeout interval is adjustable; you can modify this machinewide setting by selecting a computer from the MTS Explorer's tree view and opening its Properties dialog box.)

When the MTS run time calls down to create the physical transaction, the DTC creates a transaction object and passes the MTS run time an *ITransaction* reference. The MTS run time holds onto this reference for the lifetime of the logical MTS transaction. The *ITransaction* interface lets the MTS run time call *Commit* or *Abort*. As you can see, the MTS run time can control the outcome of the transaction.

As a Visual Basic programmer, you cannot obtain an *ITransaction* reference to the transaction object and call *Commit* or *Abort* yourself. So now you're asking, "How do I control the transaction?" The answer lies in knowing when the MTS run time calls *Commit* and *Abort* and seeing how you can influence its decision. The MTS run time decides to commit or abort the transaction when the root object is deactivated. Before this time, you can do quite a lot to change the state of the transaction. You can invoke methods on the object context that allow you to vote on whether you think the transaction should succeed.

The Three Flags: Happy, Done, and Doomed

Figure 10-5 shows a diagram of the root object, its context wrapper, and the MTS transaction in which they are running. It also shows some important internal flags that are maintained by MTS. These variables aren't directly exposed to you, but you should understand how they influence the MTS run time's decision to complete or abort the transaction.

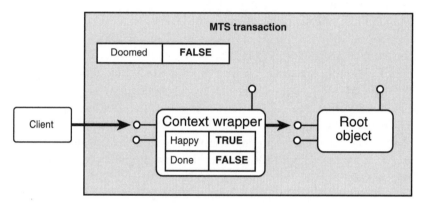

Figure 10-5. *The doomed flag tells the MTS transaction whether to commit or abort the transaction when the root object is deactivated. The happy flag indicates whether the object wants to commit its changes. The done flag indicates whether the object is ready to be deactivated.*

The transaction as a whole maintains a Boolean value that indicates whether the transaction must be aborted. We'll call this the *doomed flag*. This value is initially set to False when the MTS transaction is created. When this flag is set to True, the MTS run time knows to abort the transaction. Now you must answer two important questions:

- When does the MTS run time inspect the doomed flag?

- How can you change the value of the doomed flag?

To answer these questions, you must understand that the root object plays an important role in every MTS transaction. There are two cases in which the MTS run time inspects the doomed flag. Let's look at these cases to see what the MTS run time does after inspecting the doomed flag.

In the first case, the MTS run time inspects the doomed flag whenever the root object returns control to its caller. Remember that the flow of execution always passes through the context wrapper first. When control passes through the context wrapper, the MTS run time checks the doomed flag. If the doomed flag is False, the MTS run time doesn't do anything. However, if the MTS run time finds that the doomed flag has been set to True by one of the objects inside the transaction, it aborts the transaction and deactivates all its objects except for the root object. As you will see, this situation is undesirable. The transaction has been aborted, but the root object remains activated in a futile state. You can prevent this from happening by following the rules outlined later in this chapter.

In the second case, the MTS run time inspects the doomed flag when the root object is deactivated. When the root object is deactivated during an active transaction, the MTS run time inspects the doomed flag and releases the transaction by calling either *Commit* or *Abort*. If the doomed flag is set to False, the MTS run time calls *Commit*. If the flag is set to True, the MTS run time calls *Abort*. Note that the deactivation of the root object should always cause the end of the transaction's life cycle. When the root is deactivated, the transaction will always be released. However, as long as the root object remains activated, the transaction can remain alive and can hold all of its locks.

Now let's look at the two flags maintained inside the context wrapper for every MTS transactional object. The first one is the *happy* flag. It has an initial value of True when the context wrapper is created. When an object running inside an MTS transaction is deactivated, the MTS run time examines its happy flag. If the happy flag is set to False, the MTS run time sets the transaction's doomed flag to True. Once the transaction's doomed flag is set to True, it can't be reversed. This has a powerful implication. If the root object or any other object inside a transaction is deactivated in an unhappy state, the transaction is doomed to failure.

Let's look at a few scenarios to see how all this works. First, imagine that a base client creates an object from a component marked as Requires A Transaction and invokes a method call. This results in the creation of an MTS transaction and triggers the MTS run time to call down to the DTC to create the physical transaction as well. What happens if the base client simply releases its reference to the MTS object? When the MTS object is deactivated, the MTS run time inspects its happy flag. The happy flag still has its initial value of True. Therefore, the MTS run time doesn't change the doomed flag. The doomed flag remains False, and the MTS run time calls *Commit* on the transaction. You can run a simple example and confirm these results by examining the Transaction Statistics in the MTS Explorer.

So that's pretty easy. You create an object inside a transaction, activate it, and then release it. All it takes is three steps to successfully begin and commit a transaction with the DTC. Even though we haven't done anything interesting yet, such as writing to a database, this example shows how and when the MTS run time interacts with the DTC. We didn't write any code to explicitly begin or commit the transaction. The MTS model of declarative transaction does all of that for you.

Now let's abort a transaction. All you do is set the happy flag inside the root object's context wrapper to False. One way to do this is by calling *DisableCommit* in a method of the root object, as shown in the code on the following page.

```
Dim ObjCtx As ObjectContext
Set ObjCtx = GetObjectContext()
ObjCtx.DisableCommit()
```

When the base client invokes a method on the root object with this code, the MTS run time changes the value of the happy flag to False. Now, when the base client releases its connection, the root object is deactivated. During the object's deactivation, the MTS run time sees that the happy flag is False and changes the value of the transaction's doomed flag to True. When the root object is deactivated, the MTS run time calls *Abort* on the transaction.

DisableCommit is complemented by another method named *EnableCommit*, which simply returns the happy flag to True. You can call each of these methods repeatedly. The happy flag is just a Boolean value, so whichever method is called last before the object is deactivated determines how the MTS run time handles the transaction. When you call one of these methods, you simply vote on whether the transaction should succeed. Note that because MTS looks at these bits only after your method has returned control to the context wrapper, you can call *EnableCommit* and *DisableCommit* as many times as you like within a given method. Only the last call that your object's method makes prior to returning control to the context wrapper will actually matter.

Calling *SetComplete* and *SetAbort*

In addition to *DisableCommit* and *EnableCommit*, two other important methods let you control your transaction: *SetComplete* and *SetAbort*. Like the other two methods, these cast a vote by modifying the happy flag. *SetComplete* sets the happy flag to True, while *SetAbort* sets it to False. However, *SetComplete* and *SetAbort* are different from the other two methods because they set the done flag to True. As you'll see, the done flag has a dramatic effect.

As you'll recall from Chapter 9, the context wrapper provides a basis for interception. Interception lets the MTS run time conduct preprocessing and postprocessing on a call-by-call basis. When a method call returns from an MTS object through the context wrapper, the MTS run time inspects the done flag. If the done flag is set to True, the MTS run time deactivates the object. Therefore, when an MTS object calls *SetComplete* or *SetAbort*, the MTS run time deactivates it upon return of the method call. Because *SetAbort* also sets the happy bit to false, this has the effect of dooming the transaction. If, on the other hand, an object that is the root of a transaction calls *SetComplete*, the context wrapper no longer waits for the client to release its reference and tries to commit the transaction immediately. The MTS run time inspects the other flags and decides whether to commit or abort the transaction in the same way it does when calling *EnableCommit* and *DisableCommit*. *SetComplete* and *SetAbort* simply force the MTS run time to end the transaction much faster, which means those expensive locks that your transaction was holding get released earlier, allowing greater scalability. You don't have to wait for the client to release the root object.

It's important to use *SetComplete* and *SetAbort* at the appropriate times. When you cast your vote by calling *DisableCommit* or *EnableCommit*, the transaction and all its locks are held until the base client releases the root object. Calling *SetComplete* or *SetAbort* is much better because the root object forces the MTS run time to release the transaction. It's faster and more reliable. When you work in an OLTP environment, the most important thing you can do to improve concurrency and throughput is to reduce the amount of time that any transaction holds its locks.

You've seen that the MTS run time deactivates the root object and releases the transaction when you call *SetComplete* or *SetAbort*. This leads to another important question: How does the deactivation of the root object affect the client? When a base client invokes a method that includes a call to *SetComplete* or *SetAbort*, the object is deactivated and destroyed. If the client had to deal with the fact that the object has died, you'd have a messy problem. Fortunately, the MTS run time can hide the object's demise from the client. Let's look at how this is possible.

The base client thinks that it's connected directly to the object, but it's really holding a reference to the context wrapper. This allows the MTS run time to perform a little trickery. When the object is deactivated, the client remains connected to the context wrapper. When the base client invokes another method call, the MTS run time creates another instance from the same component and activates it inside the context wrapper. This just-in-time activation policy makes the base client think that it's dealing with a single object across method calls. However, behind the context wrapper, the MTS run time creates and destroys objects on every call.

If a base client continues to call methods that call either *SetComplete* or *SetAbort*, the MTS run time creates and releases a new root object and a new transaction each time. All of this occurs within the window of time that starts with the method call's preprocessing and ends with the postprocessing. This is how you should write your MTS transactions. An MTS transaction and the objects inside it should be flashes in the pan. In the world of OLTP, shorter transactions result in better concurrency and throughput.

Next we'll examine how to add secondary objects to an MTS transaction. The core concepts are the same. The root object still calls *SetComplete* or *SetAbort*. This forces the MTS run time to release the transaction and all the locks that it holds before returning control to the base client. When you program in an OLTP environment, you must adopt a "get in and get out" philosophy. Acquire your locks late and release them early. The MTS programming model gives you plenty of support for this new mind-set.

Multiobject Transactions

As you know, the root object can create secondary objects inside the same transaction by calling *CreateInstance* on components that are marked as either Requires or Supports. Figure 10-6 shows a root object and three secondary objects inside an MTS transaction. If you create these secondary objects correctly, each will have its own context wrapper and thus its own happy flag and done flag.

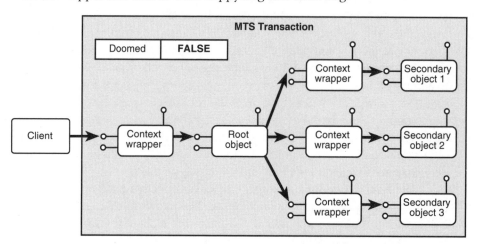

Figure 10-6. *The root object can propagate secondary objects into its transaction by calling* CreateInstance *on components that are marked as Requires or Supports.*

An MTS transaction is a democratic community in which each object gets to vote on whether the transaction should succeed. A secondary object follows the same rules as the root object. When a secondary object is deactivated, the MTS run time inspects its happy flag. If the happy flag is set to False, the MTS run time sets the transaction's doomed flag to True. When this happens, the transaction is doomed to failure. There is nothing that any other object can do to set the doomed flag back to True. As you can see, any object inside a transaction can prevent the transaction from committing.

You'll often write methods in the root object to create secondary objects. Once the secondary objects have been created, the root object can call their methods to complete the work for the transaction. You need to understand how things work inside a transaction so that you can coordinate communication among all these objects.

Let's look at the case in which the root object makes several successful method calls on a secondary object. As long as the secondary object doesn't call *SetComplete* or *SetAbort*, it remains activated until it's released by the root object. The root object can make several successful calls on the secondary object and then call *SetComplete* to commit the transaction. When the root calls *SetComplete*, both objects are deactivated. The secondary object is deactivated first, followed by the root object. As long as neither object sets its happy flag to False by calling *SetAbort* or *DisableCommit*, the transaction is committed.

What happens if the secondary object wants to abort the transaction? If the secondary object calls *SetAbort* and returns, the MTS run time deactivates the object and sets the doomed flag to True. At this point, the root object gets control back and must decide how to deal with the situation. Since the doomed flag is set to True, the root object can't save the transaction. Once a secondary object has been deactivated and has set the doomed flag to True, the root object shouldn't call *SetComplete*. If it does, the base client receives an *mtsErrCtxAborted* error from the MTS run time. Moreover, if the root object tries to activate another object inside the transaction after the doomed flag is set to True, it experiences an *mtsErrCtxAborting* error.

If the root object simply returns control to its caller at this point without calling *SetComplete* or *SetAbort*, the MTS run time sees that the doomed flag has been set to True and it releases the transaction and deactivates all the secondary objects. This results in an unfortunate situation. The root object is left activated in a crippled state. Future method calls on the root object will more than likely result in *mtsErrCtxAborted* and *mtsErrCtxAborting* errors being raised by the MTS run time.

These problems should lead you to one conclusion. When a secondary object calls *SetAbort*, the root object should also call *SetAbort* and halt any attempt to complete additional work. However, there's one small hitch. The root cannot examine the doomed flag. It can't ask the MTS run time whether a secondary object has called *SetAbort*. Therefore, your secondary objects must communicate with the root object when it calls *SetAbort*. You can use the return value or output parameters in the methods of your secondary objects to indicate whether they called *SetAbort*, or you can raise errors from the secondary objects back to the root object.

For example, if a secondary object decides to roll back the entire transaction in *Method1*, it can use the following sequence of calls:

```
Dim ObjCtx As ObjectContext
Set ObjCtx = GetObjectContext()
ObjCtx.SetAbort
Dim ErrorCode As Long, Description As String
ErrorCode = myErrorEnum1 ' Something like (vbObjectError + 3)
Description = "The requested quantity is not available"
Err.Raise ErrorCode, , Description
```

If you follow this convention, a method in the root object can assume that all secondary objects raise an error after calling *SetAbort*. This means that an error handler in the root object should call *SetAbort* and raise its own error to forward the secondary object's error message back to the base client. If the root object can call methods on the secondary objects without experiencing an error, it can assume that everything is fine and call *SetComplete*. You can see what a method call in the root object looks like on the following page.

```
Sub RootMethod1()
    On Error GoTo MyRootMethod_Err
    Dim ObjCtx As ObjectContext
    Set ObjCtx = GetObjectContext()
    Dim Secondary1 As CSecondary
    Set Secondary1 = ObjCtx.CreateInstance("MyDll.CSecondary")
    Secondary1.Method1
    ' Commit transaction if call completes successfully.
    ObjCtx.SetComplete
Exit Sub
MyRootMethod_Err:
    ' Roll back transaction and get out ASAP on error.
    ObjCtx.SetAbort
    ' Forward error information back to base client.
    Err.Raise Err.Number, , Err.Description
End Sub
```

Of course, this code shows one of many possible approaches. If you take a different approach, be sure you carefully coordinate the communication between the secondary objects and the root object.

At times, you might call *DisableCommit* in a secondary object and return control to the root. If you do this, the secondary object indicates that it can't commit its work in its present state. However, *DisableCommit* doesn't deactivate the secondary object upon return to the root object. This is different from a call to *SetAbort*, in which the MTS run time deactivates the secondary object before the root object gets control back. A call to *SetAbort* dooms the transaction to failure. When a secondary object calls *DisableCommit*, it says, "I am currently unhappy, but perhaps the root object can invoke another method and make me change my mind."

As you might imagine, using *DisableCommit* requires you to design a more elaborate communication protocol among the objects inside a transaction. When a secondary object calls *DisableCommit*, the root object can try to persuade the object to change its mind by executing additional methods. However, the root object must ultimately call *SetComplete* or *SetAbort*. Therefore, the root object must find a way to make the secondary object happy or determine that the transaction can't be saved.

You should avoid calling *DisableCommit* from the root object. You don't want to pass control back to the base client when a transaction is pending. Never allow the base client to control when the locks are released. This will probably result in locks being left on data items for longer than necessary. It also makes the transaction vulnerable to the 60-second timeout used by MTS. This conflicts with your newfound "get in and get out" mind-set. OK, enough said.

Enlisting Connections to Resource Managers

Now that we've covered the basics of how to commit and roll back an MTS transaction, let's discuss how to write your changes. You must connect one or more of the objects that you create inside a transaction to a resource manager, as you see illustrated in Figure 10-7. Once these connections are established, you must enlist them with the DTC. This involves setting up a line of communication between the DTC for your MTS application and the DTC of each resource manager. As you saw earlier in this chapter, these lines of communication are used to execute the two-phase commit protocol.

Enlisting a connection in an MTS application is actually quite simple. You just have to follow two rules. First, make sure you establish the connection from an object running inside a transaction. Second, make sure that the RM and the RM proxy you're using support OLE Transactions. If you follow these rules, the MTS run time will automatically interact with the RM proxy and the DTC to enlist the connection.

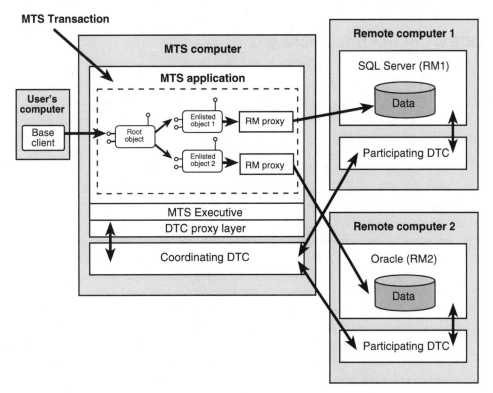

Figure 10-7. *When you create a connection to a resource manager such as SQL Server or Oracle from an object inside an MTS transaction, the MTS run time and the RM proxy automatically enlist the resource manager with the DTC. When the root object is deactivated, the MTS run time calls Abort or Commit to begin executing the two-phase commit protocol.*

When you make a typical connection using ADO, RDO, or ODBC, your write and read operations are automatically part of a distributed transaction. It couldn't be easier. Let's look at an example. If you're working with SQL Server 6.5 and connecting through ADO with an ODBC driver, you can connect with this code:

```
Dim conn As ADODB.Connection, sConnectString As String
Set conn = New ADODB.Connection
sConnectString = "DSN=MyDatabase;UID=BusAccount1;PWD=rosebud"
conn.Open sConnectString
```

As you can see, this is the same code that you'd write to create any ADO connection. The MTS run time has prepared the ODBC Driver Manager to auto-enlist any ODBC connection made from inside an MTS transaction. The RM proxy (the ODBC driver in this case) interacts with the DBMS to establish a connection between the DTCs running on two different nodes, as shown in Figure 10-7 on the preceding page. You simply make your connections and begin accessing data. All of your changes are charged against a single distributed transaction that's being controlled by the MTS run time.

ODBC Connection Pooling

The ODBC Driver Manager is an *MTS resource dispenser*. The MTS programming model uses the abstraction of resource dispensers to model plug-in modules that work with the MTS run time to efficiently share resources among MTS objects. The MTS SDK has a specification that details the requirements of writing resource dispensers for MTS applications. The ODBC Driver Manager has been written to pool both standard connections and enlisted connections and to share them across MTS objects.

Here's how standard connection pooling works. When you initially establish an ODBC connection in one of your MTS objects, the ODBC Driver Manager goes through a handshake with the DBMS that involves passing a user ID and password. When the application logs on, the DBMS verifies the security profile of the user and returns a connection handle. This connection handle allows the application to submit SQL statements to the database. Establishing an ODBC connection consumes processing cycles on both computers and requires at least one round-trip between the connecting application and the DBMS.

When your object releases a connection, the ODBC driver doesn't drop the connection to the DBMS. Instead, it places the connection handle in a pool for future use by other objects. When another object attempts to connect to the same DBMS, the ODBC Driver Manager looks through the pool to see whether a connection is available. It compares the connect string of the requested connection with the connect string of the connections in the pool. If it finds a match, it allocates a connection without going through the logon process again. This speeds things up and significantly improves the scalability of any middle-tier application that is handling concurrent requests from multiple clients. You should note that this standard connection pooling isn't unique to MTS. The ODBC Driver Manager offers this capability to other applications, such as the Web server process for Internet Information Server (IIS).

The ODBC Driver Manager manages the connection pool dynamically. It creates additional connections as the traffic in your application picks up. It also dynamically releases connections to the DBMS when things slow down. It's great that all this happens behind the scenes. Just remember that objects can share a pooled connection only if they all agree on the same server, user name, and password. Be sure that every component in an MTS application uses the same connect string when it opens a connection to a particular DBMS.

The ODBC resource dispenser provides one other feature in the MTS run-time environment that is not available to other applications that use ODBC connection pooling. The ODBC resource dispenser is capable of pooling enlisted connections. As you have already seen, when a connection is established, it requires a round-trip to and from the DBMS. Likewise, when a connection is enlisted in a distributed transaction, it requires another round-trip to and from the DBMS. The pooling of enlisted connections is a further optimization to reduce round-trips. And as you remember from Chapter 6, round-trips are inherently evil. You should always be looking for ways to reduce the number of round-trips it takes to complete an operation. The pooling of enlisted connections is a great way to enhance performance.

When you close an enlisted connection from an object running inside a transaction, the ODBC resource dispenser returns it to the pool. If another object inside the same transaction requests a connection using the same connect string, the ODBC resource dispenser can use the same preenlisted connection. This means that several objects inside a single transaction can open and close ODBC connections without incurring redundant round-trips to and from the same DBMS for enlistment. The MTS run time takes care of cleaning up the enlisted connection when the transaction is released.

All this affects the way you write data access code because the way you write data access code for MTS is very different from the way you write it for a two-tier application. The two-tier style of writing data access code promotes conducting as many operations as possible through a single open connection because opening connections is very expensive in the absence of connection pooling. In the MTS programming model, you'll be opening and closing connections much more frequently, often within the scope of a single method.

A secondary object usually opens and closes a connection inside each method that is called from the root object. The secondary object should always close the connection before returning control to the root object. Here's what can happen if you don't follow this rule: When one secondary object returns to the root object without closing its connection, the connection will not be returned to the pool. If the root object calls upon another secondary object to perform other operations in the same database, another physical connection must be used. The second connection will require at least one unnecessary round-trip to and from the DBMS for enlistment and possibly another to establish the connection.

Partitioning Business Logic and Data Access Code

Figure 10-7, shown earlier, provides an example of two secondary objects that have each enlisted a connection in an MTS transaction. One connection is to a SQL Server database and the other to an Oracle database. Such a design lets you package the data access code for one connection in one Visual Basic class module and the data access code for the other connection in a second class module. This is a common way to write an MTS application, but it is only one of many possibilities. The approach you take is largely a matter of programming style.

You can also establish a connection to an RM directly from the root object. The root object can enlist a connection and make changes just as secondary objects can. This might result in a simpler design. However, if you do this, you'll create a single class that contains both your business logic and your data access code. In larger designs, it is common to run your business logic in the root object and run your data access code in secondary objects. The root object models the high-level composer of a transaction's workflow. The root object composes a transaction by delegating data access to secondary objects.

If you use this style of programming, each secondary object represents a connection to a DBMS or possibly a more granular entity inside the DBMS, such as a table. Each secondary object directly connects to and enlists with a resource manager. With this approach, secondary objects are also known as enlisted objects.

In an MTS application, each enlisted object should acquire and release its own connection. Don't try to share an open connection by passing an ADO connection reference between objects. Acquiring and releasing connections doesn't impose a performance penalty because the ODBC resource dispenser will reuse a preenlisted connection if one is available. Also keep in mind that no problems will arise because of concurrency. As you remember, each MTS transaction lives inside a single activity, which means that there's a single flow of control. No two objects inside the same transaction will ever be running a method call at the same time. As long as all secondary objects close their connections before returning control, the transaction as a whole will never require more than a single connection to any data source.

While MTS can help you avoid round-trips to and from the DBMS when you're establishing and enlisting connections, it doesn't automatically optimize the data access code that you write. When you open a connection and begin to perform read and write operations, your code will result in round-trips to and from the DBMS. As you design your MTS applications, you should be aware of how many round-trips you're making to the DBMS and back. Reducing round-trips in data access code is one of the best ways to increase the scalability of a distributed application.

Let's look at an example. Suppose you're writing a method in a secondary object to remove a requested quantity of a certain product from inventory. It's natural for a secondary object to accomplish this in two discrete database operations. First, the secondary object can run a SELECT statement to open an ADO recordset on the Products table. This allows the secondary object to determine whether the quantity currently in inventory is enough to satisfy the order request. If the requested quantity is greater than the inventory quantity, the secondary object should call *SetAbort* and raise an error back to the root object. Then, if the requested quantity is less than or equal to the inventory quantity, the secondary object can complete its mission by running an UPDATE statement against the Products table. The upside to this approach is that it allows you to maintain your logic inside your MTS component by using Visual Basic. The downside to this approach is that it takes two round-trips to and from the DBMS to complete an operation that could be completed in one.

So how can you conduct multiple operations in a single round-trip to and from the DBMS? Unfortunately, the answer is usually writing more logic in SQL and less logic in Visual Basic. You can either submit SQL batches or execute stored procedures to conduct multiple operations in a single round-trip. This means that stored procedures are as important to an MTS application as they are to a two-tier application. Some people claim that stored procedures don't have a place in three-tier development. They don't understand the importance of reducing round-trips between the middle-tier application and the DBMS.

Let's look at one more example. Suppose you create a separate MTS component for each table in the database. If you are dealing with the Products table, the Customers table, and the Orders table, you can create a separate Visual Basic class for each table. This provides great modularity and a pure object-oriented design because it creates a natural one-to-one mapping between tables and classes. However, because each component is conducting its operations independently, your transaction will require at least one round-trip to and from the DBMS per component.

You can further reduce the number of your round-trips by modeling a single Visual Basic class for each database connection. This will give you the ability to conduct all your operations in as few round-trips as possible. If you take this to the extreme, you'll have one stored procedure for each connection. The upside to this approach is that it will give you the best performance and scalability. The downside is that you'll write and maintain more of your logic in SQL and less in Visual Basic. Additionally, you'll have to deal with raising errors in SQL and propagating them back to your Visual Basic code. This is more complicated than raising errors between two Visual Basic objects.

As you can see, you must make some difficult decisions when you design your data access code. From the perspective of application design and code maintenance, it's desirable to create an MTS component for each table in the database and write as much logic as possible in Visual Basic. From a scalability point of view, it's better to conduct multiple operations inside stored procedures. Unfortunately, there's no single answer that will lead to object-oriented design purity and scalability. Then again, scalability is usually an important requirement of an OLTP application, while a pure object-oriented design is not.

Avoiding Deadlocks

Creating an OLTP application typically requires balancing two antagonistic forces. On one hand, you want the highest possible levels of concurrency. On the other hand, you must have isolation to guarantee the consistency of your data. This means that the system must place locks on data items to block certain transactions while other transactions perform their work. Unfortunately, in an OLTP application concurrency and consistency are always in conflict.

As you've seen, an MTS application runs its transactions with an isolation level of Serializable. This means that the integrity of the system's data is the primary concern. If you write your business logic and data access code correctly, the two-phase commit protocol will make sure that your data stays in a consistent form. Most of the time when a transaction is blocked, it simply waits its turn and then gets to do its work. However, sometimes the locks acquired by a transaction don't have the desired effect.

In some situations, the locks held by two or more transactions conflict in such a way that the conflict can't be resolved by waiting. This is known as a *deadlock*. For example, suppose *transaction A* has acquired a write lock on *data item X* and is attempting to acquire a write lock on *data item Y* to complete its work. If *transaction B* has acquired a write lock on *data item Y* and is waiting on the write lock held on *data item X*, the two transactions have hit a stalemate. Without intervention, both transactions will wait indefinitely for the other to release its locks.

A single DBMS such as SQL Server can detect a deadlock situation. SQL Server resolves a deadlock by terminating one of the transactions and sending an error message to the victim. When the locks of the victim are released, the other transaction can complete its work. In a distributed transaction, some deadlock situations can't be detected by any single resource manager. This is why MTS transactions have a timeout of 60 seconds. If a transaction cannot be completed within a minute, the DTC assumes that a deadlock has occurred. In either case, your code must be ready to deal with deadlock errors when they arise.

To prevent deadlocks in your MTS applications, you can employ a few techniques. For example, a *cyclic deadlock* can occur when two programmers have written separate transactions for the same system. For example, one programmer might write a transaction that modifies the Products table and then the Customers table. If another programmer writes a second transaction that accesses the same tables in reverse order, the chance of a deadlock is greater. You can reduce the chances of cyclic deadlocks by maintaining a consistent flow of data access across all the transactions that run in a single system.

Deadlocks resulting from lock conversion are also common and require your attention. Let's say that you're writing a transaction that removes a specific quantity of a product from inventory. Your transaction starts by running a SELECT statement against the Products table to find out whether the requested quantity is in stock. If the inventory quantity is equal to or greater than the requested quantity, you then run an UPDATE statement to remove the quantity from inventory. We'll assume that the SELECT statement and the UPDATE statement are both run against the same record in the Products table.

In a high-volume OTLP application, there's a good chance that two separate transactions will both run the SELECT statement and acquire read locks before either can acquire the write lock required for the UPDATE statement. This results in a deadlock. Each transaction waits for the other to remove its read lock so that it can acquire a write lock. The problem is that the transaction first acquires a read lock on a data item and then tries to convert the lock to a write lock. If two transactions acquire the read lock at the same time, neither party can convert the lock to a write lock.

SQL Server supports another type of lock called an *update lock,* which solves this problem. You should use an update lock whenever you need to escalate a read lock to a write lock during a transaction. An update lock conflicts with write locks and with other update locks. A transaction will block while trying to acquire an update lock if another transaction has already acquired a write lock or an update lock. However, unlike a write lock, an update lock doesn't conflict with read locks. If a transaction holds a read lock on a data item, another transaction can acquire an update lock. Likewise, if one transaction holds an update lock, other transactions can acquire read locks.

An update lock can solve the lock conversion problem without having as dramatic an impact on concurrency as a write lock. You can explicitly ask for an update lock by using the (UPDLOCK) hint in a Transact-SQL SELECT statement. Here's an example of using an update hint in a SELECT statement with ADO:

```
Dim sSQL As String
sSQL = "SELECT Quantity" & _ .
       " FROM Products (UPDLOCK)" & _
       " WHERE Product = 'Dog'"
Dim rs As ADODB.Recordset
Set rs = New ADODB.Recordset
rs.CursorLocation = adUseClient
rs.CursorType = adOpenForwardOnly
rs.LockType = adLockReadOnly
' Assume conn is an open connection.
rs.Open sSQL, conn
```

(continued)

229

```
Dim Quantity As Long
Quantity = rs.Fields("Quantity")
' The update lock is now in place.
' Execute UPDATE statement if appropriate.
```

Be sure to use parentheses when you use a hint with SQL Server. If you forget them, SQL Server will interpret the hint as an alias for the table name.

The ODBC driver for SQL Server 6.5 also uses update locks if you use pessimistic locking with server-side cursors. The following code doesn't use the (UPDLOCK) hint, but it has the same effect:

```
Dim sSQL As String
sSQL = "SELECT Quantity" & _
       " FROM Products " & _
       " WHERE Product = 'Dog'"
Dim rs As ADODB.Recordset
Set rs = New ADODB.Recordset
rs.CursorLocation = adUseServer
rs.CursorType = adOpenDynamic
rs.LockType = adLockPessimistic
' Assume conn is an open connection.
rs.Open sSQL, conn
Dim Quantity As Long
Quantity = rs.Fields("Quantity")
' The update lock is now in place.
' Execute UPDATE statement if appropriate.
```

Both of these examples show how to eliminate deadlocks caused by lock conversion. While you can write your applications to eliminate some types of deadlocks, other types are unavoidable in a large OLTP system. Some deadlocks will be caught by the DBMS; others will be caught when an MTS transaction reaches its timeout value.

You must plan to trap deadlock errors when they occur and handle them as gracefully as possible. Sometimes you can handle a deadlock by resubmitting the transaction. This can hide the deadlock from the user of the application. At other times, you might be forced to return an error to the caller along with instructions to "try again later."

Much Ado About Statelessness

As I've said, to reach higher levels of system concurrency and performance, your locks must be released as quickly as possible. With MTS, transactions stay alive, locks and all, until you release them by calling *SetComplete* or *SetAbort* in the root object. When you use these functions, MTS also destroys all the objects associated with the transaction as part of the cleanup process. Therefore, the root object and any enlisted objects live for only the duration of a single method call. This programming model is much different from those of classic object-oriented programming (OOP) and COM and requires a new way of thinking.

The OOP and COM programming paradigms fail to address scenarios in which state is discarded at the completion of each method call. Object-oriented clients assume that they can obtain a persistent reference to a long-lived object. If a client modifies a state within an object, object-oriented programmers assume that the object will hold these changes across multiple method calls. This isn't the case with transactional objects in the MTS environment. Each object must die as part of the transaction's cleanup, and its state must go along with it.

This transparent destruction of transactional objects is known as *stateless programming*. In the short history of MTS, there has been a good deal of confusion about why statelessness is an essential aspect of the programming model. Quite a few books and articles have suggested that stateless programming is about reclaiming memory on the computer running the MTS application. They argue that destroying objects and reclaiming memory results in higher levels of scalability because of more efficient resource usage. This argument is both confusing and inaccurate.

MTS supports stateless programming to ensure the semantics of a transaction. This has nothing to do with reclaiming memory on the computer running your MTS application. The idea is that an object in an MTS application can see a data item in a consistent state only while the RM is holding a lock. If an MTS object holds a copy of this data item after the lock has been released, another transaction can modify the original data item inside the RM. The original data item and the copy can thus get out of sync and violate the ACID rules of a transaction. The point of stateless programming is that any copy of a data item must be thrown away when the RM releases its locks. This is why MTS requires that all transactional objects be destroyed when a transaction is released.

If you have an object that isn't involved in a transaction and doesn't acquire locks on an RM, having the object retain state across method calls is no problem. If you set a component's transaction support property to Does Not Support Transactions and don't call *SetComplete* or *SetAbort*, you can create stateful MTS objects.

Consider the disadvantages of statelessness: If you can't maintain state in an object, you must pass initialization parameters in every method call. For example, if you use a customer object, you must pass the primary key or some other logical ID for the customer in each method call. This isn't only tedious when it comes to defining methods but can actually decrease a system's scalability. Method calls require more parameters, which results in more network traffic. Every call requires additional processing cycles from the server for the creation, initialization, and activation of a physical object. If just-in-time activation requires complex calculations or database access, statelessness can reduce scalability.

As you can see, you must carefully weigh the pros and cons when you decide whether you really need a stateless object. Objects that are stateful definitely have a place in MTS programming as long as they aren't part of a transaction. Stateful objects can retain their logical identity and save processing cycles that are required to create and initialize new instances. You can also use stateful objects to accomplish many programming tasks that are impossible with stateless objects.

Writing Transactions for MTS

This book's companion CD contains a sample MTS project named the Market application, which demonstrates many of the principles presented in this chapter. The application includes an ActiveX DLL with a few MTS components that you can install with the MTS Explorer. It also includes a form-based Visual Basic application that runs as a base client and the required setup scripts to create the Market database in SQL Server. This application should help reinforce the concepts in this chapter and give you ideas about creating your own OLTP applications.

You should try to gain a solid understanding of the database APIs and resource managers that you will use to create your applications. Visual Studio includes many productivity features for writing data access code with ADO and for creating SQL Server databases. For instance, you can create and debug stored procedures inside the Visual Basic IDE. To learn what's available with Visual Basic 6, pick up a copy of the sixth edition of *The Hitchhiker's Guide to Visual Basic and SQL Server,* by Bill Vaughn (Microsoft Press). This book also has excellent coverage of both ADO and SQL Server. I highly recommend it as a desktop reference.

You should also take the time to learn how to optimize your applications for each resource manager you will work with. You'll find many ways to tune a DBMS such as SQL Server and Oracle to gain significantly higher levels of concurrency and throughput. In most cases, tuning a DBMS requires that you understand how the lock manager works and how to tune your data access code and stored procedures to find the best balance between isolation and concurrency.

Chapter 11

Programming with Microsoft Message Queue

Message queuing has traditionally been an integral part of distributed application programming. Products such as IBM's MQSeries are popular because they add an extra dimension that can't be achieved with a synchronous, connection-oriented communications mechanism such as Remote Procedure Call (RPC). This chapter explains why and when you should use queues in a distributed application and how queues can add responsiveness and reliability to an online transaction processing (OLTP) application that can't be achieved by other means.

You'll also learn about message passing and Microsoft Message Queue (MSMQ) programming, as well as how to send and receive messages with Microsoft Visual Basic. You'll learn common techniques for managing queues and messages, and you'll learn how to pack parameterized information into a message body and unpack it on the receiving side.

The chapter also explains transactional programming with MSMQ. You must send transacted messages to transactional queues in order to be guaranteed exactly one delivery. You'll learn two straightforward techniques for sending and receiving transactional messages with MSMQ and Visual Basic: You can leverage MSMQ's internal transactioning mechanism, or you can use a Microsoft Transaction Server (MTS) transaction.

The chapter concludes with a description of the queue types that you can use to create an MSMQ application: response queues, administration queues, journal queues, and dead letter queues.

WHY ARE QUEUES IMPORTANT?

The basic idea behind message queues is simple. A queue is a named, ordered repository of messages. Figure 11-1 shows how a queue is typically used in a distributed application. A message is a request or some other type of notification that is sent from one application to another in the same system.

A sender application creates and prepares a message by setting various properties in the message header and packing parameterized information into a payload, which is called the message body. After preparing the message, the sender application writes it to the queue. A receiver application reads the message and removes it from the queue so that it's processed only once. The receiver application then interprets the request, unpacks the parameters from the body, and carries out whatever processing is required.

Message queues also support the concept of a reader application. This type of application can examine a message in a queue without removing it. This is known as *peeking*. Peeking allows an application to be selective about the messages it removes from a queue.

Any application can assume more than one of these roles. It's common for an application to act as both a reader and a receiver on a single queue. The application can look at what's in the queue and remove only those messages that meet certain criteria. It is also common for one application to receive messages from one queue while sending messages to a second queue.

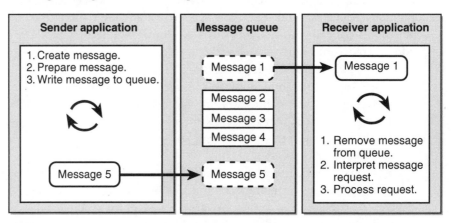

Figure 11-1. *A sender application creates and prepares a message and then writes it to the queue. A receiver application removes the message from the queue, interprets the message's request, and executes whatever processing the message requires.*

A message queue is a valuable building block in a distributed system because it allows applications to submit requests and send information to other applications in a connectionless, asynchronous manner. In some ways, message passing is like RPC, and in other ways it's very different. As you've seen throughout this book, COM uses RPC to issue interprocess requests between clients and objects. Let's compare using messages to using RPC for communicating between applications in a distributed system.

Every RPC actually requires two distinct messages. A request message that carries inbound parameters is sent from the client to the object. After executing the method implementation, the object sends a response message to the client that carries the return value and output parameters. One of the best things about Distributed COM and RPC is that they hide the complexities of passing these messages between the client and the object. You simply create an object and invoke a method. You don't have to think about sending and receiving messages. The proxy and the stub work together with the RPC layer to marshal the data back and forth and control the flow of execution. COM and RPC make sending the request, executing the method implementation, and receiving the response seem like a single operation to the caller.

While COM and RPC simplify interprocess communication, they have a few notable limitations because RPC bundles the request message, the method execution, and the response message into one indivisible operation. Queues let you overcome some of the shortcomings of RPC, but programming with queues requires more work because you have to explicitly send and receive messages.

Let's look at five common problems with RPC that you can solve by using message queues. The first problem is that the client's thread of control is blocked while the object executes a method call. In other words, method calls based on COM and RPC are synchronous. If an object takes considerable time to process a method call, the client's thread is held hostage by the underlying RPC layer until it receives the object's response. If you use a message queue, a client can post an asynchronous request to the queue. The client doesn't have to wait for a server's response before continuing its work; it can continue its work immediately after submitting a request. Furthermore, the server application that receives the client's message can process the request and send an asynchronous message to the response queue being monitored by the client. While this style of asynchronous programming adds complexity to the interaction between a client application and a server, it can increase efficiency.

A second problem with RPC is that it requires an established connection between the client and the server. Both the client application and the server must be on line at the same time for the application as a whole to be operational. For example, if the server is off line, the client can't submit a request. Likewise, if the client is off line, the server can't process any requests. In essence, neither side can get any work done unless the other side is up and running. This poses an unacceptable constraint for many distributed applications. Think about what this means to a large N-tier information system. A middle-tier application or a database management system (DBMS) might go off line due to a system crash or scheduled maintenance. If the system is based on RPC, clients must wait until all the servers come back on line before they can resume making requests.

A queue can solve this problem because it acts as a buffer between the client application and the server. The client application can continue to send request messages to a queue regardless of whether the server is on line. When the server comes back on line, it can resume responding to the requests that have accumulated. A server can also continue its work after client applications have gone off line. The queue acts as a buffering mechanism that allows either side to accomplish its work in the absence of the other.

A third problem with RPC is that a client application must make a connection to a specific server. RPC has no built-in capacity to distribute the load of processing client requests across a group of servers. If you need load balancing in an RPC-based system, you must typically write code that directs some users to one server and other users to another server. However, most load balancing schemes used in RPC-style applications are vulnerable to problems because the users who are connected to one server might submit a lot of requests while the users connected to a second server aren't sending any requests. One server will become overloaded while the other server sits idle. A queue can provide a much better solution.

Figure 11-2 shows a queue-based approach to load balancing. If every client application sends requests to a single queue, a group of servers can work together to

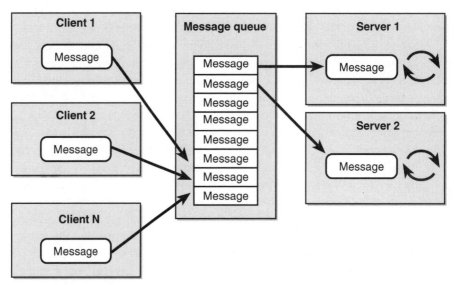

Figure 11-2. *A queue provides an easy way to balance the processing load across a group of servers. This style of load balancing is less complex and more efficient than the algorithms used in most RPC-based systems.*

process these messages. The queue acts as a central clearinghouse for every request in the application. One server will never be overloaded while another server sits idle.

A fourth problem with RPC is that all requests are processed on a first come, first served basis. There is no way to prioritize calls. A high-priority request must wait its turn if low-priority requests were submitted ahead of it. A queue can solve this problem by assigning priority levels to messages. Messages with a higher priority level are placed at the head of the queue, while lower-priority messages are placed at the tail. The server can thus respond to the most important messages first.

The fifth (and arguably the most significant) problem with RPC is that it is vulnerable to failures that lead to inconsistent results in OLTP applications. Let's look at what can go wrong when a base client invokes an RPC-based method call to run an MTS transaction. There are three possible cases for failure. First, the method call's request message might fail between the client and the server. Second, the MTS application might crash while the method call is executing a transaction. In both of these scenarios, the intended changes of the transaction are not committed. The third failure scenario is that the method call's response message to the client might fail or be lost after the method call has successfully run and committed the transaction.

So here's the trouble. What if a client submits a transaction through RPC but doesn't get a successful response? The client application has no way of knowing whether the transaction has been committed. If the client submits the same request a second time, the transaction might be committed a second time. As you can see, this creates a problem that RPC can't solve by itself.

Transactional message queues provide a way to submit a transaction request with exactly-once delivery semantics. You can run a transaction with exactly-once semantics by breaking it down into three distinct phases in which messages are sent and received from transactional queues. Figure 11-3 shows these three phases.

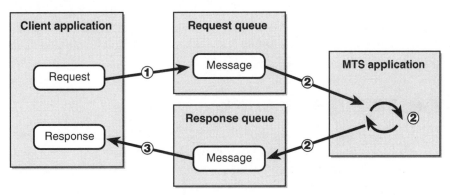

Figure 11-3. *Running a transaction with exactly-once semantics involves using a transactional queue in three distinct phases.*

First the client submits a message to a queue that is known as the *request queue*. In the second phase, the server carries out three steps within a single high-level transaction. It receives the message from the request queue, processes the transaction requested by the client, and writes a message to a *response queue*.

In this second phase, the server must successfully accomplish all three steps, or the high-level transaction will be rolled back. If the high-level transaction in phase two is rolled back, the client's message is returned to the request queue. This means that if phase two fails, the application that's running transactions can start phase two from scratch by receiving the message from the request queue a second time. When phase two completes successfully, it means the requested transaction has been committed. It also means that you'll find a corresponding message in the response queue. In the third phase, the client application receives a message from the response queue indicating that the transaction has been successfully committed.

This example doesn't address all the complexities you'll face in a transactional application, but it reveals the essence of why message passing is superior to RPC. Queues give the client the ability to determine which of three possible states a request is in. A request can be waiting to be processed, in the state of being processed, or finished being processed. If the client sees that the original message is still in the request queue, the request hasn't been processed. If the client finds a corresponding message in the response queue, it knows the request has been processed. If there isn't a message in either queue, the client knows the request is currently being processed. RPC isn't as good as message passing because it doesn't allow the client to determine the exact status of a request.

Now that you know how queues can improve your distributed applications, let's put this knowledge to work using MSMQ. As you program with MSMQ, you'll see that it requires more effort than writing COM-based method calls. When you use Distributed COM and RPC, you basically get all of your interprocess communication for free. When you use MSMQ, you have to invest more time in both application design and programming. However, when you consider the limitations of RPC, MSMQ is well worth the time and energy you invest.

THE MSMQ NETWORK

Without going into the level of detail that an MSMQ administrator would require, I'll explain how to set up MSMQ in a network environment. You'll learn enough about how MSMQ works in a production environment to get started if you need to set up MSMQ on one or more development workstations. We'll begin with some high-level concepts and general MSMQ terminology.

An *MSMQ enterprise* is a set of computers that send and receive messages to and from a common set of queues. While it's possible to pass messages across enterprises, this can cause unnecessary problems. So a company should typically configure all of its computers to run within a single MSMQ enterprise.

An enterprise can be divided into *MSMQ sites*. A site is typically a set of computers in the same physical location. For example, a company with a single MSMQ enterprise can set up sites in London, Boston, and Los Angeles. The communication between computers in a site should be fast and inexpensive. Messages sent between sites must pass across *site links*. An MSMQ administrator can tune these links to optimize performance.

MSMQ also lets you assign a set of computers to a *connected network* (CN), a collection of computers that run the same protocol and can therefore communicate directly with one another. When a message is sent between two computers that do not belong to the same CN, the message must be routed through other computers. A computer can be a member of more than one CN. A CN is usually set up to run within a single site, but this isn't a requirement. You can create a CN that spans multiple sites.

The computers that are responsible for managing an MSMQ enterprise maintain administrative information in a distributed database known as the *MSMQ Information Store* (MQIS). The MQIS holds information such as a list of all the computers in the enterprise and a list of all the public queues. The MQIS is physically stored in one or more SQL Server databases. Complicated enterprises use the replication features of SQL Server to keep the information in each SQL Server database up to date.

The first installation of MSMQ in any enterprise must be on a computer that will serve as the *primary enterprise controller* (PEC). This computer must run both Windows NT Server and SQL Server. It also acts as the controller for its site. When you create another site, you should configure a second computer to act as a *primary site controller* (PSC). Each PSC uses a SQL Server database to hold a copy of the MQIS. To improve fault tolerance and load balancing, you can configure additional computers to act as *backup site controllers* (BSCs). A BSC maintains a read-only copy of the MQIS.

You can also configure a computer to run as an *MSMQ routing server*. A routing server can accept a message from one computer and forward it to its destination queue. You can thus pass messages between computers that aren't in the same CN. For example, if the sending computer is running only the IP protocol and the destination queue is on a computer running only the IPX protocol, the routing server can use its store-and-forward capabilities to get the message to its destination. A routing server also acts as a clearinghouse that stores messages until the computer with the destination queue comes back on line. Every PEC, PSC, and BSC acts as a routing server in addition to its other responsibilities. You can add more routing servers to the network to handle higher volumes of message traffic.

The four types of MSMQ computers that I've described so far are all examples of MSMQ servers. You can also configure a computer running MSMQ to run as an independent client or a dependent client. An independent client, like a server, can manage its own local queues. This is a good choice for remote computers because a sender application can send messages to a local queue when the user isn't connected to the network. Later, when the remote computer establishes a connection to the network, MSMQ will automatically forward the messages to their destination queue.

A dependent client can't maintain queues locally. It must be directly connected to an MSMQ server in order to send and receive messages. A computer that's always connected to MSMQ servers across a LAN is typically the only type of machine that you would run as a dependent client.

Before installing MSMQ, you should consider which version you need. One version of MSMQ is part of the Windows NT Option Pack, and the other version is part of Windows NT Server Enterprise Edition. You can use the option pack version for developing MSMQ applications in a small production environment. The version included with Windows NT Server Enterprise Edition can accommodate many more users and offers more flexibility in terms of installation and intersite routing. Consult the MSMQ documentation for more details.

INSTALLING MSMQ

Let's say you want to use to use the option pack version of MSMQ so that you can start developing MSMQ applications. First you must configure a computer to play the role of the PEC. You should install Windows NT Server and SQL Server (including the latest service packs) before you install MSMQ.

To begin the PEC installation, run the Windows NT Option Pack setup program and indicate that you want to install MSMQ. MSMQ isn't part of the default installation for the option pack. When you're asked what type of MSMQ configuration you want to run, indicate that you want to install a PEC. (Any other type of installation requires an existing PEC.) During the installation of the PEC, you'll be prompted for three names: an enterprise name, a site name, and the name of at least one CN. For the CN, you must also select a network protocol, such as IP.

After you configure the PEC, you can install MSMQ on other computers to run within the same enterprise. When you select another configuration such as a PSC or an independent client, the MSMQ installation will prompt you to enter the computer name of the PEC. (Note that you enter the computer name, not the enterprise name or the site name.) The computer on which you install MSMQ must be connected to the PEC or some other MSMQ server that has a copy of the MQIS.

The main administration tool for MSMQ is the MSMQ Explorer. This tool provides an easy-to-use interface, as shown in Figure 11-4. You should become familiar with this tool because it makes it easy to create and manage queues during development. Note that a computer must be able to connect to the MQIS in order to run the

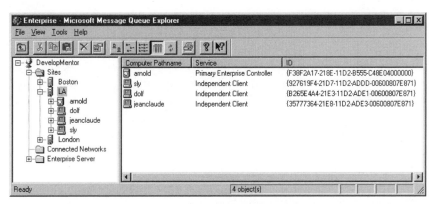

Figure 11-4. *You can use the MSMQ Explorer to quickly create, purge, and delete queues. You can also use it to examine the properties of messages that have been sent to a particular queue.*

MSMQ Explorer. For example, if your development machine is configured to run as an independent client, you can run the MSMQ Explorer only while you are connected to the network.

After installing the PEC, you have a few choices when you install MSMQ on other computers. If you are installing MSMQ on Windows NT Workstation with the Windows NT Option Pack, you can configure your computer to run only as an independent client or a dependent client. Installing MSMQ as an independent client is a good choice when your development workstation is always connected to the network. As long as an independent client is connected to the PEC, a PSC, or a BSC, it can do things that require the MQIS, such as run queries to find public queues and use the MSMQ Explorer.

If you develop on a laptop computer, you might not want to configure your computer as an independent client. If you want the full functionality of MSMQ when your computer is disconnected from the network, you must have a local copy of the MQIS. This means that you must configure your computer as a PEC, a PSC, or a BSC. In each case, your laptop computer must run Windows NT Server and SQL Server. You therefore need a fast computer and at least 128 MB of memory. As you can see, you must weigh quite a few issues before you configure your development workstation with MSMQ.

OK, that's enough administrative overhead to give you one heck of a headache. MSMQ involves lots of networking complexity, and it takes a lot of experience to design and deploy MSMQ in a large enterprise. However, the good news is that this undertaking is usually the responsibility of network engineers and administrators. At this point, you should have enough information to install MSMQ on the computers in your development environment. Now let's start writing MSMQ applications that send and receive messages.

PROGRAMMING MSMQ OBJECTS

You can choose from two ways to program with MSMQ. MSMQ exposes a C-level API as well as a set of ActiveX components. As a Visual Basic programmer, you're much better off using the ActiveX components when you program MSMQ. Note that some MSMQ functionality is accessible only through the C-level API. Fortunately, you can meet most of the common requirements for message passing in a distributed application by using the ActiveX components. In the rare circumstances in which you need to use the C-level API, you can use Visual Basic *Declare* statements and call into the API directly. However, this chapter will examine only the use of ActiveX components. Once you include a reference to MSMQ's type library (the Microsoft Message Queue Object Library) in your Visual Basic project, you can use these ActiveX components in your code.

I won't cover every possibility for programming with MSMQ's ActiveX components. MSMQ provides several ActiveX components, and each one has quite a few properties and methods. Instead, I'll simply get you started by offering MSMQ programming examples that demonstrate the most common types of code required in a distributed application. You should use the HTML document *MSMQ Programmer's Reference* to complement the material presented in this chapter.

Creating a Public Queue

Let's begin our tour of MSMQ programming by creating a queue. MSMQ lets you create both public queues and private queues. We'll start by creating a public queue. In this chapter, you should assume that all queues are public unless I indicate they are private.

You can create a public queue in one of two ways. You can create a queue by hand using the MSMQ Explorer, or you can create a queue programmatically. We'll create one by hand first. Simply right-click on a computer in the MSMQ Explorer, and choose Queue from the New menu. You must give the queue a name and specify whether you want the queue to be transactional. I'll defer a discussion of transactional queues until later in this chapter. For now, just create a queue by giving it a name, and leave the Transactional check box deselected. Click OK to create the queue.

After you create the queue, you can examine its attributes by right-clicking on it and choosing Properties. You'll see a tabbed dialog box in which you can modify various properties of the queue. When you examine the queue properties, you'll notice that MSMQ has automatically generated a GUID to identify the queue.

You can also create a queue programmatically using an *MSMQQueueInfo* object. First you must create the object and assign it a valid *PathName*. A queue's *PathName* should include the name of the computer and the name of the queue. For example, look at the following code:

```
Dim qi As MSMQQueueInfo
Set qi = New MSMQQueueInfo
qi.PathName = "MyComputer\MyQueue"
qi.Label = "My Queue"
qi.Create
```

This example uses an *MSMQQueueInfo* object to create a new queue. Once you set the *PathName* property, you can create a queue by invoking the *Create* method. This example also sets the *Label* property of the new queue. A label is optional, but it can be helpful when you need to locate the queue later on.

The *Create* method takes two optional parameters. The first parameter indicates whether the new queue is transactional. The second parameter, *IsWorldReadable*, lets you indicate whether the queue will be readable to users other than the owner. The default value for this parameter is False, which means that only the queue's owner is able to receive messages from the queue. If you pass True to this parameter, the queue can be read by all users. Whatever you pass, all users can send messages to the queue. You can also set queue security permissions by modifying the discretionary access control list (DACL) for the queue. You do this by opening the queue's Properties dialog box and navigating to the Security tab in the MSMQ Explorer.

Note that you can abbreviate the *PathName* for a local queue so that you don't have to hardcode the name of the computer. You must do this when you want to write generic code that will run on many different computers. A single dot (as in *.\MyQueue*) signifies that the queue path is defined on the local computer. You can use this abbreviated form when you create and open a local queue. For example, you can rewrite the previous code as follows:

```
Dim qi As MSMQQueueInfo
Set qi = New MSMQQueueInfo
qi.PathName = ".\MyQueue"
qi.Label = "My Queue"
qi.Create
```

In addition to creating queues, you can use an *MSMQQueueInfo* object when you want to search for or open an existing queue. Let's say you want to get a little tricky and create a queue when one with a predefined caption doesn't already exist. First, you can run a query against the MQIS with an *MSMQQuery* object to determine whether a queue with a certain label already exists. You run a query by invoking the *LookupQueue* method, which returns an *MSMQQueueInfos* object. The *MSMQ-QueueInfos* object is a collection of *MSMQQueueInfo* objects that match your lookup criteria. Here's an example of conducting a lookup by a queue's caption:

```
Dim qry As MSMQQuery
Set qry = New MSMQQuery
Dim qis As MSMQQueueInfos
```

(continued)

243

```
Set qis = qry.LookupQueue(Label:="MyComputer\MyQueue")
Dim qi As MSMQQueueInfo
Set qi = qis.Next
If qi Is Nothing Then
    ' The queue did not exist.
    Set qi = New MSMQQueueInfo
    qi.PathName = "MyComputer\MyQueue"
    qi.Label = "MyComputer\MyQueue"
    qi.Create
End If
```

In this example, a new queue is created only if a queue with the label *MyComputer\MyQueue* doesn't already exist. Note that you can also use other types of criteria when you run a lookup query.

Now let's open a queue and send a message. The next object you need to understand is an *MSMQQueue* object. At first, the relationship between *MSMQQueueInfo* objects and *MSMQQueue* objects can be a little confusing. It's reasonable to conclude that an *MSMQQueue* object represents a physical queue because of its name. However, you're better off thinking of it as a queue handle. For example, you can open three different *MSMQQueue* objects on the same physical queue:

```
Dim qi As MSMQQueueInfo
Set qi = new MSMQueueInfo
qi.PathName = ".\MyQueue"
Dim qSend As MSMQQueue
Set qSend = qi.Open(MQ_SEND_ACCESS, MQ_DENY_NONE)
Dim qPeek As MSMQQueue
Set qPeek = qi.Open(MQ_PEEK_ACCESS, MQ_DENY_NONE)
Dim qReceive As MSMQQueue
Set qReceive = qi.Open(MQ_RECEIVE_ACCESS, MQ_DENY_NONE)
```

You can see that an *MSMQQueueInfo* object represents a physical queue and that an *MSMQQueue* object actually represents an open handle to the queue. When you call *Open*, you must specify the type of access you want in the first parameter. You can peek at as well as receive from a queue when you open it with *MQ_RECEIVE_ACCESS*. However, if you want to send messages while also peeking at or receiving from the same queue, you must open two *MSMQQueue* objects. Remember to invoke the *Close* method on an *MSMQQueue* object as soon as you've finished using it.

You can use the second parameter to *Open* to specify the share mode for the queue. The default value of this parameter is *MQ_DENY_NONE*, which means that the queue can be opened by more than one application for receive access at the same time. You must use this setting when you open a queue using *MQ_PEEK_ACCESS* or *MQ_SEND_ACCESS*. However, when you open a queue with receive access, you can set the share mode to *MQ_DENY_RECEIVE_SHARE* to prevent other applications from receiving messages at the same time. When one application opens a queue with both *MQ_RECEIVE_ACCESS* and *MQ_DENY_RECEIVE_SHARE*, no other application can open the queue in receive mode. An application using this mode will be the only one that can remove messages from the queue.

Using a Private Queue

When you create a public queue, MSMQ assigns it an identifying GUID and publishes it in the MQIS. This allows other applications to open the queue by assigning the computer name and queue name to the *PathName* property. This also allows other applications to find the queue by running queries against the MQIS. However, the process of publishing a public queue takes up time and disk space and is sometimes unnecessary.

Imagine an application that consists of hundreds or thousands of independent clients that all require a local response queue. In this situation, it makes sense to use private queues. Private queues must be created locally, and they are not published in the MQIS. They're published only on the computer on which they reside.

As you'll see later in this chapter, you can send the information about a private response queue in the header of a request message. This lets you establish bidirectional communication between a client application and the server. More important, using private queues means that you don't have to publish all those response queues, which saves both time and disk space. You can create a private queue by adding *Private$* to the queue's *PathName*, like this:

```
Dim qResponseInfo As MSMQQueueInfo
Set qResponseInfo = New MSMQQueueInfo
qResponseInfo.PathName = ".\Private$\MyResponseQueue"
qResponseInfo.Create
```

MSMQ applications can send messages to private queues on other machines as long as they can find the queues. This isn't as easy as locating public queues because you can't open a private queue using a *PathName*—it isn't published in the MQIS. Later in this chapter, I'll show you a technique for passing the response queue's information to another application in a request message.

Another way that you can send messages to private queues on another computer is by using the *FormatName* property. This technique is valuable when you are dealing with private queues on disconnected clients. When a queue is created, MSMQ creates a *FormatName* for it. Here's an example of two different *FormatName* properties for a public queue and a private queue:

```
PUBLIC=067ce2cb-26fc-11d2-b56b-f4552d000000
PRIVATE=f38f2a17-218e-11d2-b555-c48e04000000\00000022
```

The *FormatName* of a public queue includes the GUID that identifies the queue in the MQIS. A private queue doesn't have its own GUID. Instead, its *FormatName* includes the GUID that identifies the local computer and an extra computer-specific queue identifier. An application can send messages to a private queue across the network by assigning the *FormatName* before invoking the *Open* method. Of course, the application must know the *FormatName* ahead of time.

Sending a Message

Let's send our first message. MSMQ makes this task remarkably easy. You can create a new *MSMQMessage* object and prepare it by setting a few properties. You can then invoke the *MSMQMessage* object's *Send* method, and MSMQ will route your message to its destination queue. Here's a simple example:

```
Dim qi As MSMQQueueInfo
Set qi = New MSMQQueueInfo
qi.PathName = ".\MyQueue"
Dim q As MSMQQueue
Set q = qi.Open(MQ_SEND_ACCESS, MQ_DENY_NONE)
' Create a new message.
Dim msg As MSMQMessage
Set msg = New MSMQMessage
' Prepare the message.
msg.Label = "My superficial label"
msg.Body = "My parameterized request information"
msg.Priority = MQ_MAX_PRIORITY
' Send message to open queue.
msg.Send q
q.Close
```

As you can see, MSMQ's ActiveX components make it pretty easy to open a queue and send a message. The message in the last example was prepared by setting three properties. The *Caption* is a string property of the message header that distinguishes or identifies a particular message. The two other message properties are the message body and the message priority.

In MSMQ, a message *body* is stored as an array of bytes. The body is typically used to transmit parameterized data between the sender and the receiver. This example demonstrates that you can simply assign a Visual Basic for Applications (VBA) string to a message body. The receiver can read this string from the message body just as easily. However, in many cases you'll use a message body that is more complex. For example, you might need to pass multiple parameters from the sender to the receiver. I'll revisit this topic later in this chapter and discuss how to pack parameterized information into the message body.

The last property used in the example is the message *priority*. A message has a priority value between 0 and 7; the higher the value, the higher the priority. MSMQ stores messages with higher priority levels at the head of the queue. For example, a message with a priority level of 6 is placed in the queue behind all messages of priority 7 and behind messages of priority 6 that have already been written to the queue. The new message is placed ahead of any message of priority 5 or lower. The MSMQ type library contains the constants *MQ_MAX_PRIORITY* (7) and *MQ_MIN_PRIORITY* (0). The default priority for a new message is 3.

You can use the MSMQ Explorer to examine the messages in a queue, as shown in Figure 11-5. You should see a list of all the messages that have been sent to the queue but have not been received. As you can see, messages with the highest priority are placed at the head of the queue. The message at the head is usually the first one to be received.

You must have read permissions for a queue in order to see the messages in it with the MSMQ Explorer. There might be times when your installation of MSMQ doesn't give you these read permissions by default. You can modify the access permissions for a queue by right-clicking on it in the MSMQ Explorer and choosing Properties. If you navigate to the Security tab, you can change both the owner and the permissions for the queue so you can see the messages inside it. It's especially useful to look at the header attributes and bodies of messages when you're beginning to program with MSMQ.

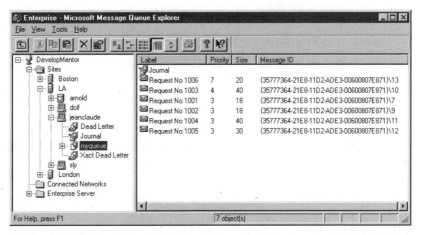

Figure 11-5. *You can examine the messages in a queue using the MSMQ Explorer. Messages with the highest priority are at the head of the queue.*

Other Message Properties

Before I move on to the next section, I want to introduce a few other important message properties. The first is the *Delivery* property, which has two possible settings. The default setting is *MQMSG_DELIVERY_EXPRESS*, which means that the message is sent in a fast but unreliable fashion. Express messages are retained in memory only while they're being routed across various computers toward their destination queue. If a computer crashes while holding express messages, the messages could be lost.

To ensure that a message isn't lost while being routed to its destination queue, you can set the *Delivery* property to *MQMSG_DELIVERY_RECOVERABLE*. The message will be flushed to disk as it is passed from one computer to another. The disk I/O required with recoverable messages results in significant performance degradation, but the message won't be lost in the case of a system failure. When you send non-transactional messages, you must explicitly set the *Delivery* property if you want recoverable delivery. When you send transactional messages, the *Delivery* property is automatically set to *MQMSG_DELIVERY_RECOVERABLE*.

When a message is sent to a queue, MSMQ assigns it an ID property. This property is a 20-byte array that uniquely identifies the message. MSMQ generates the ID by using two different values. The first 16 bytes of the ID are the GUID of the sending computer. (MSMQ assigns an identifying GUID to every computer during installation.) As you can see in Figure 11-5 (shown earlier), the first part of the message ID is always the same for any message sent from the same computer. The last 4 bytes of the ID are a unique integer generated by the sending computer. In most cases, you don't need to worry about what's inside the Byte array. However, if you need to compare two IDs to see whether they represent the same message, you can use VBA's *StrComp* function with the *vbBinaryCompare* flag.

Each message also has a *CorrelationID* property. Like the ID, this property is also stored as a 20-byte array. Let's look at a problem to see why this property is valuable. Let's say that a client application sends request messages to a server. The server processes the requests and sends a response message for each request. How does the client application know which request message is associated with which response message? The *CorrelationID* property solves this problem.

When the server processes a request, it can assign the ID of the incoming request message to the *CorrelationID* of the outgoing response message. When the client application receives a response message, it can compare the *CorrelationID* of the response message with the ID from each request message. This allows the sender to correlate messages. As you can see, the *CorrelationID* is useful when you create your own response messages. As you'll see later in this chapter, MSMQ also assigns the proper *CorrelationID* automatically when it prepares certain system-generated messages, such as an acknowledgment message.

Receiving and Peeking at Messages

To receive a message, you first open an *MSMQQueue* object with receive access, and then you invoke the *Receive* method to read and remove the first message in the queue:

```
Dim qi As MSMQQueueInfo
Set qi = New MSMQQueueInfo
qi.PathName = ".\MyQueue"
Dim q As MSMQQueue
Set q = qi.Open(MQ_RECEIVE_ACCESS, MQ_DENY_NONE)
Dim msg As MSMQMessage
' Attempt to receive first message in queue.
```

```
Set msg = q.Receive(ReceiveTimeout:=1000)
If Not (msg Is Nothing) Then
    ' You have removed the first message from the queue.
    MsgBox msg.Body, vbInformation, msg.Label
Else
    ' You timed out waiting on an empty queue.
End If
q.close
```

There's an interesting difference between sending and receiving a message with MSMQ. You invoke the *Send* method on an *MSMQMessage* object, but you invoke the *Receive* method on an *MSMQQueue* object. (This doesn't really cause problems; it's just a small idiosyncrasy of the MSMQ programming model.) If a message is in the queue, a call to *Receive* removes it and returns a newly created *MSMQMessage* object. If there's no message in the queue, a call to *Receive* behaves differently depending on how the timeout interval is set.

By default, a call to *Receive* has no timeout value and will block indefinitely if no message is in the queue.

If you don't want the thread that calls *Receive* to block indefinitely, you can specify a timeout interval. You can use the *ReceiveTimeout* parameter to specify the number of milliseconds that you want to wait on an empty queue. If you call *Receive* on an empty queue and the timeout interval expires before a message arrives, the call to *Receive* returns with a null reference instead of an *MSMQMessage* object. The code in the last example shows how to set a timeout value of 1000 milliseconds. It also shows how to determine whether a message arrived before the timeout expired. If you don't want to wait at all, you can use a *ReceiveTimeout* value of 0. A *ReceiveTimeout* value of ?1 indicates that you want to wait indefinitely. (This is the default if you don't pass a timeout value.)

You can call *Receive* repeatedly inside a *Do* loop to synchronously remove every message from a queue. The following example shows how to receive all the messages from a queue and fill a list box with message captions:

```
Dim qi As MSMQQueueInfo
Set qi = New MSMQQueueInfo
qi.PathName = ".\MyQueue"
Dim q As MSMQQueue
Set q = qi.Open(MQ_RECEIVE_ACCESS, MQ_DENY_RECEIVE_SHARE)
Dim msg As MSMQMessage
Set msg = q.Receive(ReceiveTimeout:=0)
Do Until msg Is Nothing
    lstReceive.AddItem msg.Label
    Set msg = q.Receive(ReceiveTimeout:=0)
Loop
q.Close
```

You can set the share mode for *MQ_DENY_RECEIVE_SHARE* so that your application won't have to contend with other applications while removing messages from the queue. Use a timeout value of 0 if you want to reach the end of the queue and move on to other business as soon as possible.

Sometimes you'll want to inspect the messages in a queue before removing them. You can use an *MSMQQueue* object's peek methods in conjunction with an implicit cursor to enumerate through the message in a queue. After opening a queue with either receive access or peek access, you can call *Peek*, *PeekCurrent*, or *PeekNext*.

Peek is similar to *Receive* in that it reads the first message in the queue. However, *Peek* doesn't remove the message. If you call *Peek* repeatedly, you keep getting the same message. Another problem with *Peek* is that it has no effect on the implicit cursor behind the *MSMQQueue* object. Therefore, it is more common to work with *PeekCurrent* and *PeekNext*.

You can move the implicit cursor to the first message in a queue with a call to *PeekCurrent*. As with a call to *Receive*, you should use a timeout interval if you don't want to block on an empty queue. After an initial call to *PeekCurrent*, you can enumerate through the rest of the messages in a queue by calling *PeekNext*:

```
Dim qi As MSMQQueueInfo
Set qi = New MSMQQueueInfo
qi.PathName = ".\MyQueue"
Dim q As MSMQQueue
Set q = qi.Open(MQ_PEEK_ACCESS, MQ_DENY_NONE)
Dim msg As MSMQMessage
Set msg = q.PeekCurrent(ReceiveTimeout:=0)
Do Until msg Is Nothing
    ' Add message captions to a list box.
    lstPeek.AddItem msg.Label
    Set msg = q.PeekNext(ReceiveTimeout:=0)
Loop
q.Close
```

The *ReceiveCurrent* method is often used in conjunction with *PeekCurrent* and *PeekNext*. For example, you can enumerate through the messages in a queue by peeking at each one and comparing the properties of the current message against criteria of the messages you want to receive and process. For example, after calling *PeekCurrent* or *PeekNext*, you can compare the label of the current message with a specific caption that you're looking for. If you come across a message with the caption you're looking for, you can call *ReceiveCurrent* to remove it from the queue and process it.

Using MSMQ Events

The examples I have shown so far of peeking and receiving messages have all used synchronous techniques for examining and removing the messages in a queue. These techniques are easy ways to read or remove all the messages that are currently in a queue. They also let you process future messages as they are sent. The following code doesn't use a timeout interval; it blocks until a message is sent to the queue. It processes all messages until the queue is empty and then blocks until more messages arrive:

```
' Assume q is an open MSMQQueue object with receive access.
Dim msg As MSMQMessage
Do While True ' Loop forever.
    ' Wait indefinitely for each message.
    Set msg = q.Receive()
    ' Process message.
Loop
```

While this style of coding allows you to process messages as they arrive, it also holds the calling thread hostage. If you have a single-threaded application, the application can't do anything else. However, you can use MSMQ events as an alternative to this synchronous style of message processing. MSMQ events let your application respond to asynchronous notifications that are raised by MSMQ as messages arrive at a queue. You can therefore respond to a new message without having to dedicate a thread to block on a call to *Receive* or *PeekNext*.

Let's look at how MSMQ events work. The MSMQ eventing mechanism is based on the *MSMQEvent* component. To use events, you must first create an *MSMQEvent* object and set up an event sink. Next you must associate the *MSMQEvent* object with an *MSMQQueue* object that has been opened for either peek access or receive access. You create the association between the two objects by invoking the *Enable-Notification* method on the *MSMQQueue* object and passing a reference to the *MSMQ-Event* object. After you call *EnableNotification*, MSMQ notifies your application when a message has arrived by raising an *Arrived* event.

You learned how to set up an event sink with Visual Basic in Chapter 6. As you'll recall, to create an event sink you must use the *WithEvents* keyword and declare the source object's reference variable in the declaration section of a form module or a class module. The following code shows how to set up an event sink for a new *MSMQEvent* object and associate it with an open *MSMQQueue* object:

```
Private qPeek As MSMQQueue
Private WithEvents qPeekEvents As MSMQEvent

Private Sub Form_Load()
    Dim qi As MSMQQueueInfo
    Set qi = New MSMQQueueInfo
    qi.PathName = ".\MyQueue"
    Set qPeek = qi.Open(MQ_PEEK_ACCESS, MQ_DENY_NONE)
    Set qPeekEvents = New MSMQEvent
    qPeek.EnableNotification qPeekEvents
End Sub
```

This example uses peek access, but events work in a similar manner for receiving messages. Once you set up the *MSMQEvent* object's event sink and call *Enable-Notification*, you will be notified with an *Arrived* event as soon as MSMQ finds a message in the queue. Here's an implementation of the *Arrived* event that adds the caption of new messages to a list box as they arrive in the queue:

```
Sub qPeekEvents_Arrived(ByVal Queue As Object, ByVal Cursor As Long)
    Dim q As MSMQQueue
    Set q = Queue   ' Cast to type MSMQQueue to avoid IDispatch.
    Dim msg As MSMQMessage
    Set msg = q.PeekCurrent(ReceiveTimeOut:=0)
    If Not (msg Is Nothing) Then
        lstPeek.AddItem msg.Label
    End If
    q.EnableNotification qPeekEvents, MQMSG_NEXT
End Sub
```

Note that this example calls *EnableNotification* every time an *Arrived* event is raised. This is required because a call to *EnableNotification* sets up a notification for only the next message. If you want to receive notifications in an ongoing fashion, you must keep calling *EnableNotification* in the *Arrived* event. It is also important to pass the appropriate cursor constant when you call *EnableNotification*. This example passes the constant *MQMSG_NEXT* in order to advance the implicit cursor. The next time an *Arrived* event is raised, a call to *PeekCurrent* examines the next message in the queue.

You should also note that the code in the example above peeks at every message that was stored in the queue when the *MSMQEvent* object was set up. In other words, MSMQ raises events for existing messages as well as future messages. If you care only about future messages, you can synchronously advance the implicit cursor to the last existing message before calling *EnableNotification*.

Packing Parameters into the Message Body

When you prepare a message, you must often pack several different pieces of parameterized information into the body before sending it to a queue. On the receiving side, you must also be able to unpack these parameters before you start processing the sender's request. Up to this point, I've shown you only how to pass simple VBA strings in a message body. Now we'll look at how to pass more complex data structures.

A message body is a Variant that is stored and transmitted as a Byte array. You can read and write the usual VBA data types to the body, such as Boolean, Byte, Integer, Long, Single, Double, Currency, Date, and String. MSMQ tracks the type you use in the message header. This makes it quite easy to store a single value in a message body. However, it doesn't solve the problem of packing in several pieces of data at once.

To pack several pieces of data into a message, you must understand how to use the Byte array behind the message body.

Using an array behind the message body is tricky because it must be an array of bytes. If you assign another type of array to the message body, MSMQ converts it to a Byte array. Unfortunately, once your data has been converted to a Byte array, there's no easy way to convert it back to the original array type on the receiving side. This means that a simple technique such as sending your parameters in a String array won't work as you might hope. A Byte array is flexible because it can hold just about any binary or text-based data. If you don't mind working with a Byte array directly, you can pack the message body using code like this:

```
Dim msg As MSMQMessage
Set msg = New MSMQMessage
Dim data(11) As Byte
' Fill the array with parameterized data.
data(0) = 65: data(1) = 66
data(2) = 67: data(3) = 68
data(4) = 49: data(5) = 51
data(6) = 53: data(7) = 55
data(8) = 57: data(9) = 97
data(10) = 98: data(11) = 99
msg.Body = data
msg.Send q
```

Figure 11-6 on the following page shows the Body tab of the message's Property dialog box, which you can view using the MSMQ Explorer. The message body shown in the figure is the same one that was generated in the last code example. The Body tab shows the contents of the message in both hexadecimal format and ANSI format.

How do you unpack this Byte array from the message body in a receiver application? It's pretty easy. All you have to do is create a dynamic array reference and assign the message body to it, like this:

```
Dim msg As MSMQMessage
Set msg = q.Receive()
Dim d() As Byte
d = msg.Body
' Now the Byte array is populated.
' For example, to inspect value in position 2
Dim Val As Byte
Val = d(2)
```

While it's important for you to understand that the message body is always stored as a Byte array, the technique I have just shown isn't always the best way to pack and unpack your parameterized information. Writing and reading Byte arrays gives you as much flexibility as MSMQ can offer, but it doesn't offer high levels of productivity.

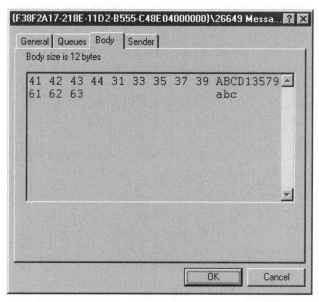

Figure 11-6. *A message body is always stored as a Byte array. The left side shows the hexadecimal value of each byte in the array; the right side displays the ANSI character that represents the value of each byte. The first byte in this body has the decimal value 65 and the hexadecimal value 41, and the letter A is its ANSI character representation.*

It can also be tricky and time consuming to write the code for packing and unpacking several pieces of parameterized information into a Byte array. Several other techniques are easier and faster to program. You should work directly with Byte arrays only when the data being packed is fairly straightforward or no other technique can give you the results you need.

OK, let's put your knowledge of Byte arrays to work and pack several parameters into a single message body. Suppose you want to send a request message to submit a sales order. The body of the request message must include a customer name, a product name, and a requested quantity. How do you pack these three pieces of information into a message body? We'll look at three different techniques: using a string parsing technique, using a Visual Basic *PropertyBag* object, and using a persistent Visual Basic class to read and write an entire object into the message body.

Using a String Parsing Technique

You've already seen that it's easy to write and read a VBA string to and from a message body. As you'll recall from Chapter 6, a VBA string is stored internally using a COM data type known as a basic string (BSTR). A BSTR maintains the actual string data with an array of Unicode characters. Because a BSTR is based on Unicode, it requires 2 bytes per character; ANSI strings require only 1 byte per character.

Packing a VBA string into a message body is easy because MSMQ does the Byte array conversions for you behind the scenes. When you assign a string to a message body, MSMQ simply converts the Unicode characters array to a Byte array. On the receiving side, when you assign the message body to a string variable, MSMQ creates a new BSTR and populates it with the Unicode characters from inside the Byte array. The conversion going on behind the scenes is somewhat complicated, but things couldn't be easier in terms of the Visual Basic code that you must write.

Now let's look at a simple string parsing technique to write the three parameters to a message body. You can simply create a long string by concatenating your parameters and using a character such as a semicolon (;) to delimit each one. This string can be easily written to and read from the message body. The only tricky part is writing the code to pack and unpack the string. Let's begin by packing the string:

```
Function PackMessage1(ByVal Customer As String, _
                      ByVal Product As String, _
                      ByVal Quantity As Long) As String
  PackMessage1 = Customer & ";" & Product & ";" & CStr(Quantity)
End Function
```

The *PackMessage1* method takes three parameters and embeds them in a single VBA string. The embedded semicolons are used by the receiving code to unpack the string. The sending application can now use *PackMessage1* to pack up a message and send it on its way:

```
Dim MsgBody As String
MsgBody = PackMessage1("Bob", "Ant", 100)
msg.Body = MsgBody
msg.Send q
```

On the receiving side, you must provide the code to unpack the string. The following *UnpackMessage1* method walks the string and pulls out the packed parameter values one by one:

```
Private Sub UnpackMessage1(ByVal MsgBody As String, _
                           ByRef Customer As String, _
                           ByRef Product As String, _
                           ByRef Quantity As Long)
    Dim StartPosition As Integer, Delimiter As Integer
    StartPosition = 1
    Delimiter = InStr(StartPosition, MsgBody, ";")
    Customer = Mid(MsgBody, StartPosition, Delimiter - StartPosition)
    StartPosition = Delimiter + 1
    Delimiter = InStr(StartPosition, MsgBody, ";")
    Product = Mid(MsgBody, StartPosition, Delimiter - StartPosition)
    StartPosition = Delimiter + 1
    Quantity = CLng(Mid(MsgBody, StartPosition, Len(MsgBody) - Delimiter))
End Sub
```

Now that you have the code to unpack the string, the rest is fairly straightforward. You can receive or peek at a message and extract the request parameters from the body. Here's an example of using the *UnpackMessage1* method in the receiving application:

```
Set msg = q.Receive()
Dim PackedMsg As String
PackedMsg = msg.Body
Dim Customer As String, Product As String, Quantity As Long
UnpackMessage1 PackedMsg, Customer, Product, Quantity
' Customer, Product, and Quantity are now populated.
```

Parsing strings offers much higher productivity than using a Byte array directly. While the code might be tedious to write, it usually isn't very complicated. It's also much easier than working with Byte arrays. However, Visual Basic 6 has a few new options that you should consider before you decide how to pack and unpack your parameters. In the following sections, I'll present two other Visual Basic 6 techniques that offer higher levels of productivity than this parsing technique.

Using *PropertyBag* Objects

PropertyBag objects aren't new with Visual Basic 6. You might have used them if you programmed ActiveX controls with version 5. However, Visual Basic 6 is the first version that allows you to create *PropertyBag* objects with the New operator. This means you can create a stand-alone *PropertyBag* object to pack and unpack your parameters.

A *PropertyBag* object is useful because it can automate most of the tedious work of packing and unpacking your parameterized information. Each *PropertyBag* object has a *Contents* property, which represents a Byte array. You can write named values into this Byte array using the *WriteProperty* method. Once you write all your parameters into a *PropertyBag* object, you can use the *Contents* property to serialize the Byte array into the message body:

```
Function PackMessage2(ByVal Customer As String, _
                      ByVal Product As String, _
                      ByVal Quantity As Long) As Byte()
    Dim PropBag As PropertyBag
    Set PropBag  = New PropertyBag
    PropBag.WriteProperty "Customer", Customer
    PropBag.WriteProperty "Product", Product
    PropBag.WriteProperty "Quantity", Quantity
    PackMessage2 = PropBag.Contents
End Function
```

This method takes three parameter values and returns a Byte array. (Note that Visual Basic 6 can use the array type as a method return value.) The *PropertyBag* object writes your named values into a stream of bytes using its own proprietary algorithm.

You can use the *PackMessage2* method in the sender application to pack a message body, like this:

```
Dim msg As MSMQMessage
Set msg = New MSMQMessage
msg.Body = PackMessage2("Bob", "Ant", 100)
msg.Send q
```

Once you pack up a Byte array in the sender application, you need a second *PropertyBag* object on the receiving side to unpack it. The *UnpackMessage2* method unpacks the message using the *ReadProperty* method of the *PropertyBag* object:

```
Sub UnpackMessage2(ByRef MsgBody() As Byte, _
                   ByRef Customer As String, _
                   ByRef Product As String, _
                   ByRef Quantity As Long)
    Dim PropBag As PropertyBag
    Set PropBag = New PropertyBag
    PropBag.Contents = MsgBody
    Customer = PropBag.ReadProperty("Customer")
    Product = PropBag.ReadProperty("Product")
    Quantity = PropBag.ReadProperty("Quantity")
End Sub
```

Now you can use the *UnpackMessage2* method in the receiver application to unpack the message:

```
Set msg = q.Receive()
Dim Customer As String, Product As String, Quantity As Long
UnpackMessage2 msg.Body, Customer, Product, Quantity
' Customer, Product, and Quantity are now populated.
```

As you can see, the *PropertyBag* object makes your life much easier because it packs and unpacks your parameters for you. This technique does carry some overhead compared to the string parsing technique, however. The *PropertyBag* object writes proprietary header information into the Byte array in addition to the name of each property. To give you an idea of how much overhead is involved, let's compare the two code examples above. The code for the string parsing technique created a message body 22 bytes long, and the *PropertyBag* technique created a message body 116 bytes long.

The overhead of the *PropertyBag* technique depends on the size of the parameters being passed. The overhead becomes less noticeable as your parameter values become larger. Also keep in mind that the header information for each MSMQ message is quite large itself. An MSMQ message header typically contains 136 bytes or more no matter how big the body is. You must weigh the trade-offs between productivity and efficiency.

Using Persistent Objects

The last technique for passing parameterized information in a message body is perhaps the most exciting. MSMQ lets you read and write entire objects to the message body. However, the object must belong to a certain category. MSMQ can serialize the properties of an object into and out of a message body if the object implements either *IPersistStream* or *IPersistStorage*. These are two standard COM interfaces that derive from *IPersist*.

The interface definitions for *IPersistStream* and *IPersistStorage* contain parameters that are incompatible with Visual Basic. You can't implement these interfaces in a straightforward manner using the *Implements* keyword. Fortunately, Visual Basic 6 has added persistable classes. When you create a persistable class, Visual Basic automatically implements *IPersistStream* behind the scenes. Persistable classes let you read and write objects in and out of the message body directly.

Every public class in an ActiveX DLL and ActiveX EXE project has a *Persistable* property. You must set this property to *Persistable* at design time to make a persistent class. When you make a class persistent, the Visual Basic IDE lets you add a *ReadProperties* and a *WriteProperties* method to the class module. You can add the skeletons for these two methods using the wizard bar. (The wizard bar consists of two combo boxes at the top of the class module window.) You can also add the *InitProperties* method, although it isn't required when you use MSMQ.

You can use the *ReadProperties* and *WriteProperties* methods to read your properties to an internal *PropertyBag* object. Visual Basic creates this *PropertyBag* object for you behind the scenes and uses it to implement *IPersistStream*. Remember, your object must implement *IPersistStream* in order for MSMQ to write it to a message body. When MSMQ calls the methods in the *IPersistStream* interface, Visual Basic simply forwards these calls to your implementations of *ReadProperties* and *WriteProperties*.

Using persistable classes with MSMQ is a lot easier to use than it sounds. For example, you can create a new persistable class and add the properties you want to pack into the message body. Next you provide an implementation of *ReadProperties* and *WriteProperties*. Here's a Visual Basic class module that does this:

```
' COrderRequest: a persistable class.
Public Customer As String
Public Product As String
Public Quantity As Long

Private Sub Class_ReadProperties(PropBag As PropertyBag)
    Customer = PropBag.ReadProperty("Customer", "")
    Product = PropBag.ReadProperty("Product", "")
    Quantity = PropBag.ReadProperty("Quantity", "")
End Sub
```

```
Private Sub Class_WriteProperties(PropBag As PropertyBag)
    PropBag.WriteProperty "Customer", Customer
    PropBag.WriteProperty "Product", Product
    PropBag.WriteProperty "Quantity", Quantity
End Sub
```

As you can see, it's pretty easy. Once you have a persistable class like the one shown above, you can pack it into a message body, like this:

```
Dim msg As MSMQMessage
Set msg = New MSMQMessage
' Create and prepare object.
Dim Order As COrderRequest
Set Order = New COrderRequest
Order.Customer = txtPCS1
Order.Product = txtPCS2
Order.Quantity = txtPCS3
' Assign the object to the message body.
' Your WriteProperties is called.
msg.Body = Order
msg.Send q
```

When you assign an object to the message body, MSMQ performs a *Query-Interface* on the object to see whether it supports either *IPersistStream* or *IPersist-Storage*. Since your object supports *IPersistStream*, MSMQ knows that it can call a method on this interface named *Save*. Visual Basic forwards the call to *Save* to your implementation of *WriteProperties*. You write your parameters into the *PropertyBag*, and these values are automatically copied into the message body as an array of bytes.

In the receiver applications, things are just as easy. You can rehydrate a persistent object from a message body by creating a new reference and assigning the message body to it:

```
Set msg = q.Receive(ReceiveTimeOut:=0)
Dim Order As COrderRequest
Set Order = msg.Body
Dim Customer As String, Product As String, Quantity As Long
Customer = Order.Customer
Product = Order.Product
Quantity = Order.Quantity
```

When you assign a message body to a reference using the *Set* keyword, MSMQ creates a new instance of the object and calls the *Load* method of *IPersistStream*. Visual Basic forwards this call to your implementation of *ReadProperties*. Once again, you use the *PropertyBag* object to extract your data.

You should keep a few things in mind when you use persistable classes with MSMQ. First, this parameter-packing technique uses a bit more overhead than the technique using a stand-alone *PropertyBag* object, and it uses considerably more overhead than the string parsing technique. Second, you should create your persistable classes in ActiveX DLLs so that every application that sends and receives messages can leverage the same code.

One last thing to note is that you can use persistable classes with MSMQ only after you have installed Windows NT Service Pack 4. Earlier versions of MSMQ aren't compatible with Visual Basic's implementation of *IPersistStream*. In particular, your code will fail when you try to assign an object created from a persistable class to an MSMQ message body. This means you must install Windows NT Service Pack 4 (or later) on all your production machines as well as your development workstations when you start working with persistable classes.

USING TRANSACTIONAL MESSAGES

When you send a message inside a transaction, you get a few guarantees that you don't get with a nontransactional message. First, MSMQ provides exactly-once delivery semantics. It takes some extra precautions so that messages that are on their way to a destination queue are not lost or duplicated. MSMQ also ensures that messages inside the same transaction are delivered in the order in which they were sent. MSMQ doesn't use message priorities in transactional queues for this reason. Every message in a transaction queue has a priority level of 0.

Let's look at an example of in-order delivery. Let's say that you send message A and then you send message B to the same queue. Message A will arrive before message B as long as they are part of the same transaction. This means that message A will be placed closer to the head of the queue. However, you should note that other messages from other transactions might be interleaved with yours. MSMQ guarantees the ordering of messages only within a single transaction.

In MSMQ, transactional messages must be sent to transactional queues. You can't change the transactional attribute after a queue has been created. It is therefore important to indicate whether you want a queue to be transactional when you create it. You can use the first parameter of the *MSMQQueueInfo* component's *Create* method to indicate whether you want a transactional queue. If you don't pass this parameter, a nontransactional queue will be created by default. It's also easy to indicate that you want a transactional queue when you create one by hand using the MSMQ Explorer.

You can send and receive transactional messages with MSMQ in two ways. You can use MSMQ's internal transactioning mechanism, or you can use external transactions that are coordinated by the Distributed Transaction Coordinator (DTC) with the two-phase commit protocol (described in Chapter 10). Each technique offers distinct advantages.

MSMQ provides its own internal transactioning mechanism, which provides the best performance. However, when you use internal transactions, MSMQ can't coordinate the transaction with any other type of resource manager, such as a SQL Server database. Internal transactions do not use the DTC or the two-phase commit protocol. Instead, MSMQ uses a more efficient protocol that is especially tuned for transactional messaging. Consequently, internal transactions are much faster than externally coordinated transactions.

Because MSMQ supports the OLE Transactions protocol, you can use it along with another resource manager when you create DTC-based transactions. Your connection to a transactional queue can be enlisted with the DTC. External transactions are also known as *coordinated transactions* because they are managed by the DTC. While external transactions are slower than internal transactions, they let you define transactions that include message passing along with operations to other resource managers. For example, you can write a transaction that receives a request message, modifies a SQL Server database, and sends a response message. Because the three operations are part of a single transaction, the DTC enforces the ACID rules (described in Chapter 10).

MSMQ lets you explicitly begin and control an external DTC-based transaction. However, it's hard for you to do much in Visual Basic with the DTC without using MTS because you have to enlist any other resource manager connection yourself. Fortunately, you can send and receive messages from inside an MTS transaction and let MTS deal with enlisting the connection to a DBMS. This makes it easy to mix message passing and DBMS access inside a single transaction. The MTS run time will enlist all the resource managers (including MSMQ) for you behind the scenes.

MSMQ Internal Transactions

MSMQ provides a shortcut when you want to send only a single transacted message. To send a single message in its own transaction, pass the constant *MQ_SINGLE_MESSAGE* when you call *Send*. Here's what a call to *Send* looks like:

```
msg.Send q, MQ_SINGLE_MESSAGE
```

You'll often want to send single messages inside a transaction because you'll want to guarantee exactly-once delivery. If you don't send the message inside a transaction, it might be lost or duplicated.

If you want to send multiple messages inside an internal transaction, you must create a new *MSMQTransactionDispenser* object. You can then invoke its *BeginTransaction* method to start a new transaction. A call to *BeginTransaction* returns an *MSMQTransaction* object. You can pass a reference to this *MSMQTransaction* object when you call a message writing operation such as *Send, Receive,* or *ReceiveCurrent*. The code at the top of the next page is an example of sending two messages to one transactional queue while performing a *Receive* operation on another transactional queue.

```
Dim td As MSMQTransactionDispenser
Set td = New MSMQTransactionDispenser
Dim tx As MSMQTransaction
Set tx = td.BeginTransaction()
' Send and receive message from transactional queues.
msg1.Send q1, tx
msg2.Send q1, tx
Set msg3 = q2.Receive(Transaction:=tx, ReceiveTimeOut:=0)
' Commit the transaction.
tx.Commit
```

The messages are not sent to the queue until the transaction has been committed. In this example, you can be sure that *msg1* will be placed in the queue ahead of *msg2*. When you receive a message inside a transaction, it is removed from the queue immediately. Another application won't see the message in the queue, even though the transaction hasn't been committed. However, if the transaction is aborted, the message is returned to the queue. This behavior is the same for transactional queues whether you are using internal transactions or external transactions.

You must follow certain rules when you program against transactional queues. If you violate one of the rules, you will experience a run-time error.

- You can't send a message from inside a transaction to a nontransactional queue.

- You can't send a message to a transactional queue if the message isn't part of a transaction.

- You can't receive messages from and send messages to the same queue from inside the same transaction.

- You can receive transactional messages only when the receiving application is running on the same computer as the transactional queue.

Another thing to keep in mind is that MSMQ transactions run at a lower isolation level than those in SQL Server. As you remember from Chapter 10, SQL Server will always conduct the operations inside an MTS transaction with an isolation level of Serializable. MSMQ doesn't support the Serializable isolation level because of the way it manages locks during a transaction.

MSMQ provides an isolation level of Read Committed between a receiving transaction and a sending transaction. The receiver can see messages from the committed send transaction even if the send transaction started after the receive transaction. If MSMQ were to run transactions with an isolation level of Serializable, it would have to put a lock on the queue and block send operations until the receiving transaction was complete. A locking scheme such as this would pose an unacceptable concurrency restraint in a queuing system.

With respect to two receiving transactions, however, the isolation level is Read Uncommitted. Let's look at an example to demonstrate this point. Assume there is a single message in a transactional queue. If transaction A receives the message from the queue, transaction B will see the queue as empty. If transaction A later aborts, the message will be written back to the queue. The queue was really never empty. However, transaction B saw the queue as empty because it read the queue in an uncommitted state. You shouldn't see the inability to run serializable transactions as a flaw in MSMQ. It's really just an inherent problem with transactional queuing. Isolation is sacrificed to maintain higher levels of concurrency. This means you can't make as many assumptions as you can when working with a DBMS that runs its operations with an isolation level of Serializable.

External Transactions with MTS

MSMQ includes an ActiveX component for creating DTC-based transactions named the *MSMQCoordinatedTransactionDispenser*. This component's interface is identical to the *MSMQTransactionDispenser* component that you saw earlier in this chapter. Both components expose a single method, *BeginTransaction*, which returns an *MSMQTransaction* object. In fact, in most of your code you can use these two components interchangeably.

The difference between the two components is that the coordinated dispenser works with the DTC, while the internal dispenser doesn't. When you commit an external transaction, the DTC executes the two-phase protocol against MSMQ, which acts as a resource manager. The coordinated dispenser also lets you enlist a resource manager other than MSMQ into a transaction. There's currently no straightforward way, however, to enlist another resource manager such as SQL Server using the *MSMQTransaction* object. This means that most Visual Basic programmers can't benefit from using the coordinated dispenser directly.

Fortunately, you can get the same benefits of external transactions by sending and receiving messages from within an MTS transaction. The MTS run time can enlist MSMQ as well as other resource managers such as SQL Server and Oracle into a single transaction. Here's an example of sending a message inside a transactional MTS component:

```
Dim ObjCtx As ObjectContext
Set ObjCtx = GetObjectContext()
' First, write a few records to a SQL Server database.
' Second, send a message to MSMQ.
Dim qi As MSMQQueueInfo
Set qi = New MSMQQueueInfo
qi.PathName = ".\MyResponseQueue"
Dim q As MSMQQueue
```

(continued)

```
Set q = qi.Open(MQ_SEND_ACCESS, MQ_DENY_NONE)
Dim msg As MSMQMessage
Set msg = New MSMQMessage
msg.Body = "The database has been updated"
msg.Send q, MQ_MTS_TRANSACTION
q.Close
ObjCtx.SetComplete ' Or call SetAbort.
```

You can pass the constant *MQ_MTS_TRANSACTION* in a call to *Send*, *Receive*, or *ReceiveCurrent* to indicate that you want your writing operation to be part of the current MTS transaction. If you don't pass a transaction parameter, this value is also the default. Note that passing *MQ_MTS_TRANSACTION* results in a transacted operation if you make the call from within an MTS transaction.

Passing *MQ_MTS_TRANSACTION* results in a *Wrong Transaction Usage* error if your program attempts to send a message inside MTS outside the scope of a transaction. Passing *MQ_MTS_TRANSACTION* will result in a nontransacted receive if your program calls *Receive* or *ReceiveCurrent* inside MTS outside the scope of a transaction.

As in the case of an internal transaction, messages inside an MTS transaction are not actually sent until the transaction has been committed. When you receive messages inside a transaction, they are removed from the queue right away. If you call *SetAbort* to roll back a transaction, your messages are written back to the queue. Remember, there are no guarantees that the message will be placed back in the same positions. The previous description of MSMQ isolation levels applies to external transactions as well as internal transactions.

USING AUXILIARY QUEUES

This section provides a brief overview of the well-known queue types that are available to MSMQ programmers. Some of these queues, such as journal queues and dead letter queues, are created automatically by MSMQ. Others, such as administration queues and response queues, let you tell MSMQ and other applications where you want them to send messages that correspond to a message that you have sent.

Journal Queues

MSMQ includes an auditing feature called *journaling*. Journaling allows you to store a copy of a message for auditing purposes. You can thus easily track messages that have already been sent and received. Two types of journaling are available: target journaling and source journaling.

Target journaling lets you make copies of incoming messages from the perspective of the destination queue. You can enable this feature on a queue-by-queue basis either programmatically or using the MSMQ Explorer. When you set the *Journal* property of a queue to True, MSMQ makes a copy of each message as it's removed from the queue. MSMQ places this copy in the queue's journal, which is another system-supplied queue inside the destination queue. When you create a queue, MSMQ creates a journal queue inside it. You can inspect a queue's journal programmatically or manually with the MSMQ Explorer to audit the messages that have been sent and received.

Source journaling lets you make copies of outgoing messages from the perspective of the message sender. You turn on source journaling by setting the *Journal* property of a message. Each computer has its own journal queue. A dependent client maintains its journal queue on an MSMQ server, but all other MSMQ computers maintain their journal queue locally. To enable source journaling on a message-by-message basis, you can write the following code:

```
msg.Journal = MQMSG_JOURNAL
msg.Send q
```

Nontransactional messages are journaled as soon as the message is sent from the sender's computer to the next computer in the routing scheme. The message might have reached the computer holding the destination queue, but it's also possible that the message has only made it to a routing server on its way to the destination queue. A journal entry for a nontransactional message doesn't guarantee that the message has been delivered or will be delivered. When you journal a transactional message, however, the message isn't journaled until the message has reached its destination queue.

Dead Letter Queues

Dead letter queues keep a copy of messages that couldn't be delivered. Many things can prevent a message from being delivered. For example, a message might have been sent to an unknown destination queue, or the destination queue's quota might have been reached. Another reason for failed delivery is that a message can expire. For example, the sender of a message can assign a maximum time for the message to be delivered and a maximum time for it to be received. Look at the following code:

```
msg.MaxTimeToReachQueue = 10
msg.MaxTimeToReceive = 120
msg.Journal = MQMSG_JOURNAL + MQMSG_DEADLETTER
msg.Send q
```

If this message doesn't arrive at its destination queue within 10 seconds or the message isn't received within 2 minutes, it expires. When a message expires, it is sent to a dead letter queue.

When the computer holding a nontransactional message has determined that the message can't be delivered, it stores the message in its local dead letter queue.

The computer that stores the message in its dead letter queue can be the sender's computer, the destination computer, or any MSMQ server in between. This situation makes it fairly hard to use dead letter queues for nontransactional messages in a large enterprise.

When a transactional message can't be delivered, it is sent to a special queue on the sender's computer named the Xact Dead Letter queue. The sender of a transactional message can examine its Journal queue and its Xact Dead Letter queue to determine the status. The sender can thus determine whether the message has been delivered, has failed, or is still en route.

Administration Queues

Administration queues are somewhat like journal queues and dead letter queues in that they let you determine when a message has been delivered or has failed. However, administration queues can provide a lot of other information as well. These queues are unlike journal queues and dead letter queues because you create them yourself. Once you designate a queue as an administration queue, you can prepare an *MSMQQueueInfo* object and assign it to the *AdminQueueInfo* property of a message:

```
Set q = qi.Open(MQ_SEND_ACCESS, MQ_DENY_NONE)
' Set up admin queue.
Dim qiAdmin As MSMQQueueInfo
Set qiAdmin = New MSMQQueueInfo
qiAdmin.PathName = ".\MyAdminQueue"
msg.Ack = MQMSG_ACKNOWLEDGMENT_FULL_RECEIVE
Set msg.AdminQueueInfo = qiAdmin
' Send message.
msg.Send q
```

The *Ack* property of a message tells MSMQ which type of acknowledgment messages you want to receive in the administration queue. Consult the *MSMQ Programmer's Reference* to see what other possibilities are available. Note that MSMQ places the ID of your message into the *CorrelationId* of any message that it sends to the administration queue.

Response Queues

The last type of queue I'll cover is a response queue. When an application sends a message to a queue, it is often desirable to have the receiver send a response message back to the sender. When you send a message, you can pass information in the message header that lets the receiver open a response queue on the sender's computer.

Each *MSMQMessage* object has a *ResponseQueueInfo* property. You must set up this property using an *MSMQQueueInfo* object, just as you would with the *Admin-QueueInfo* property. The receiving application can use the *ResponseQueueInfo* to open the queue and send a response message. It's usually a good idea to place the ID of the original message into the *CorrelationId* of the response message. You should consider using private queues instead of public queues when setting up response queues in an application that has many clients.

The following code listings show how to set up the sending application and the receiving application to get all of this working. The first listing shows the code for setting up the sending application with a request queue. The listing that immediately follows shows the code that is required in the receiving application to receive the message, open the response queue, and send a response message. This example also includes several other programming techniques that were presented in this chapter, including using private queues, events, and internal transactions.

```
'*******************
Const sRequestPath = "MyServer\MyRequestQueue"
Private qRequest As MSMQQueue

Private qResponseInfo As MSMQQueueInfo
Private qResponse As MSMQQueue
Private WithEvents qResponseEvents As MSMQEvent

Private Sub Form_Load()
    ' Open request queue.
    Dim qi As New MSMQQueueInfo
    qi.PathName = sRequestPath
    Set qRequest = qi.Open(MQ_SEND_ACCESS, MQ_DENY_NONE)
    ' Open response queue (creating it if required).
    Set qResponseInfo = New MSMQQueueInfo
    qResponseInfo.PathName = ".\Private$/MyResponseQueue"
    qResponseInfo.Label = "Local Response Queue"
    On Error Resume Next ' Ignore error if queue exists.
    qResponseInfo.Create True ' Create transactional queue.
    On Error GoTo 0 ' Turn standard error handling back on.
    Set qResponse = qResponseInfo.Open(MQ_RECEIVE_ACCESS, _
                                       MQ_DENY_NONE)
    ' Set up event to monitor incoming response messages.
    Set qResponseEvents = New MSMQEvent
    qResponse.EnableNotification qResponseEvents
End Sub

Private Sub cmdSendMessage_Click()
    Dim q As MSMQQueue
    Dim msg As New MSMQMessage
```

Programming Distributed Applications with COM and Microsoft Visual Basic

```
    msg.Body = txtBody.Text
    Set msg.ResponseQueueInfo = qResponseInfo
    msg.Send qRequest, MQ_SINGLE_MESSAGE
End Sub

Sub qResponseEvents_Arrived(ByVal Queue As Object, ByVal Cursor As Long)
    Dim q As MSMQQueue, msg As MSMQMessage
    Set q = Queue
    Set msg = q.Receive(Transaction:=MQ_SINGLE_MESSAGE, _
                    ReceiveTimeOut:=0)
    If Not msg Is Nothing Then
        lstResponses.AddItem msg.Label & " : " & msg.Body
    Else
        MsgBox "something went wrong"
    End If
    Queue.EnableNotification qResponseEvents
End Sub
'************************


'************************
Const qRequestPath = "MyServer\MyRequestQueue"

Dim qr As MSMQQueue
Private WithEvents qRecEvents As MSMQEvent

Private Sub Form_Load()
    Dim qi As New MSMQQueueInfo
    qi.PathName = qRequestPath
    Set qr = qi.Open(MQ_RECEIVE_ACCESS, _
                MQ_DENY_RECEIVE_SHARE)
    Set qRecEvents = New MSMQEvent
    qr.EnableNotification qRecEvents
End Sub

Sub qRecEvents_Arrived(ByVal Queue As Object, ByVal Cursor As Long)
    ' Set up transaction.
    Dim td As MSMQTransactionDispenser
    Set td = New MSMQTransactionDispenser
    Dim tx As MSMQTransaction
    Set tx = td.BeginTransaction()
    ' Receive message.
    Dim msg As MSMQMessage
    Set msg = Queue.Receive(Transaction:=tx, ReceiveTimeout:=0)
    If msg Is Nothing Then
        ' Something went wrong.
        MsgBox "oops!"
        tx.Abort
```

```
    Else
        ' Process the request.
        lstRequests.AddItem msg.Label & " : " & msg.Body
        lstRequests.Refresh
        Dim qResp As MSMQQueue
        Set qResp = msg.ResponseQueueInfo.Open(MQ_SEND_ACCESS, _
                                        MQ_DENY_RECEIVE_SHARE)
        Dim msgResp As New MSMQMessage
        msgResp.Label = "Receipt for: " & msg.Label
        msgResp.Body = msg.Body
        msgResp.CorrelationId = msg.Id
        msgResp.Send qResp, tx
        tx.Commit
    End If
    Queue.EnableNotification qRecEvents
End Sub
```

This chapter showed you many basic techniques for programming queues and messages with MSMQ. ActiveX components make some things remarkably easy. However, as you get deeper and deeper into an MSMQ project, you'll find yourself constantly scanning the MSMQ type library with the Object Browser and the *MSMQ Programmer's Reference* to find some new method, property, or constant. And every new release of MSMQ is sure to add more to what is already available. In this chapter, you saw the nuts and bolts of MSMQ programming. In Chapter 12, I'll show you how to incorporate MSMQ applications into a large information system based on MTS.

Chapter 12

Designing Distributed Applications

This chapter begins by covering a few more important aspects of Microsoft Transaction Server (MTS). It explains how MTS extends COM security with its own role-based security model, and it shows you how to share global data among MTS objects using the shared property manager. The chapter also explains how to create Web-based applications that leverage the COM and MTS techniques that you've learned in this book. I describe the IIS/ASP architecture and show you how to create Visual Basic objects from an Active Server Pages (ASP) page. You can create ASP applications that allow Web clients to run your MTS transactions. I also show you some techniques for programming against the built-in ASP objects from inside a Visual Basic DLL.

The chapter concludes with a description of important design issues that you should consider when you build a distributed application. As you know, MTS provides a transaction processing monitor and a few other critical middle-tier services. However, you must provide many other essential pieces of middleware yourself. This chapter explains how to create a scalable event-based notification system and a middle-tier application that monitors a queue for incoming messages. It also explains how to design a system that balances the processing load for hundreds of client applications across a group of servers. You'll learn about some of the high-level design issues involved and examine some of the new services that will be available in COM+.

THE MTS SECURITY MODEL

Chapter 8 described the security models of Microsoft Windows NT and COM as they existed before the introduction of MTS. As you'll recall, each Windows NT user account and group account has an associated security ID (SID). When a user tries to access a distributed application from across the network, the system authenticates the user's credentials and checks whether the user has the proper authorization. Administrators authorize access to users in a distributed application by granting *access permissions* and optionally *launch permissions* to Windows NT user accounts and group accounts, using a tool such as Dcomcnfg.exe. This tool's editor lets you modify the discretionary access control list (DACL) associated with the application's *AppID*.

Identity is also an important concept in COM security. An administrator should configure the *AppID* for each distributed application using a *RunAs* setting so that the system knows which Windows NT user account to use as the application's security principal. (An application that hasn't been explicitly assigned a *RunAs* setting runs under the identity of the launching user.) When the Service Control Manager (SCM) launches an application, it uses the *RunAs* setting to assign an identity to the application's process. Objects created inside the application run with the same credentials as the application's security principal. Identity is also known as *activation security* because it's set up when the application is activated.

Chapter 8 also explained how COM offers both declarative security and programmatic security. Declarative security is beneficial because it transfers the responsibility for securing a distributed application from programmers to administrators. Programmatic security provides more control and flexibility than declarative security. However, there's little you can do on the programmatic side of COM security using Visual Basic. Unless you're prepared to write some supporting code in a C++ DLL, you must run your Visual Basic applications using declarative security settings stored in the local Registry.

As you know, COM security is built on top of Windows NT security and the Remote Procedure Call (RPC) layer. COM can leverage the accounts database and SID management as well as authentication and authorization checking from the underlying system. It's important to understand how all this works because MTS security is layered on top of COM security. MTS uses COM authentication to validate users. MTS also uses COM's activation security to control which Windows NT user account serves as the identity for a server package.

However, MTS doesn't use the same authorization scheme as COM. One shortcoming of the access control provided by COM is that it lacks sufficient granularity. You can configure only two types of permissions for an application: access permissions and launch permissions. This means that access control is an all-or-nothing proposition. You can either grant or deny access permissions on an application-wide basis for each Windows NT user or group. Once you let a user in the door, you can't control what the user can do. MTS replaces COM's access scheme with its own to provide a greater degree of granularity and control.

In Windows NT 4, every COM application should be configured with its own *AppID*. An MTS application is no exception. (An MTS server package is an MTS application.) MTS creates and manages a hidden *AppID* for every server package. Using the MTS Explorer, you can easily change the authentication level and identity settings for a server package. When you change these settings, MTS modifies the hidden *AppID* for you.

The designers of MTS decided to replace COM access control with their own version. The *AppID* behind an MTS server package is configured to use the default machinewide launch permissions; however, when the package is launched, MTS grants access permissions to all users. In effect, MTS turns off COM's access control. All users must be able to get past the security checkpoints of COM in order to reach those of MTS.

MTS Roles

MTS extends COM security with its own security model using the concept of a *role*. A given user can be assigned to multiple roles. A role is a set of users within an MTS application that have the same security profile. Whenever you design a secured MTS application, you should define an appropriately named role for each type of user. For example, you can design an application with three roles: Reader, Writer, and Manager. In MTS, both declarative and programmatic security checks are performed on the roles you define instead of on SIDs, as in COM. The MTS security model thus offers more control and flexibility than does COM.

Let's look at declarative security first. When you create a new server package, declarative authorization checking is turned off by default. You can turn it on by selecting the Enable Authorization Checking option on the Security tab of the server package's Properties dialog box. You can then configure which roles (and therefore which users) have permission to invoke methods on objects running inside the application. There are four steps to configuring declarative security checks with roles in an MTS server package. Using the MTS Explorer, you do the following:

1. Enable authorization checking for the package.

2. Create a set of roles inside the server package.

3. Add a role to the role membership of each component you want to permit access to. You can also add roles to the membership of an interface of a component.

4. Associate Windows NT user accounts and group accounts with the roles you created. (An administrator usually does this at deployment time.)

One of the biggest benefits of roles is that you can preconfigure the permissions for the entire application in the development environment. Permissions in MTS have no dependencies on the SIDs from the Windows NT accounts database. This makes the role-based model much more flexible than the COM security model, in which access permissions are assigned directly to SIDs. The concept of roles is more natural for developers, and the use of roles eases deployment of a single package in multiple production environments.

Another benefit of this model is that you can configure access permissions on a component-by-component as well as an interface-by-interface basis. This declarative security scheme provides much more control than COM security. You can also configure declarative security at the interface level, which provides yet another motivation to base the design of your Visual Basic applications on user-defined interfaces.

For example, you can create a *CCustomers* component that implements two user-defined interfaces, *IQueryCustomer* and *IUpdateCustomer*. When you set up the permissions for your application, you can configure every role in the package to have access to the *IQueryCustomer* interface but restrict access to the *IUpdateCustomer* interface for every role except Writer. Stop and think about the implications of this example. I simply can't overemphasize how powerful declarative security checks are at the interface level.

Yes, I know that user-defined interfaces bring along some additional complexity, which makes many Visual Basic programmers run and hide. It's easy to fall back on Visual Basic's ability to create and implicitly cast to the default interface behind the scenes. And certainly the Visual Basic team itself can be justly accused of de-emphasizing the importance of user-defined interfaces in COM programming, given the fact that their integrated development environment (IDE) has very little support for them. But here's my point. Even if you don't care to design applications that take advantage of polymorphism and run-time type information (covered in Chapter 2), you should consider implementing user-defined interfaces because of the advantages they bring to declarative security.

You always have the ability to define user-defined interfaces and implement them in your Visual Basic components. As you remember, Chapter 6 covered what your options are in terms of using Interface Definition Language (IDL) as well as using the Visual Basic IDE. The key point is that when you design your components in terms of user-defined interfaces, you have created far more control for your administrators at deployment time.

Secured MTS Applications

A role is defined within the scope of an MTS server package. That is, each role exists within a single MTS application (running process). When a server package is launched, the MTS container application (mtx.exe) and the MTS executive (mtxex.dll) work together to set up the role-based authorization checking scheme.

Package security isn't available with library packages. Library packages aren't secured because they're loaded into the address space of an unknown client application. You can't be sure that the client application will be a secured MTS application. Furthermore, you must set up role-based authorization checking when the hosting process is launched. You can't do this with library packages because of their passive nature.

What this boils down to is that roles and role membership have no meaning within an MTS library package. When you attempt to create a role or assign role membership in a library package, the MTS Explorer displays a dialog box indicating that package security isn't available. You must be careful because a client application can defeat the MTS security model by creating objects directly from a library package. When a non-MTS client creates objects from a library package, the application is unsecured and the role-based security features of MTS won't function properly.

As you've seen, each class and interface can have one or more associated roles in its membership. If authorization checking is enabled, the caller must be in at least one role in order to successfully invoke a method, as shown in Figure 12-1. If MTS discovers that the caller doesn't belong to any role associated with the component or the interface in use, it fails the call and returns the well-known HRESULT *E_ACCESSDENIED*. If the caller is a Visual Basic application, the Visual Basic run time catches the HRESULT *E_ACCESSDENIED* and raises a trappable "Permission denied" error with an error number of 70.

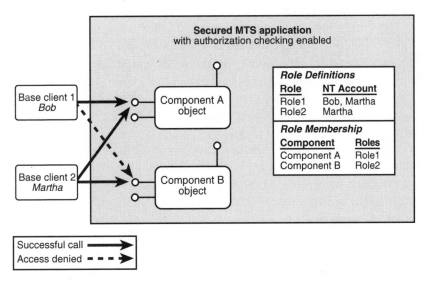

Figure 12-1. *MTS performs security checks for access control when a call arrives at a secured MTS application.*

MTS performs authorization checks only on calls from outside the package, not on intrapackage (intraprocess) calls. Intraprocess calls are therefore much faster. However, because intraprocess calls are assumed to be secure, you must protect your applications from unintended security holes.

Let's say that you have component A and component B inside a server package in which you have enabled authorization checking. You've placed Role1 in the membership of component A and Role2 in the membership of component B, as shown in Figure 12-1 on page 275. Any user who is a member of Role1 can directly invoke a method on objects of type A but not on objects of type B. But what happens if a Role1 user invokes a method on an object of type A, which in turn invokes a method on an object of type B? The call will succeed because there are no intraprocess security checks. You should understand the implications of this example when you design components that make intraprocess calls.

Calls between server packages can also be tricky. For example, what happens if client A makes a call on server package B, which then makes a call on server package C? You might expect server package C to perform its security checks using client A's security credentials, but this isn't the case. MTS performs its security checks from hop to hop as opposed to performing them from end to end. This means you must understand the difference between the *direct caller* and the *original caller*. The direct caller is the party one hop up the call chain, while the original caller is the party at the top of the call chain. MTS always performs its security checks using the credentials of the direct caller.

In this example, client A is the original caller and server package B is the direct caller. Server package C conducts its security checks using the Windows NT user account that serves as the identity for server package B. As you can see, you must be careful. When you grant a role access permissions to a component, you must be certain that the component itself doesn't make any intraprocess calls or interprocess calls that will permit access to other components that should be off-limits to the role in question.

As you've seen, the declarative security available in MTS (in its current release) offers access control at both the component and the interface level. COM+ will likely extend this control down to the method level. However, if you need method-level granularity now, you must resort to programmatic security. Fortunately, programmatic security is much easier in MTS than it is in COM. MTS exposes a handful of properties and methods through the *ObjectContext* interface, making programmatic security easily accessible to Visual Basic programmers.

MTS Programmatic Security

MTS offers programmatic security to complement and extend what is possible through declarative security. You can write your own security checks using the *ObjectContext* interface. For example, you can test a call to see whether it's running inside a secured MTS application before you attempt a secured operation:

```
Const E_ACCESSDENIED = &H80070005
Dim ObjCtx As ObjectContext
Set ObjCtx = GetObjectContext()
If ObjCtx.IsSecurityEnabled() Then
    ' Conduct secured operation.
Else
    ' Raise an access-denied error to caller.
    Err.Raise E_ACCESSDENIED, _
            "MyDll.MyClass.MyMethod", _
            "Permission denied"
End If
```

IsSecurityEnabled tells you whether the current call is running inside a secured MTS application. This method always returns True when it's called from a component in an MTS server package. It also returns True when it's called from a library package that has been loaded by a server package. However, if the library package has been loaded into an unsecured client application, it will return False. If you want your code to run only within a secured MTS application, you can use the code in the previous example to raise a "Permission denied" error back to the caller if the library package has been loaded into an unsecured application.

You can also write code to test whether the caller belongs to a particular role. The *IsCallerInRole* method accepts a single string parameter of the role you want to test. This method returns True if either the Windows NT user account or one of the Windows NT group accounts of the caller maps to this role. *IsCallerInRole* always returns True when it's called inside an unsecured application. You should therefore call *IsCallerInRole* together with *IsSecurityEnabled*, like this:

```
Dim ObjCtx As ObjectContext
Set ObjCtx = GetObjectContext()
If ObjCtx.IsSecurityEnabled() And _
    ObjCtx.IsCallerInRole("Manager") Then
    ' Conduct a secured, manager-only operation.
Else
    Err.Raise E_ACCESSDENIED, _
            "MyDll.MyClass.MyMethod", _
            "Permission denied"
End If
```

As you can see, *IsCallerInRole* lets you perform access checking at the method level. It also lets you perform conditional access checks. For example, you can write the *SubmitOrder* method so that only users in the role of Manager can submit a purchase order if the request exceeds $5,000, as you can see in the following code.

```
Const E_ACCESSDENIED = &H80070005
Dim ObjCtx As ObjectContext
Set ObjCtx = GetObjectContext()
Dim Amount As Currency
' Determine the purchase amount.
Amount = GetAmount()
' Check for manager role on any amount that exceeds $5,000.
If Amount > 5000 Then
    If Not ObjCtx.IsSecurityEnabled() Or _
        Not ObjCtx.IsCallerInRole("Manager") Then
        ' The caller isn't a manager, and the amount is more than $5,000.
        ObjCtx.SetAbort
        Dim ErrDesc As String
        ErrDesc = "Manager required when amount exceeds $5,000"
        Err.Raise E_ACCESSDENIED, , ErrDesc
    End If
End If
' Now conduct secured operation.
```

You can call *IsCallerInRole* from a component inside a library package, but such a call can check only against the roles defined inside the server package in which the library package has been loaded. MTS also generates an *mtsErrCtxRoleNotFound* error if you call *IsCallerInRole* inside a secured MTS application and pass a role name that doesn't exist.

In addition to the role-based programmatic security you've just seen, MTS can provide the names of the Windows NT user accounts for both the object's creator and the object's caller. This is the code required to retrieve the original caller's Windows NT user account name:

```
Dim ObjCtx As ObjectContext
Set ObjCtx = GetObjectContext()
Dim Caller As String
Caller = ObjCtx.Security.GetOriginalCaller()
```

This example shows how to use the *Security* property of the *ObjectContext* interface. The *Security* property lets you call the *GetOriginalCallerName* method. This method returns the caller's account name in an *Authority\User* format, as in *MyDomain\TedP*. In addition to *GetOriginalCallerName*, the Security object also exposes *GetDirectCallerName*, *GetDirectCreatorName*, and *GetOriginalCreatorName*. The concepts of original creator and direct creator work in exactly the same way as those of original caller and direct caller explained earlier in this chapter.

SHARING GLOBAL DATA
ACROSS MTS OBJECTS

The MTS programming model uses *resource dispensers* to model plug-in modules that work with the MTS run time. A resource dispenser shares nondurable resources across objects in an MTS application in a way that promotes efficiency and scalability. The MTS SDK details the requirements of writing resource dispensers for MTS applications. As you saw in Chapter 10, the ODBC Driver Manager is an MTS resource dispenser. One other resource dispenser ships with MTS—the Shared Property Manager (SPM). (Real COM programmers call it "the spam.")

The SPM is a resource dispenser that facilitates the sharing of global memory among objects running inside the same MTS application (process). This is great news for Visual Basic programmers. As you'll recall from Chapter 7, Visual Basic doesn't provide an easy, reliable way to share global data in a multithreaded application. When you declare a public variable in a BAS module, Visual Basic stores the data in thread local storage. Consequently, a set of Visual Basic objects can share BAS-module variables only when they're running in the same single-threaded apartment (STA). If two Visual Basic objects from the same project are running in different STAs, they see a separate instance of each BAS-module variable.

With MTS, you should assume that every activity runs in a separate STA. This means that Visual Basic alone doesn't provide a reasonable way to share data across objects running in separate MTS activities. However, at times you might want all the objects in an MTS application to share a set of global variables. You can solve this problem using the SPM.

Before I explain how to use the SPM, you should note that accessing global data from multiple threads introduces concurrency issues. As you saw in Chapter 7, concurrent access to global data usually requires synchronization. Failure to properly synchronize access to global data can lead to data inconsistency and data corruption in a multithreaded environment.

The SPM provides a simple yet effective form of synchronization. Instead of having stand-alone properties, the SPM requires you to define each property within the scope of a *property group*. A property group provides a namespace for a set of properties and also lets you indicate how to synchronize access to your data. Figure 12-2 on the following page shows how things look from a high-level perspective. The shared property group implements an internal lock manager to synchronize access to property objects inside a group.

The SPM is a name/value dictionary that lets you create and retrieve properties and property groups by name. Let's look at an example. To use the SPM, you must reference the Shared Property Manager Type Library (mtxspm.dll) in your MTS DLL

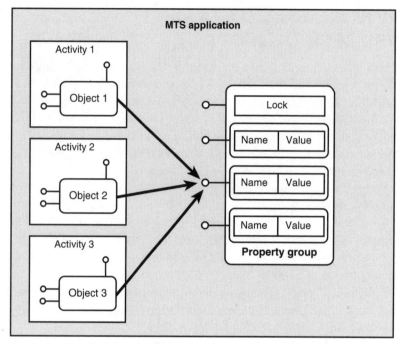

Figure 12-2. *The shared property manager provides synchronized access to global data through shared properties inside a property group. When you create a property group, you should indicate how you want it to manage locking and its lifetime.*

project. Before you can create and retrieve properties and property groups, you must create an instance of the shared property group manager, like this:

```
Dim ObjCtx As ObjectContext
Set ObjCtx = GetObjectContext()
' Create shared property group manager instance.
Dim spgMgr As SharedPropertyGroupManager
Dim spgMgr_ProgID As String
spgMgr_ProgID = "MTxSpm.SharedPropertyGroupManager.1"
Set spgMgr = ObjCtx.CreateInstance(spgMgr_ProgID)
```

You can then create a shared property group:

```
Dim MyGroup As SharedPropertyGroup
Dim GroupAlreadyExists As Boolean
Set MyGroup = spgMgr.CreatePropertyGroup("MyGroup", _
                                         LockMethod, _
                                         Process, _
                                         GroupAlreadyExists)
```

The *CreatePropertyGroup* method takes four parameters. The first parameter lets you pass the name of the property group. If a property group of the same name already exists, the SPM binds you to it. If the property group doesn't exist, the SPM creates it and then binds you to it. The last parameter of *CreatePropertyGroup* is a Boolean output parameter that tells the caller whether the property group existed before the call.

The second and third parameters let you specify an *isolation mode* and a *release mode* for your property group. The isolation mode allows you to establish the locking behavior for the group, while the release mode tells the SPM how long you want the group to remain in memory. Note that both these parameters are passed *ByRef* and that the SPM ignores their input values if the property group already exists. Only the client that creates the group can set these values. If the property group already exists, the SPM returns the current isolation mode and release mode to the caller in these two parameters as output values.

You can pass the isolation mode value *LockSetGet* or *LockMethod*. If you pass *LockSetGet*, the SPM locks individual properties when they're accessed by a client. This ensures that two clients never read and write to the same property at the same time. In other words, it prevents concurrent access to a shared property object's data, which can result in inconsistency and corruption. However, *LockSetGet* doesn't prevent other clients from concurrently accessing other properties in the group.

You should pass *LockMethod* when you want each client to acquire a groupwide exclusive lock across a set of operations. There are a few reasons why you might need to do this. You might want to read a property and then update its value without the risk of another client updating its value between your two operations. Or you might have interdependencies among the properties in a group. In this case, each client might require a higher level of isolation when running a series of updates.

When you create a property group using *LockMethod*, a client will acquire an exclusive lock that prevents other clients from reading or writing to any property in the group. This lock is held for the duration of the client's method call. When another client attempts to access a property inside a locked group, its call blocks until the lock is released. As with transactions, higher levels of isolation in the SPM result in more blocking and lower levels of concurrency.

When you set the release mode for a group, you can pass a value of either *Process* or *Standard*. The value *Process* indicates that you want the property group to remain in memory for the lifetime of the MTS application. The value *Standard* indicates that you want the property group to manage its lifetime using standard reference counting. When you pass *Standard*, the property group releases itself from memory as soon as the last client drops its connection.

Of course, the SPM isn't really useful until you start creating and using shared properties. Now that you know how to create a property group, you can create a property using the *CreateProperty* method or the *CreatePropertyByPosition* method. Following is an example of creating a property and setting its default value.

```
Dim MyProperty As SharedProperty
Dim PropertyAlreadyExists As Boolean
' Create and/or bind to property.
Set MyProperty = MyGroup.CreateProperty("MyProperty", _
                                        PropertyAlreadyExists)
' Give property a default value when created.
If (PropertyAlreadyExists = False) Then
    MyProperty.Value = "My favorite initial value"
End If
```

As in the case of *CreatePropertyGroup*, *CreateProperty* simply binds you to a property if it already exists. You can retrieve an existing property by name or by position. If the property doesn't already exist, the SPM creates it and assigns the default value 0 (as a long integer) to its *Value* property. If you want a different default value, you should explicitly set it when the property is created.

The *Value* property of a shared property object is stored as a variant. This situation gives you quite a bit of flexibility. You can store any variant-compliant data type in a shared property such as *Integer*, *Long*, *Double*, or *String*. You can also store a variant-compliant array. Here is an example of storing an array of strings in a shared property:

```
Dim data() As String
ReDim data(3)
data(0) = "Bob"
data(1) = "Carol"
data(2) = "Ted"
data(3) = "Alice"
MyProperty.Value = data
```

After you create the property, it's pretty easy to read and write to it. You might even be tempted to assign a Visual Basic object reference to a shared property. However, this is a very bad idea. Shared COM objects don't fit into the MTS programming model very well. Because of their problems with thread affinity, shared Visual Basic objects don't fit in at all. In MTS, every object should be owned by one and only one client. However, you can store the state that defines a logical object inside the SPM using primitive data types and arrays. If you do this, you can simply rehydrate objects on an as-needed basis as long as each one lives entirely within the scope of a single activity.

You should also keep in mind that read and write operations in the SPM aren't transacted. While the SPM can provide isolation, it doesn't provide any rollback facilities. If you modify a property from inside an MTS transaction, your changes are permanent, even when you call *SetAbort*. And don't be fooled into thinking that your property group locks are held to the end of your transactions. The locks in the SPM have nothing to do with the current transaction. The SPM releases its locks as soon as the current method finishes, which in most cases is before the end of your MTS transaction.

COM+ will introduce a new service called the In-Memory Database (IMDB), which will let you share data among objects as the SPM does today. However, the IMDB will be exposed as an OLE DB provider. It will also be a resource manager that can enlist your connections inside an MTS transaction. Your read and write operations to the IMDB will thus be enlisted and reversible in addition to being isolated. A call to *SetAbort* will undo any change you've made.

CREATING WEB-BASED APPLICATIONS

Many companies have adopted Web-based solutions because of the advantages of using a browser in the presentation tier. HTML and HTTP let you create scalable applications that are both cross-platform and self-distributing. Web-based applications also let companies move beyond the LAN and WAN to reach new audiences. A client needs only a Web browser, a TCP/IP address, and an Internet connection.

When you design a Web-based application, you must make assumptions about your user base. In particular, you must decide between developing an application for the majority of users on the Internet and developing an intranet-style application. If you can assume that every client will run a recent version of Microsoft Internet Explorer, you can develop your application using browser-specific features such as ActiveX controls and ActiveX documents. However, this generally limits your audience to intranet users.

This section focuses on cross-platform development for the Web. If you want to reach clients using all types of browsers, you must avoid techniques that involve client-side COM. However, cross-platform development doesn't prevent you from running COM code on the server. You can create Web-based applications that let clients running different browsers on Macintosh and UNIX platforms use your MTS applications just as clients running Internet Explorer and Windows can.

Internet Information Server (IIS) makes it relatively easy to create Web-based applications that interact with your server-side COM components. The key to making everything work is ASP. An ASP page is an HTML page that can contain server-side processing instructions. Once you understand how ASP works, you can write Web pages that create Visual Basic objects and run MTS transactions.

ASP Architecture

Let's examine how things work inside an ASP application. ASP pages are simple HTML text files that have an .asp extension instead of the .htm or .html extension used by standard Web pages. When the IIS Web server determines that a client has requested a page with an .asp extension, it creates an ASP filter to parse out all of the server-side processing instructions. This makes it remarkably easy to embed server-side logic in an HTML page using a scripting language such as VBScript or JavaScript. Following is a simple example of an ASP page that uses VBScript.

```
<%@ LANGUAGE="VBSCRIPT" %>
<HTML>
<!-- MyPage.asp -->
<!-- Use VBScript for inline scripts -->
<HEAD>
<TITLE>My ASP Page</TITLE>
</HEAD>
<BODY>
<!--- Inline server-side script -->
<%
Dim sMsg
sMsg= "The current time is " & FormatDateTime(Now(), vbLongTime)
Response.Write sMsg
%>
</BODY>
</HTML>
```

This example shows how easy it is to write a simple ASP page. Note that the ASP filter recognizes the inline tags <% and %> as the beginning and the end of a server-side script. When you create an ASP page, you can program against the five built-in ASP objects: *Request, Response, Session, Application,* and *Server.* I won't cover the fundamentals of ASP programming here because many excellent resources are available on this topic. I'll simply assume that you have a basic knowledge of writing ASP pages, and I'll show examples only of the VBScript code that you can write inside an ASP script.

The Windows NT 4 Option Pack provides a new level of integration between IIS and MTS. This integration amounts to a melding of the two run-time environments. Figure 12-3 shows a diagram of the IIS Web server process (inetinfo.exe). As you can see, the Web server process loads the MTS Executive (mtxex.dll). The installation of the Windows NT 4 Option Pack automatically creates an MTS library package named

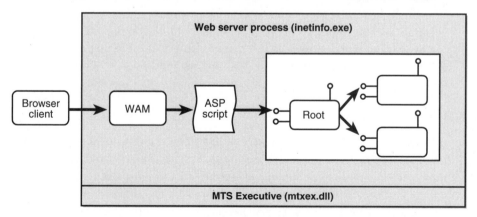

Figure 12-3. *A WAM object is responsible for creating an ASP filter when it processes an ASP page request. This filter parses server-side scripts from the page and runs them before returning control to the client.*

IIS In-Process Applications. If you locate this package in the MTS Explorer, you can see that it is preconfigured with a set of Web application manager (WAM) components. WAM components are registered with the MTS Explorer, which means that WAM objects are MTS objects. Each WAM object has a context wrapper and can talk to the MTS run time through its object context.

IIS uses WAM objects to handle incoming requests. (The manner in which WAM objects work is undocumented, so my descriptions here contain some degree of speculation.) Although Figure 12-3 shows a simplified picture of a single WAM object creating an ASP filter, in most cases a client request for an ASP page passes between several WAM objects before being processed. WAM objects are also very sophisticated in their use of thread pooling and thread dispatching. While the low-level details of how WAM objects work shouldn't concern you, you should understand that a WAM object is ultimately responsible for creating an ASP filter when a client requests a Web page with an .asp extension.

IIS 4 also lets you configure an ASP application (a virtual directory) to run in its own dedicated process. You can thus isolate your ASP application from the IIS Web server process as well as from other ASP applications. The way to configure an ASP application to run as a separate process is by using the Internet Service Manager and selecting the Run In Separate Memory Space (Isolated Process) option in the Properties dialog box for the ASP application's virtual directory.

Running an ASP application in isolation can provide greater isolation and fault tolerance in a production environment. Running in isolation can also be quite handy during development as well. When you create Visual Basic DLLs for an ASP application, you'll find that you need to unload the application before rebuilding the DLL. This is a real pain if you've loaded a DLL into the IIS Web server process because you have to shut down two separate IIS services before you can rebuild your DLL. However, the Properties dialog box for an isolated ASP application gives you the option of unloading the ASP application's process from memory. Once you unload the ASP application, you can rebuild any DLLs that it has loaded.

When you configure your ASP application to run in an isolated process, IIS launches your ASP application in a new instance of the MTS container application (mtx.exe), as shown in Figure 12-4 on the following page. IIS also creates a new MTS package dedicated to the isolated ASP application. For example, if you mark a virtual directory named Market to run in isolation, a package named IIS-Default Web Site//Root/Market will be created for you automatically.

Whether you run your ASP applications in isolation or in the IIS Web server process, a WAM object is responsible for processing each request for an ASP page. When a WAM object processes an ASP request, it creates a COM object that serves as the ASP filter. We'll call this object an ASP *scripting object*. The scripting object scans the ASP page and parses out any server-side processing instructions. Once these server-side processing instructions run, IIS returns an HTML stream to the client.

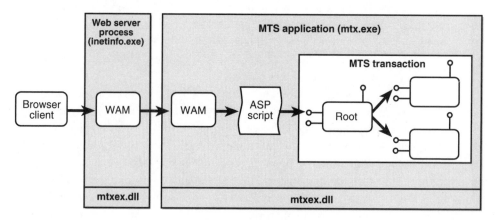

Figure 12-4. *When you run an ASP application as an isolated process, it's launched using the MTS container application (mtx.exe). IIS redirects incoming requests from WAM objects running in the IIS Web server process to a WAM object running in the isolated ASP application.*

Calling Visual Basic objects from ASP

You enjoy a few benefits when you move your business logic and data access code out of ASP pages and into a Visual Basic DLL. First, ASP is great for creating small programs, but managing an application that contains thousands of lines of code becomes increasingly difficult. Using a class-based object-oriented programming language such as Visual Basic offers much higher levels of encapsulation and code reuse. Second, writing code in the Visual Basic IDE offers enhancements such as IntelliSense and compile-time type checking that you don't get when writing VBScript code. This can make a huge difference when you're writing lots of data access code against the ActiveX Data Objects (ADO) type library. Third, today's multitier designs encourage the use of business objects to decouple the user interface code from the data access code. One of the benefits of this separation is that it eliminates the need for SQL in your ASP code. Finally, COM-based DLLs created with Visual Basic can take full advantage of the integration between IIS and the MTS run-time environment. Using MTS components in an ASP application gives you an infrastructure for building a reliable Web-based OLTP system.

The easiest technique for creating a Visual Basic object from an ASP page is to use the *CreateObject* method of the built-in ASP *Server* object:

```
<%
Dim obj
Set obj = Server.CreateObject("MyDll.CMyClass")
Response.Write obj.MyMethod()
%>
```

Server.CreateObject takes a ProgID and creates a new object. You should note that this ASP call is similar to calling the *CreateInstance* method in the *ObjectContext* interface in MTS. A call to *Server.CreateObject* always creates an MTS with its own context wrapper.

Once you've created an object from an ASP page using *Server.CreateObject*, you can then invoke methods and access properties on the object as usual. Figures 12-3 and 12-4 on the preceding pages show how you can run an MTS transaction from an ASP page. If you want to run an MTS transaction in an isolated ASP application, you should install your MTS components in the special MTS server package that was created for you when you marked the application to run in isolation. If you want to run an MTS transaction in the IIS Web server process, you should install your MTS components in a library package.

When you run an MTS transaction from an ASP page, you might consider running the transaction in a separate MTS application for security reasons. When you run your transaction in the same process as the ASP code, you rely on IIS to authenticate each user. If the ASP application has been configured to allow anonymous access, any Internet user can run your transactions. If you run your transactions in a separate MTS application, you can use the MTS role-based security model to give you more control over which users can run your transactions.

You should note a few strange things about writing ASP code with VBScript. First of all, all variables must be variants. This takes some getting used to. Second, VBScript can currently retrieve output parameters only when they are declared as variants. If you try to call a method on a Visual Basic object that has an output parameter defined as *String* or *Double*, the VBScript code will fail and generate a fairly confusing error message.

Let's look at an example of running a transaction to submit an order in an ASP page. The following ASP code does three things: First, it scrapes the user's input off the HTML form using ASP's built-in *Request* object. Second, it creates an instance of a Visual Basic component named *CBroker* and calls the *SubmitOrder* method. You should assume that this component and all the secondary components it uses have been properly written and registered with the MTS Explorer. Third, the code checks to see whether an error was raised during the call to *SubmitOrder* and sends the appropriate response to the client using ASP's built-in *Response* object.

```
<%
On Error Resume Next
' Get input from user form.
Dim Customer, Product, Quantity
Customer = Request.Form("txtCustomer")
Product = Request.Form("cboProduct")
Quantity = Request.Form("txtQuantity")
' Submit order to Visual Basic object.
```

(continued)

```
Dim Broker, OrderStatus
Set Broker = Server.CreateObject("WebMarket.CBroker")
Broker.SubmitOrder Customer, Product, Quantity, OrderStatus
' Test to see whether transaction was successful.
If Err.Number = 0 Then
    Response.Write OrderStatus
Else
    Response.Write "Your order submission was not accepted<br>"
    Response.Write "Error: " & Err.Description
End If
%>
```

Error handling isn't as graceful in VBScript as it is in Visual Basic. You must conduct error handling by using an *On Error Resume Next* statement and checking the error number after each call. This is cumbersome, but it works. VBScript has no problem handling the errors generated by the root object inside a transaction. In Chapter 10, I suggested a way to write the methods for the root object in an MTS transaction. When you can commit the transaction, you should return the call without raising an error. If you abort the transaction, the root object should raise an error back to the caller with an informative error message. The ASP code above assumes that the *SubmitOrder* method follows this convention.

Transactional ASP pages

The integration between ASP and MTS allows you to mark an ASP page with a transaction support property, just as you can do with a registered MTS component. This means that an ASP scripting object can serve either as the root object or as a secondary object inside an MTS transaction. ASP also adds another built-in ASP object named *ObjectContext*, which gives you the ability to call *SetComplete* or *SetAbort* directly from your VBScript code. A transactional ASP page even provides two events that you can use to handle the conditional logic when a transaction has been committed or rolled back. Here's a simple example of a transactional ASP page:

```
<%@ TRANSACTION=Required LANGUAGE="VBScript" %>
<%
Main
Sub Main()
    ' Execute some ADO code.
    ' Execute some more ADO code.
    If (ThingsAreGood) Then
        ObjectContext.SetComplete
    Else
        ObjectContext.SetAbort
    End If
End Sub
' ASP supplies events for handling conditional commit/abort logic.
Sub OnTransactionCommit()
```

```
    Response.Write "transaction succeeded"
End Sub
Sub OnTransactionAbort()
    Response.Write "transaction failed: " & Err.Description
End Sub
%>
```

While transactional ASP pages give you yet another transaction-programming option, they don't offer you the same advantages of writing your transactions with Visual Basic. You will experience far more control and much better performance with compiled Visual Basic components that have been registered with the MTS Explorer. Transactional ASP pages are most valuable to Web programmers who want the benefits of MTS transactions without having to resort to using a compiled language, such as Visual Basic or C++. Since you've made it to the last chapter of this book, I assume that you're more than capable of creating MTS components with Visual Basic and that transactional ASP pages won't be of much interest to you.

Calling built-in ASP objects from Visual Basic

When you program against the five built-in ASP objects in an ASP page script, you are actually calling methods on an implicit scripting object. However, you can also program against these built-in ASP objects from inside your Visual Basic DLLs. Figure 12-5 shows the lines of communication that you must set up between the scripting object and a Visual Basic object. Once you create the connection from your Visual Basic object back to the scripting object, you can program against built-in ASP objects such as *Request* and *Response* from inside your Visual Basic DLL.

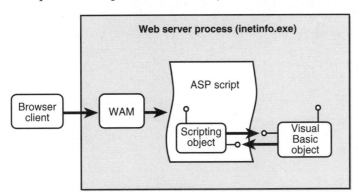

Figure 12-5. *When you create a Visual Basic object from an ASP page using* Server.CreateObject, *the Visual Basic object can program against the built-in ASP objects.*

An ASP scripting object exposes an interface named *ScriptingContext*, which lets you get at the five built-in ASP objects. However, before you can use any ASP objects in your Visual Basic project, you must reference the ASP type library. Figure

12-6 shows the ASP type library as seen through the Object Browser. As you can see, the built-in ASP objects are exposed as COM objects.

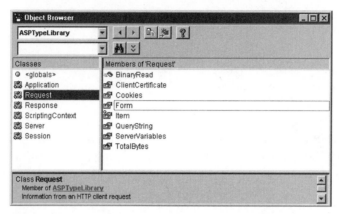

Figure 12-6. *When you program against the ASP type library, you have access to all the built-in ASP objects from a Visual Basic DLL.*

IIS 3 was the first version of IIS that let you program against the built-in ASP objects. The trick is to use the scripting object's *ScriptingContext* interface, which lets you navigate to the five other ASP objects. However, you need a little assistance to get to the *ScriptingContext* interface.

When you call *Server.CreateObject* from an ASP page, IIS creates the object and attempts to call into it through a special method named *OnStartPage*. If the call to *OnStartPage* succeeds, IIS passes a *ScriptingContext* reference to the new object. If the object doesn't implement a method named *OnStartPage*, the call fails and IIS ignores the error. If you implement this method, you can cache and use this *ScriptingContext* reference. The following code shows a Visual Basic class that does exactly this.

```
Private ScriptCtx As ScriptingContext

Sub OnStartPage(sc As ScriptingContext)
    ' Cache reference when called by IIS.
    Set ScriptCtx = sc
End Sub

Sub MyMethod()
    ' Retrieve built-in ASP objects.
    Dim req As Request, rsp As Response
    Set req = ScriptCtx.Request
    Set rsp = ScriptCtx.Response
    ' Get input from HTML form.
    Dim Customer As String
    Customer = req.Form("txtCustomer")
```

```
' Write reply back to browser.
rsp.Write "Thanks for your business"
End Sub
```

This example shows how to retrieve the *Request* object and the *Response* object from the *ScriptingContext* interface. Once you retrieve a reference to a built-in ASP object, you can program against it as if you're in an ASP page. However, Visual Basic provides many advantages over writing ASP code with VBScript. The Visual Basic IDE provides IntelliSense and compile-time type checking because you're programming against a type library. Your code will also run faster than VBScript code because it is compiled.

The technique I've just shown you, of using *OnStartPage* to get at the built-in ASP object, became obsolete with the release of IIS 4. Now you can get at the five built-in ASP objects without using the *ScriptingContext* interface. The built-in ASP objects are available through MTS's *ObjectContext* interface.

When you call *Server.CreateObject* from an ASP page, the new object is created as an MTS object with a context wrapper and an object context. *Server.CreateObject* also populates the object context's *Item* collection with the five built-in ASP objects. The following code shows how to retrieve the *Request* object and the *Response* object using the *ObjectContext* interface.

```
Sub MyMethod()
    Dim ObjCtx As ObjectContext
    Set ObjCtx = GetObjectContext()
    ' Retrieve built-in ASP objects.
    Dim req As Request, rsp As Response
    Set req = ObjCtx.Item("Request") ' Longhand
    Set rsp = ObjCtx("Response")      ' Shorthand
    ' Get input from HTML form.
    Dim Customer As String
    Customer = req.Form("txtCustomer")
    Dim Product  As String
    Product = req.Form("txtProduct")
    Dim Quantity As Long
    Quantity = req.Form("txtQuantity")
    ' Process client's request.
    ' Write response message back to browser.
    rsp.Write "Your order number is 1783"
End Sub
```

You can also retrieve the ASP *Session* object and the *Application* object using the same technique. However, you should avoid placing Visual Basic objects in either session variables or application variables. Shared Visual Basic objects create problems that severely hamper the thread dispatching architecture of IIS. Stick to using Visual Basic objects that are created and destroyed within the scope of a single ASP request.

Web Classes and the IIS Application Designer

Visual Basic 6 has a new Web-based productivity enhancement called the IIS Application Designer (IISAD). This extension of the Visual Basic IDE provides a new type of component known as a *Web class*. The way things work behind the scenes in an IISAD application is similar to what I just described. The IISAD lets you create cross-platform Web applications by programming against the built-in ASP objects from inside the Visual Basic IDE, as shown in Figure 12-7. However, IISAD brings even more to the table.

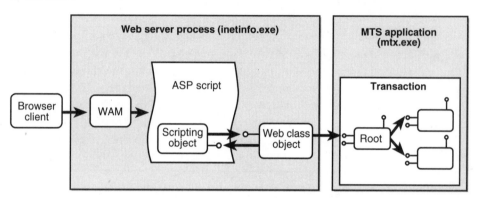

Figure 12-7. *Web classes make it simple to program against built-in ASP objects from within the Visual Basic IDE. The IISAD provides many productivity enhancing features, such as imported HTML templates with find-and-replace capabilities and integrated debugging.*

One of the biggest benefits of using the IISAD and Web classes is that they hide many of the tedious details of ASP programming from the Visual Basic developer. For example, the IISAD automatically creates the ASP page that will serve as an entry point into your ASP application. This ASP page creates an instance of a Web class manager object that controls the entire IISAD application. The ASP page calls upon the Web class manager object to create instances of your Web classes. As you can see, IISAD is a framework that is layered on top of ASP. What's more, the Web class type library adds a productive layer on top of the objects and interfaces in the ASP type library. The IISAD even gives you a way to debug your ASP code inside the Visual Basic IDE.

Another nice feature of the IISAD is that it lets you work with HTML templates. Using these templates, you can keep the HTML layout details separate from your Visual Basic code. Once you import an HTML template into your project, you can perform a search-and-replace on certain tags and stream the results back to the client. This is a great way to create an entire Web site with a single project using the Visual Basic IDE.

Because I want to finish this book sometime in 1998, I'm not going to cover the nuts and bolts of using the IISAD and Web classes. However, you should look into them if you plan to develop large-scale Web applications. Keep in mind that the IISAD framework adds complexity to an ASP application. You must plan the time to become familiar with this framework before you can expect to be productive. In some ASP applications, the complexity of this framework might be more trouble than it's worth. Remember that you still have the option of creating an ASP application with Visual Basic DLLs without the IISAD, as I showed you earlier.

CREATING MIDDLEWARE FOR A DISTRIBUTED APPLICATION

Let's examine a few common high-level design requirements in a distributed application. When you build a large information system, you must often place critical subsystems in the middle tier. While MTS 2 assists you by providing many useful middle-tier services, in a few other areas you're on your own. We'll look at some of the more common pieces of middleware that you need to obtain when you build a distributed application, and I'll also introduce some of the new services you can expect from COM+.

Creating a Scalable Notification System

One common requirement in a LAN-based application is a system that can notify a set of clients when something interesting happens. For example, in an application for stockbrokers, you might want to inform all of your users when a stock price climbs or falls beyond a preset level.

You might assume that you can create a systemwide eventing system using a straightforward technique based on Visual Basic events. However, a naive implementation using Visual Basic events won't scale to accommodate more than a handful of clients. Visual Basic events work best when a source object raises events to a single client. When you hook up multiple event sinks to a single source, Visual Basic events become slow and unreliable because events are broadcast synchronously.

For example, if you have 100 clients with event sinks hooked into one source object, an event is broadcast to client 1 and back, then client 2 and back, and so on. As you can imagine, 100 round-trips run in sequence won't provide the performance you're looking for. To make things worse, if one of the client applications crashes or raises an error in the event handler, you'll encounter problems over which you have little control.

A scalable eventing architecture requires sophisticated multithreading and asynchronous call dispatching. Figure 12-8 on the following page shows how an event is propagated in such a system.

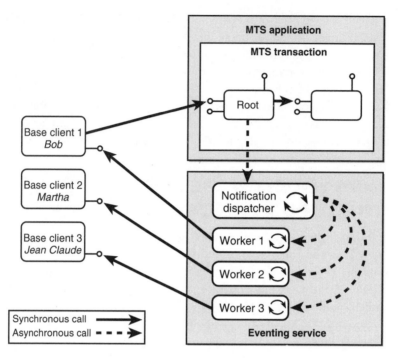

Figure 12-8. *A scalable eventing service must use multithreading and asynchronous call dispatching. COM+ will provide a similar eventing service that uses a publish-and-subscribe metaphor.*

Let's say that a client has run an MTS transaction and the root object has determined that it wants to commit the transaction. The root object then checks to see whether the transaction's modifications are worthy of raising an event. The transaction has lowered a stock price by $2.00, and the root object wants to send a notification to every client. The root object does its part by posting an asynchronous request to the eventing service. It can then return control to the client.

When the eventing service receives a request for an event, it must send a notification to every interested client. You can accomplish this by having the eventing service hold onto an outbound interface reference for each client. Such an architecture requires clients to register interface references with the eventing service. Chapter 6 showed you how to accomplish this using both Visual Basic events and a custom callback interface. Once all the clients have registered their interface references, the eventing service dispatcher can enumerate through all these references and send a notification to each client. As shown in Figure 12-8, an eventing service usually requires multiple threads and dispatches its notifications asynchronously in order to scale up appropriately when the application has hundreds or thousands of clients.

While you can build this type of an eventing service with Visual Basic, it isn't the best tool for the job. An eventing service developed with C++ offers much more flexibility when it comes to creating multiple threads and dispatching asynchronous calls. You might also consider deploying an eventing service as an actual Windows NT service. Again, C++ is much better suited for creating Windows NT services than Visual Basic.

If you don't mind waiting a little, COM+ will offer its own eventing service, which is similar to the one I've just described. This eventing service will be based on a publish-and-subscribe metaphor. Applications throughout the network can publish the types of events they expect to raise. Each client can subscribe to receive event notifications from several different applications. This approach will decouple applications that send notifications from those that receive them.

The COM+ eventing service will let clients subscribe to one or more events by registering an interface reference in the manner I've just described. It will also let you subscribe a CLSID to an event. When you do this, the eventing service will raise an event by activating an instance of the CLSID and calling a well-known method.

Creating a Queue Listener Application

Chapter 11 covered the fundamentals of message queues and Microsoft Message Queue (MSMQ) programming. As you'll recall, there are many good reasons to use queues in a distributed application. You can take advantage of MSMQ's ability to send asynchronous requests and to deal with disconnected applications, which might include WAN-based and remote clients. You also saw the benefits of exactly-once delivery, which is made possible by transactional queues.

Sending request messages from clients is relatively straightforward, but you usually have to create an application that listens in on a queue for incoming messages. Unfortunately, an MTS server package is passive—it requires a base client to activate an object before it will do anything. You usually need a middle-tier queue listener application to solve the problem of receiving request messages from the queue and directing them to the MTS application.

Figure 12-9 on the following page shows one approach to creating a queue listener application. You can monitor a queue by synchronously receiving or peeking at incoming messages, or you can use asynchronous MSMQ events. Either way, the application can react whenever a message arrives at the queue. If you have a high volume of incoming messages or if each request takes a long time to process, you should consider processing each message asynchronously. This choice leads to a more complicated design.

If you want to process messages asynchronously, the main thread of your application should listen in on the queue and dispatch a new worker thread to process each message. When the main thread determines that a new message has arrived at the queue with a call to *PeekCurrent* or *PeekNext*, it can dispatch a new worker thread and pass it the ID of the new message. The worker thread can locate the message in the queue by peeking at the message IDs and remove it with a call to *ReceiveCurrent*.

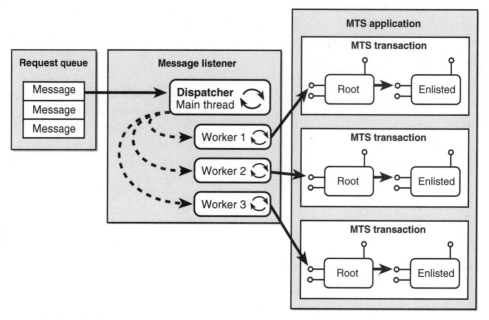

Figure 12-9. *A queue listener application monitors a queue for incoming messages. When a message arrives at the queue, the application receives it and directs the request to some destination, such as an MTS application.*

Once the worker thread receives the message, it can run an MTS transaction and send a second message to the response queue. This entire process can be wrapped inside an internal MSMQ transaction to provide the exactly-once reliability that we saw in Chapter 11. When you design a listener application, keep in mind that MSMQ requires that all transacted receive operations be conducted locally.

Because Visual Basic makes MSMQ programming easier than using any other language, it makes building a single-threaded queue listener application relatively simple. However, as with creating an eventing service, creating a sophisticated multi-threaded listener that will be deployed as a Windows NT service with Visual Basic is cumbersome at best. C++ gives you much more control in addressing all the system-level programming issues that you'll encounter.

One last thing I want to mention about message queuing is a new feature that will debut in COM+: *queued components*. A queued component is a COM component that transparently uses MSMQ as an underlying transport. You'll be able to create a client-side object from a queued component and invoke method calls as usual. Behind the scenes, the method calls will be recorded in an MSMQ message and sent to a special request queue. A complementary server-side component will receive the message and execute the method implementation.

The intention of queued components is to give you the advantages of COM and MSMQ rolled into one. Queued components are like COM components in that a client can create an object and invoke a bunch of methods. (Queued methods are asynchronous and take only input parameters.) Queued components have the advantages of message passing because they do not suffer from the limitations of RPC. Queued components will offer the benefits of priority-based messaging, asynchronous processing, communication among disconnected clients, and exactly-once delivery.

Load Balancing Across Multiple Servers

One of the most common requirements in a distributed application is the ability to scale up to accommodate more users. In most situations, the solution is to throw more hardware at the problem—to buy a bigger, faster server with multiple processors to increase throughput and concurrency or to add more servers. If you intend to scale a system by adding more servers, you must devise a scheme to balance the processing load of client requests among them.

Let's say that you start with 50 clients and 1 server. You add more servers as more users come on line, and all of a sudden you have 500 clients and 10 servers. The problem you face is how to direct clients 1 through 50 to server 1, clients 51 through 100 to server 2, and so on. One of the most common ways to balance the processing load across a group of servers is to direct different clients to different servers at activation time. A primitive approach is to hardcode the server name into the Registry of each client Registry. A more strategic approach is to add a routing server that acts as an object broker, as shown in Figure 12-10 on the following page.

Client applications request new objects from the routing server, and the routing server responds by activating an object on what it determines is the most appropriate server. A routing server can employ one of several common algorithms to balance the processing load. For example, a routing server can use a round-robin approach, in which it cycles between each server in the pool for each subsequent activation request. However, a simple algorithm like this is vulnerable to overloading one server while other servers sit around with nothing to do.

COM+ will introduce a load balancing service based on a routing server and an algorithm that selects a server based on statistical data. Each server in the pool will be responsible for sending intermittent data about its processor use and response times for fulfilling requests. This data will allow the router to make an intelligent choice about which server to use next.

In addition, the router used by COM+ will address several important fault tolerance issues. For instance, when the router tries to activate an object on a server that has crashed or gone off line, it will seamlessly activate the requested object on another server. The client will never be bothered with the details of which servers are down or where the object is actually located. The most critical computer will be the one that runs the router itself. You'll be able to make the router fault tolerant by running it on a clustered server.

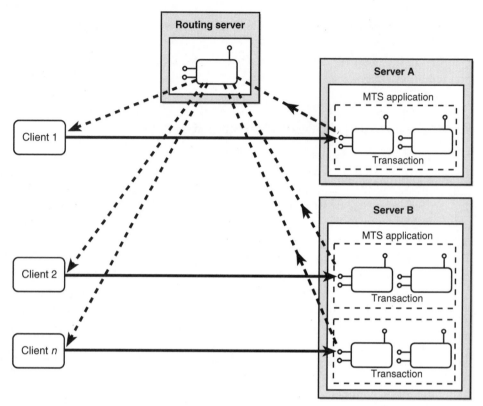

Figure 12-10. *A load balancing service based on a central routing server that connects clients to servers.*

Moving from COM to COM+

Figure 12-11 shows the middleware world in which distributed application developers live. Today many system requirements force you to build or purchase software for critical services that aren't provided by COM and MTS. As I've described, Microsoft intends to fill the demand for these pieces of middleware with a host of new services in COM+, including the following:

- An in-memory database
- An eventing service
- Queued components
- A load balancing service

I'd like to indulge myself and end this book by giving you my thoughts on the transition from COM to COM+. Today COM and MTS are two different beasts. As you

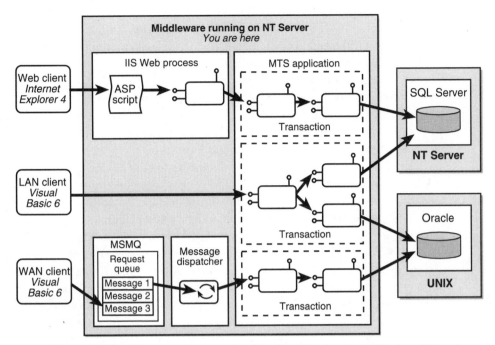

Figure 12-11. *When you design a distributed application for a Windows NT environment, you must carefully consider the type and size of your intended audience. The choices you make will affect many aspects of the application, such as flexibility, manageability, and scalability.*

learned in Chapter 9, MTS has been carefully layered on top of COM, yet COM has absolutely no knowledge of the existence of MTS. This creates quite a few problems. COM and MTS maintain their configuration information in the Registry in totally different ways. There's one security model for COM and another for MTS. There are also two different programming models. This can be confusing for a developer trying to get up to speed.

For example, when you call *CreateObject* in an MTS application, you ask COM's SCM to create an object for you. However, when you call *CreateInstance* through the *ObjectContext* interface, you ask the MTS run time to create an object for you. This creates an unnecessary level of confusion for programmers of distributed applications. What's more, calling to COM when you should be calling to MTS can get you in a load of trouble. Things would be much better if there were only one system to call into when you wanted to create an object.

COM+ will likely provide the grand unification of COM and MTS. No longer will there be the COM way of doing things vs. the MTS way. You'll have a single way to register a component and a single security model based on roles similar to the ones that exist today in MTS. You'll have one system to call into when you want to create an object. A single programming model will make it much easier for developers to get up to speed and maintain their sanity.

As COM and MTS are melded into one, the core competencies of each will continue to shine through. COM+, like COM, will use a binary component-based model centered around interface-based programming, and it will use the concept of apartments to integrate components with diverse threading capabilities. COM+ will approach interprocess communication by layering its interfaces on top of RPC, and it will leverage the accounts database and authentication scheme built into Windows NT and the underlying RPC system. As you can see, at the heart of COM+ will be the same old object model that you know and love.

In addition, a significant number of core aspects of MTS will take center stage in COM+. Code distribution will be based on packages and components. Interceptors and attribute-based programming will provide the hooks for many system services. The context wrapper and the object context will be part of the mainstream programming model. Applications will use an activity-based concurrency model. You'll be able to configure each application with its own role-based security scheme. And of course, COM+ will continue to support distributed transactions. COM+ will also provide new middleware services for critical subsystems in a distributed application. All of these advancements and the waves of technical information that they'll bring along with them should keep you and me busy well into the next millenium.

Index

TED PATTISON

Ted Pattison is an instructor and researcher at DevelopMentor (*www.develop.com*) in Los Angeles, California. He teaches professional developers how to program COM and MTS using Microsoft Visual Basic, C++, and Java. The focus of his research is distributed programming using COM, MTS, MSMQ, IIS, and ASP. He manages DevelopMentor's Visual Basic curriculum and has written several courses, including *Guerrilla VB* and *COM Programming with VB*.

Ted is a contributing editor of *MIND* magazine and has his own column dedicated to building enterprise and Internet-style applications using Visual Basic. He has published articles in *Microsoft Systems Journal* and *Visual Basic Programmer's Journal*. He is also a regular speaker at conferences such as Tech Ed, VBITs, and the NT Summit.

Ted performs consulting and mentoring services through his own firm, Subliminal Systems (*www.sublimnl.com*) in Manhattan Beach, California. He has built information systems for companies such as Hughes Aircraft and Southern California Edison using SQL Server, Visual Basic, and Microsoft Access. He also works with development teams, conducting architecture and code reviews and transferring technology to bring their programming talent up to speed on N-tier development based on Microsoft BackOffice technology. You can reach Ted at *TedP@sublimnl.com*.

The manuscript for this book was prepared using Microsoft Word 97. Pages were composed by Microsoft Press using Adobe PageMaker 6.52 for Windows, with text in Garamond and display type in Helvetica Black. Composed pages were delivered to the printer as electronic prepress files.

Cover Graphic Designer
Tim Girvin Design, Inc.

Cover Illustrator
Glenn Mitsui

Interior Graphic Artist
Joel Panchot

Principal Compositor
Peggy Herman

Principal Proofreader/Copy Editor
Shawn Peck

Indexer
Julie Kawabata

The *bible* for *Visual Basic* data access.

U.S.A. $49.99
U.K. £46.99 [V.A.T. included]
Canada $71.99
ISBN 1-57231-848-1

The HITCHHIKER'S GUIDE TO VISUAL BASIC® AND SQL SERVER, SIXTH EDITION, is the definitive guide for developers who want to use Visual Basic to access SQL Server. Whether you're using earlier versions or the latest Visual Basic 6.0 and the completely reengineered SQL Server 7.0 (which now runs on both Windows® 95 and Windows 98), this book will help you decide which of the constantly evolving data access options is best for your situation. Author William R. Vaughn provides the same depth and breadth of coverage that have made earlier editions of this book indispensable. Plus, he introduces innovations that may well change the way you think about data access!

Microsoft Press

A view of the future:
Internet business built on Windows NT.

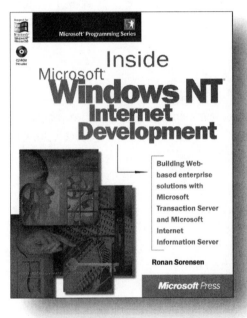

Microsoft Programming Series

Inside
Microsoft
**Windows NT
Internet
Development**

Building Web-based enterprise solutions with Microsoft Transaction Server and Microsoft Internet Information Server

Ronan Sorensen

***Microsoft** Press*

U.S.A.	**$44.99**
U.K.	£41.99 [V.A.T. included]
Canada	$64.99
ISBN 1-57231-852-X	

The Internet is a major driving force in the computer industry today. By harnessing it with the services of Microsoft® Windows NT®, you are equipped to develop the next generation of business server applications. INSIDE MICROSOFT WINDOWS NT INTERNET DEVELOPMENT delivers an authoritative overview of the complex issues involved in building these business applications and it explains why Active Server greatly simplifies their development. Content is reinforced by case study information drawn from the author's projects and clients, with sample code on CD-ROM illustrating how the various technologies are applied. Major sections of the book are devoted to Microsoft Transaction Server and to Active Server Pages. Code samples are drawn from a variety of development languages.

Microsoft *Press*

Advance
your mastery of
32-bit Windows
programming.

Microsoft Press

mspress.microsoft.com

Microsoft Press Online is your road map to the best available print and multimedia materials—resources that will help you maximize the effectiveness of Microsoft® software products. Our goal is making it easy and convenient for you to find exactly the Microsoft Press® book or interactive product you need, as well as bringing you the latest in training and certification materials from Microsoft Press.

Microsoft**press***online*

Where do you want to go today?®

Microsoft®*Press*

MICROSOFT LICENSE AGREEMENT
(Book Companion CD)

IMPORTANT—READ CAREFULLY: This Microsoft End-User License Agreement ("EULA") is a legal agreement between you (either an individual or an entity) and Microsoft Corporation for the Microsoft product identified above, which includes computer software and may include associated media, printed materials, and "on-line" or electronic documentation ("SOFTWARE PRODUCT"). Any component included within the SOFTWARE PRODUCT that is accompanied by a separate End-User License Agreement shall be governed by such agreement and not the terms set forth below. By installing, copying, or otherwise using the SOFTWARE PRODUCT, you agree to be bound by the terms of this EULA. If you do not agree to the terms of this EULA, you are not authorized to install, copy, or otherwise use the SOFTWARE PRODUCT; you may, however, return the SOFTWARE PRODUCT, along with all printed materials and other items that form a part of the Microsoft product that includes the SOFTWARE PRODUCT, to the place you obtained them for a full refund.

SOFTWARE PRODUCT LICENSE

The SOFTWARE PRODUCT is protected by United States copyright laws and international copyright treaties, as well as other intellectual property laws and treaties. The SOFTWARE PRODUCT is licensed, not sold.

1. **GRANT OF LICENSE.** This EULA grants you the following rights:

   a. **Software Product.** You may install and use one copy of the SOFTWARE PRODUCT on a single computer. The primary user of the computer on which the SOFTWARE PRODUCT is installed may make a second copy for his or her exclusive use on a portable computer.

   b. **Storage/Network Use.** You may also store or install a copy of the SOFTWARE PRODUCT on a storage device, such as a network server, used only to install or run the SOFTWARE PRODUCT on your other computers over an internal network; however, you must acquire and dedicate a license for each separate computer on which the SOFTWARE PRODUCT is installed or run from the storage device. A license for the SOFTWARE PRODUCT may not be shared or used concurrently on different computers.

   c. **License Pak.** If you have acquired this EULA in a Microsoft License Pak, you may make the number of additional copies of the computer software portion of the SOFTWARE PRODUCT authorized on the printed copy of this EULA, and you may use each copy in the manner specified above. You are also entitled to make a corresponding number of secondary copies for portable computer use as specified above.

   d. **Sample Code.** Solely with respect to portions, if any, of the SOFTWARE PRODUCT that are identified within the SOFTWARE PRODUCT as sample code (the "SAMPLE CODE"):

   i. **Use and Modification.** Microsoft grants you the right to use and modify the source code version of the SAMPLE CODE, *provided* you comply with subsection (d)(iii) below. You may not distribute the SAMPLE CODE, or any modified version of the SAMPLE CODE, in source code form.

   ii. **Redistributable Files.** Provided you comply with subsection (d)(iii) below, Microsoft grants you a nonexclusive, royalty-free right to reproduce and distribute the object code version of the SAMPLE CODE and of any modified SAMPLE CODE, other than SAMPLE CODE (or any modified version thereof) designated as not redistributable in the Readme file that forms a part of the SOFTWARE PRODUCT (the "Non-Redistributable Sample Code"). All SAMPLE CODE other than the Non-Redistributable Sample Code is collectively referred to as the "REDISTRIBUTABLES."

   iii. **Redistribution Requirements.** If you redistribute the REDISTRIBUTABLES, you agree to: (i) distribute the REDISTRIBUTABLES in object code form only in conjunction with and as a part of your software application product; (ii) not use Microsoft's name, logo, or trademarks to market your software application product; (iii) include a valid copyright notice on your software application product; (iv) indemnify, hold harmless, and defend Microsoft from and against any claims or lawsuits, including attorney's fees, that arise or result from the use or distribution of your software application product; and (v) not permit further distribution of the REDISTRIBUTABLES by your end user. Contact Microsoft for the applicable royalties due and other licensing terms for all other uses and/or distribution of the REDISTRIBUTABLES.

2. **DESCRIPTION OF OTHER RIGHTS AND LIMITATIONS.**

   - **Limitations on Reverse Engineering, Decompilation, and Disassembly.** You may not reverse engineer, decompile, or disassemble the SOFTWARE PRODUCT, except and only to the extent that such activity is expressly permitted by applicable law notwithstanding this limitation.

   - **Separation of Components.** The SOFTWARE PRODUCT is licensed as a single product. Its component parts may not be separated for use on more than one computer.

   - **Rental.** You may not rent, lease, or lend the SOFTWARE PRODUCT.

   - **Support Services.** Microsoft may, but is not obligated to, provide you with support services related to the SOFTWARE PRODUCT ("Support Services"). Use of Support Services is governed by the Microsoft policies and programs described in the user manual, in "on-line" documentation, and/or in other Microsoft-provided materials. Any supplemental software code provided to you as part of the Support Services shall be considered part of the SOFTWARE PRODUCT and subject to the terms and conditions of this EULA. With respect to technical information you provide to Microsoft as part of the Support Services, Microsoft may use such information for its business purposes, including for product support and development. Microsoft will not utilize such technical information in a form that personally identifies you.

- **Software Transfer.** You may permanently transfer all of your rights under this EULA, provided you retain no copies, you transfer all of the SOFTWARE PRODUCT (including all component parts, the media and printed materials, any upgrades, this EULA, and, if applicable, the Certificate of Authenticity), and the recipient agrees to the terms of this EULA.

- **Termination.** Without prejudice to any other rights, Microsoft may terminate this EULA if you fail to comply with the terms and conditions of this EULA. In such event, you must destroy all copies of the SOFTWARE PRODUCT and all of its component parts.

3. **COPYRIGHT.** All title and copyrights in and to the SOFTWARE PRODUCT (including but not limited to any images, photographs, animations, video, audio, music, text, SAMPLE CODE, REDISTRIBUTABLES, and "applets" incorporated into the SOFTWARE PRODUCT) and any copies of the SOFTWARE PRODUCT are owned by Microsoft or its suppliers. The SOFTWARE PRODUCT is protected by copyright laws and international treaty provisions. Therefore, you must treat the SOFTWARE PRODUCT like any other copyrighted material **except** that you may install the SOFTWARE PRODUCT on a single computer provided you keep the original solely for backup or archival purposes. You may not copy the printed materials accompanying the SOFTWARE PRODUCT.

4. **U.S. GOVERNMENT RESTRICTED RIGHTS.** The SOFTWARE PRODUCT and documentation are provided with RESTRICTED RIGHTS. Use, duplication, or disclosure by the Government is subject to restrictions as set forth in subparagraph (c)(1)(ii) of the Rights in Technical Data and Computer Software clause at DFARS 252.227-7013 or subparagraphs (c)(1) and (2) of the Commercial Computer Software—Restricted Rights at 48 CFR 52.227-19, as applicable. Manufacturer is Microsoft Corporation/One Microsoft Way/Redmond, WA 98052-6399.

5. **EXPORT RESTRICTIONS.** You agree that you will not export or re-export the SOFTWARE PRODUCT, any part thereof, or any process or service that is the direct product of the SOFTWARE PRODUCT (the foregoing collectively referred to as the "Restricted Components"), to any country, person, entity, or end user subject to U.S. export restrictions. You specifically agree not to export or re-export any of the Restricted Components (i) to any country to which the U.S. has embargoed or restricted the export of goods or services, which currently include, but are not necessarily limited to, Cuba, Iran, Iraq, Libya, North Korea, Sudan, and Syria, or to any national of any such country, wherever located, who intends to transmit or transport the Restricted Components back to such country; (ii) to any end user who you know or have reason to know will utilize the Restricted Components in the design, development, or production of nuclear, chemical, or biological weapons; or (iii) to any end user who has been prohibited from participating in U.S. export transactions by any federal agency of the U.S. government. You warrant and represent that neither the BXA nor any other U.S. federal agency has suspended, revoked, or denied your export privileges.

DISCLAIMER OF WARRANTY

NO WARRANTIES OR CONDITIONS. MICROSOFT EXPRESSLY DISCLAIMS ANY WARRANTY OR CONDITION FOR THE SOFTWARE PRODUCT. THE SOFTWARE PRODUCT AND ANY RELATED DOCUMENTATION IS PROVIDED "AS IS" WITHOUT WARRANTY OR CONDITION OF ANY KIND, EITHER EXPRESS OR IMPLIED, INCLUDING, WITHOUT LIMITATION, THE IMPLIED WARRANTIES OF MERCHANTABILITY, FITNESS FOR A PARTICULAR PURPOSE, OR NONINFRINGEMENT. THE ENTIRE RISK ARISING OUT OF USE OR PERFORMANCE OF THE SOFTWARE PRODUCT REMAINS WITH YOU.

LIMITATION OF LIABILITY. TO THE MAXIMUM EXTENT PERMITTED BY APPLICABLE LAW, IN NO EVENT SHALL MICROSOFT OR ITS SUPPLIERS BE LIABLE FOR ANY SPECIAL, INCIDENTAL, INDIRECT, OR CONSEQUENTIAL DAMAGES WHATSOEVER (INCLUDING, WITHOUT LIMITATION, DAMAGES FOR LOSS OF BUSINESS PROFITS, BUSINESS INTERRUPTION, LOSS OF BUSINESS INFORMATION, OR ANY OTHER PECUNIARY LOSS) ARISING OUT OF THE USE OF OR INABILITY TO USE THE SOFTWARE PRODUCT OR THE PROVISION OF OR FAILURE TO PROVIDE SUPPORT SERVICES, EVEN IF MICROSOFT HAS BEEN ADVISED OF THE POSSIBILITY OF SUCH DAMAGES. IN ANY CASE, MICROSOFT'S ENTIRE LIABILITY UNDER ANY PROVISION OF THIS EULA SHALL BE LIMITED TO THE GREATER OF THE AMOUNT ACTUALLY PAID BY YOU FOR THE SOFTWARE PRODUCT OR US$5.00; PROVIDED, HOWEVER, IF YOU HAVE ENTERED INTO A MICROSOFT SUPPORT SERVICES AGREEMENT, MICROSOFT'S ENTIRE LIABILITY REGARDING SUPPORT SERVICES SHALL BE GOVERNED BY THE TERMS OF THAT AGREEMENT. BECAUSE SOME STATES AND JURISDICTIONS DO NOT ALLOW THE EXCLUSION OR LIMITATION OF LIABILITY, THE ABOVE LIMITATION MAY NOT APPLY TO YOU.

MISCELLANEOUS

This EULA is governed by the laws of the State of Washington USA, except and only to the extent that applicable law mandates governing law of a different jurisdiction.

Should you have any questions concerning this EULA, or if you desire to contact Microsoft for any reason, please contact the Microsoft subsidiary serving your country, or write: Microsoft Sales Information Center/One Microsoft Way/Redmond, WA 98052-6399.

Register Today!

Return this
*Programming Distributed Applications with
COM and Microsoft® Visual Basic® 6.0*
registration card today

Microsoft Press
mspress.microsoft.com

OWNER REGISTRATION CARD   1-57231-961-5

Programming Distributed Applications with COM and Microsoft® Visual Basic® 6.0

FIRST NAME   MIDDLE INITIAL   LAST NAME

INSTITUTION OR COMPANY NAME

ADDRESS

CITY   STATE   ZIP

(   )
E-MAIL ADDRESS   PHONE NUMBER

U.S. and Canada addresses only. Fill in information above and mail postage-free.
Please mail only the bottom half of this page.

For information about Microsoft Press®
products, visit our Web site at
mspress.microsoft.com

Microsoft® *Press*

BUSINESS REPLY MAIL
FIRST-CLASS MAIL   PERMIT NO. 108   REDMOND WA

POSTAGE WILL BE PAID BY ADDRESSEE

MICROSOFT PRESS
PO BOX 97017
REDMOND, WA 98073-9830